'...part travelogue, part local history of some of the world's trouble spots and finally how one person managed to survive in those places and still achieve a level of success. It should be a must read to all who contemplate a similar career, or for the politicians who consider funding such programs.'—*Amazon reader review*

'Rarely has the world of the foreign aid worker been so fascinating. Her book is a genuine page-turner.'—John Piggott, *The Senior*

'...an important read for anyone hoping to work in development consulting or better understand it.'—Gordon Peake, *DevPolicyBlog*

Mary Venner has lived and worked as a technical adviser in Afghanistan, Kazakhstan, Kosovo, Libya, the Philippines, Somalia, East Timor, the Solomon Islands and Ukraine. Before that, she was a public servant in Canberra, Australia.

Proceeds from sales of this book will be donated to charities working to improve life for people affected by conflict and poverty.

MARY VENNER

WHERE ARE YOU THIS TIME?

*Making a Difference in
Places from Kabul to Kyiv,
Kosovo to Kazakhstan
and Kismayo to Qatar*

Where Are You This Time? by Mary Venner
Published by Late Start Publishing
© Mary Venner 2019

The moral right of the author has been asserted. All rights reserved. Without limiting the rights under copyright restricted above, no part of this publication may be reproduced, stored in or introduced into a retrieval system, or transmitted, in any form or by any means (electronic, mechanical, photocopying, recording or otherwise), without the prior written permission of both the copyright owner and the publisher of this book.

1st Edition 2019.
ISBN: 978-1-925999-39-6 (paperback)
        978-1-925999-40-2 (epub)
2nd Edition 2023, pbk.
ISBN: 978-0-646-87807-2 (paperback)
        978-0-646-87808-9 (epub)

Also available as an ebook from major ebook vendors

Acknowledgements

Many people played important roles in this story but are not mentioned due to lack of space. They include Alan and Margaret, Tony and Jan, Bill, Larry, Shukria, Anita, Nargis and Samima, Laura, Bernard and Margaret and, of course, David.

I'd also like to thank the numerous local drivers, interpreters and office staff who made it possible for me to work in these challenging places, and the government workers and officials who tolerated my endless questions and interruption to their routines.

Contents

Preface 9

PROLOGUE
Zero, Delta, Victor 15

KOSOVO
You're going where? 21
Global Village 46
The Next War in the Balkans 62
Return of the Apparatchiks 74
Bringing Westminster to Kosovo..................... 93

AFGHANISTAN
Another War, Another Project 113
1382..126
Bibi Maru 138
Ghani's tantrum.......................................152
DynCorp 162
Democracy 175

BIZARRE, TRAGIC, HOPEFUL
City of White Death, *Kazakhstan* 193
The Orange Revolution Turns Sour, *Ukraine* 211
Afghan Boy Scouts, *Kabul* 230
Seriously Weird, *Philippines* 253
Adventures in Abayaland, *Qatar*......................274
Into a Black Hole, *Libya*.............................285
A Glimmer of Hope, *Somalia* 303

EPILOGUE
Exit Report..315

Preface

A lot has happened in the world since this book was first published.

Four years ago, it seemed that the countries I was writing about would continue to go on their way once I left them behind, and for most of them, so far, that's been the case. But for some, there have been dramatic changes.

The most awful and tragic has been the unexpected return of Taliban rule in Afghanistan. Such a development was unimaginable when I worked in Afghanistan and was still a preposterous idea right up until it happened. A 'peace' agreement between the US and the Taliban, negotiated under the Trump administration without the involvement or consent of the elected Afghan government, promised the withdrawal of US troops in exchange for Taliban counter-terrorism commitments and vague plans for discussions with the government.

Against expectations, President Biden, when he took office in 2021, went ahead with the plan. It was a decisive decision from the new president, but it abandoned the people of Afghanistan to an authoritarian, theocratic regime. On 15 August 2021, as US personnel left Kabul and President Ashraf Ghani fled by helicopter, the Taliban marched in and took over the city.

Of course, the Afghan government in power at the time carries some of the blame for this disaster. I wonder, for example, who in their right mind thought Ashraf Ghani would make a good president. Almost every foreigner working in Afghanistan when I was there and who had experienced his temper tantrums, his egotism, his undisguised ambition, and his lack of administrative competence, was appalled at the idea of him ruling the country.

Once he had been elected, however, I wondered whether my criticisms of him in this book were wrong. Perhaps he had changed. Perhaps he had learned to work with others to achieve his well-intentioned grand plans. But all the reports I have read about the last days of the Ghani presidency, as the Taliban moved towards Kabul, simply reinforce my previous impressions. A western-educated academic with, as far as I know, zero experience of military issues but supreme confidence in his abilities, he proved unable to either recognise or manage the crisis that was developing.

The conflict that has erupted between Ukraine and Russia was somewhat less unexpected. The not-so-cold war that existed between Russia and the west when I left there in 2006 is now most definitely a 'hot' war. In February 2022, Russia launched an invasion of Ukraine, having previously annexed Crimea and supported breakaway Russian-speaking regions near the border. The invasion of a recognised sovereign country is never acceptable, whatever excuses and contributing factors can be identified, but based on my experiences when I was there I suspect the situation is a little more complicated than is presented in most news media. Of course, Ukraine as a country and as a political system, may have changed since that time. The fine balance between the pro-Russian and pro-western population may have shifted, the level of corruption may have moderated, and Poland's enthusiasm for welcoming Ukrainian refugees may have nothing at all to do with its historical connections to Ukrainian territory.

The juxtaposition of the developments in Afghanistan and Ukraine is telling. Ukraine has pushed the crisis in Afghanistan out of the headlines and western countries seem to have been keen to raise funds and accept refugees from a European country, while Afghans, with a genuine claim for protection but a long way away, remain in hiding or make risky, illegal journeys to find safety.

There have been changes in other countries also, but so far not as dramatic as those in Ukraine and Afghanistan. In the Philippines, the populist Rodrigo Duterte became president in 2016, followed in 2022 by the surprising return of the Marcos family to power, 36 years after the military dictator Ferdinand Marcos was overthrown. In Kazakhstan, long-term president Nursultan Nazarbayev unexpectedly retired in 2019 and the capital city, Astana, was immediately renamed 'Nursultan' in his honour. (The current president, however, has recently changed the name back to Astana.) Meanwhile, conflict continues in Somalia and Libya.

This book provides some historical background to these events. It tries to explain the context, the political challenges and the efforts made by western countries to improve the situation. It's based on the diaries and notes I made when I was working in these places as a public finance adviser to their governments. It reflects my understanding of events as I observed them. Other people may have different recollections. Some names have been changed, but others haven't.

This second edition, apart from this Introduction and a new Exit Report (all consulting assignments require an Exit Report), makes very few changes to the original text. In some places, I have modified comments that may have been, on reflection, a little harsh towards local people or colleagues. In other cases, I have doubled down.

It has been a privilege to have been able to observe history being made, and I hope that this book will give readers a better understanding of what really happens in these places.

Prologue

Zero, Delta, Victor
Kabul, Afghanistan. January 2009

'Zero Delta. This is Victor one two seven. Whisky. Bishop. Over.'

The man in the passenger seat in front of me in the British Embassy vehicle radios his coded message to the Ops Room. I presume it means, 'We're off.'

Then he turns around to look at me. 'Good morning, Mary. Have you been briefed on movement procedures before at all?' There's a Welsh lilt in his voice.

'Yes. About two times a day since I got here a week ago,' I tell him.

Nevertheless, he launches into his familiar rapid-fire script.

'Well, my name is Chris and this here in the driver's seat is Steve. You're in a B6 armoured vehicle. The doors will be locked throughout the journey. Please don't open them or get out of the vehicle unless directed to by Steve or myself.

'If there's an incident while we're moving around the city you should keep your head down and follow our instructions. We're both armed. The medical pack on the back of the seat in front of you is for self-administration should it be necessary. Do you have any allergies or conditions I should know about? Do you have any questions?'

We're only going a few blocks through the heavily guarded centre of Kabul to the Ministry of Education. When I first arrived in Afghanistan six years ago, I travelled to work every day in a battered old Corolla with a local driver. Now I have to take a close protection team with me every time.

The car drives away from the back gate of the British Embassy, past armed Ghurkha sentries and half a dozen local guards, through three successive metal boom gates and out into the streets of Kabul.

A block further on, armour or no armour, we are snarled up in Kabul's perpetual traffic jam. Taxis, minibuses and pickup trucks jostle for right of way at the intersection. At the next corner, Chris flicks down his sun visor. The red diplomatic number plate is attached to the front of it, out of sight unless needed to get past police checkpoints. I expect by now the terrorists have worked out that the diplomats' cars are the big ones without number plates.

When we arrive at the Ministry another guard lifts another boom gate and we weave around concrete barriers to the main building.

The last time I'd left Kabul I'd told everyone I wouldn't be coming back. But here I am. Afghanistan seemed to have got its hooks into me.

But so had most of the places where I'd worked during the previous decade. I still pined sometimes for the muddy chaos of post-war Kosovo, the sub-zero temperatures and bargain-priced opera tickets in Kyiv, and the crowds and noise and traffic of Manila. These places were all very different from each other, but in other ways, they were much the same in their poverty, dysfunction and insecurity.

They were also a million miles away from the comfortable life and predictable government job I'd had before I'd accepted a six-week consulting assignment all those years ago. Since then, I'd lived in a dozen different countries, most of which I'd known nothing about before I'd arrived, started learning and promptly forgotten half a dozen languages, survived without reliable electricity or even a regular water supply, and been a bystander as history unfolded in some of the most desperately troubled places in the world.

I'd been delivering international aid to those countries,

but I wasn't the kind of aid worker who looks after starving children or puts up tents for refugees. The help I bring is in the form of red tape and regulation, taxation and accounting, spreadsheets and computers.

My job is to tell governments how to raise more taxes, spend them wisely and ensure the money isn't stolen by corrupt officials, or by the very politicians I'm giving advice to. Not surprisingly, officials and politicians are not always keen to accept the changes my colleagues and I recommend. On the other hand, some of our recommendations have not always been sensible or implementable.

Chris follows me up the stairs and along the dusty Ministry of Education corridors. He's a stocky guy wearing an armoured vest under his short-sleeved shirt. He looks like Arnold Schwarzenegger with a hump. There's a curly wire coming out of one ear and a microphone pinned to the front of his shirt.

He sits outside in the corridor throughout my long and rambling two-hour meeting about the Afghan education budget. When I'm finally ready to go he leans forward and talks to his well-developed left pectoral muscle. 'Stand by. Stand by.'

Steve has the vehicle waiting outside the door by the time we get downstairs. At the exit gate he turns right. I could have told him it would be better to turn left. I've been here so many times before. But they're supposed to be the experts. They're supposed to be protecting me.

So now we are inextricably tangled in Kabul's afternoon rush hour. It's 3.30 pm, knockoff time for the city's civil servants, and the main streets are clogged with vintage buses taking them home. There's no alternative now but to follow them in a huge loop of one-way streets through the heart of Kabul, past the new mosque shimmering in the winter sunlight, around Zarnegar Park and in front of the fortified five-star Serena Hotel, just to end up almost where we started.

Steve drives aggressively. He tries to push his way through the traffic, but there's not much that pumping the clutch and spinning the steering wheel and jerking the brake pedal can do about the everyday chaos of Kabul's city streets. We are hemmed in by Afghans on bicycles, pedestrians crossing the street without looking, handcarts of fruit for sale pushing against the traffic flow, beggars looking sadly through the tinted windows and half a dozen other B6 armoured vehicles driven by aggressive close protection teams also heading in the same direction as us, towards the diplomatic safety zone.

It would definitely have been easier if we'd turned left.

Finally, we arrive at the Embassy compound, drive back through the three boom gates, and wait while the guards check under the chassis for hidden bombs.

'Zero delta. Victor one two seven. Bishop. Lincoln. Over.'

I guess that means we're home.

Kosovo

You're Going Where?
Pristina, Kosovo. February 2000

'Now let me see if I've got this straight,' Peter said as he poured more red wine into my glass, which had somehow emptied itself yet again. 'You're flying all the way to this place—how do you pronounce it?—Skopje? Which none of us have ever heard of.

'You've paid for your own business class ticket. You've been told to bring 2,000 Deutschmarks in small denomination notes. And when you get there you have to find someone called "Erol". And you're doing this on the strength of a few emails that purport to come from Washington and claim to be offering you a job?'

I looked around the dinner table at the small group of friends who'd come to say goodbye. It was the night before I was due to leave home on my big adventure. Yes, when he put it like that, it did sound a bit unlikely.

Even the travel agent, sitting in front of a huge map of the world, had never heard of Skopje. Most of her customers were more interested in holiday packages to Bali or cruises to Fiji than return business class tickets to the capital of what was then known, officially, as the Former Yugoslav Republic of Macedonia.

A day and a half later, I'd arrived in the harsh fluorescent light of Skopje Airport on a grey winter afternoon. The middle-aged men in business suits and military uniforms who'd travelled with me on the flight from Vienna had gathered their luggage and left. I was almost the only passenger still waiting for my bag to appear on the conveyor belt.

Ten years earlier, Skopje had been in a different country. Macedonia had been part of the communist, centrally-planned, bureaucratically-controlled Socialist Federal Republic of Yugoslavia. For decades, this part of Europe had been peaceful and, in relative terms, open and modern. Then ethnic nationalism, exploited by evil men, had torn the country apart. After years of chaos and war, Yugoslavia now existed more or less in name only and Skopje had become the capital of a newly created state.

Macedonia's complicated and bloody history was far from over, but there was now a new Balkan war zone just a few miles away across the border. Kosovo was the latest region to break away from the crumbling remains of Yugoslavia.

I'd watched events unfold there on the news every night during much of 1999. Dramatic footage of burning villages, Albanian Kosovars crossing snow-topped mountains to escape Serb soldiers, and the western world's intervention with nightly bombing raids on government buildings in Belgrade. After three months of conflict, peace had been declared. Other crises, some much closer to home, became the headlines and I forgot about Kosovo. Until I got the email.

Someone called Mike in Washington had found me almost by accident. He'd been given my name by someone I used to work with who'd heard from someone else I used to work with that I might be looking for a job.

Over the past few months, I'd been sending my resume to anyone I could think of and applied for dozens of jobs, which I realise now I had no hope of getting. I was starting to think the one I already had wasn't really that bad when the email landed in my inbox.

Mike worked for an American consulting firm that had been contracted by the US Agency for International Development to find people to work with the post-conflict UN Mission in Kosovo. I had no idea what that meant, but it implied overseas travel and sounded like an adventure.

The offer was only for a six-week assignment, but I jumped at it.

Precisely twenty-three days later, I was at Skopje Airport on a mid-winter afternoon with 2,000 Deutschmarks hidden in a pouch around my waist, looking for Erol, with no idea what would happen next.

At last, my suitcase rumbled along the rubber belt towards me. I dragged it to the exit door where a crowd of short men with black moustaches and leather jackets bayed like a pack of ferocious dogs at the emerging passengers.

'Taxi!'

'Taxi!'

'Lady! You need taxi?'

Ours had been the last flight of the afternoon and perhaps their last chance to make good money today.

Erol stood in the middle of the melee. He was also short and had a black moustache and a leather jacket, but he wasn't shouting, just smiling benignly and holding a sign with my name on it.

Away from the leafless trees and grey concrete buildings of Skopje, the road toiled uphill for half an hour towards the boundary between the independent country of Macedonia and the Serb province of Kosovo, a boundary that had not existed until a few years ago.

Erol didn't speak much English but that didn't stop him from talking. He told me he drove this route to Kosovo's capital, Pristina, almost every day, taking foreigners like me to a place that, until recently, almost no one had wanted to visit. In the few months since the fighting had ended, his taxi business had been booming.

When we got to the border crossing it turned out that, by some amazing coincidence, Erol was related to, or went to school with, lived next door to, or was best friends with almost every uniformed Macedonian official on duty that afternoon. They greeted him and waved us to the head of the line of waiting cars and he offered them cans of soft drink and beer.

Long before we arrived at the border, I knew we must be getting close. Hundreds of trucks lined the narrow winding road waiting for their turn at the customs checkpoint.

'Sometimes they wait here two days, three days, maybe longer.' Erol explained. With the highway from Serbia now closed, almost everything needed in Kosovo arrived along this country backroad.

It was bitterly cold in the mountains in the late afternoon gloom. The heavily armed Macedonian police and NATO soldiers in their thick uniforms looked bored and miserable as they directed traffic in the fog, but inside Erol's Mercedes it was warm and a Macedonian radio station played sunny Caribbean reggae. Young boys with empty wheelbarrows waited beside the road hoping someone would need them to carry their luggage through the checkpoint for a small fee.

Erol drove like a maniac once we were on the Kosovo side of the border and swerved violently to avoid the potholes in the crumbling road. In previous centuries there would have been a good chance of being ambushed by bandits on this narrow, lonely mountain pass. Perhaps not even that long ago. There was little likelihood of that on this day. Military convoys travelled with us all the way. British, Italian, Swedish, Polish and Greek army trucks, tanks, jeeps and buses passed in both directions, and from time to time, a helicopter flew low overhead.

On the other side of the mountains, the flat fields on either side of the road were covered with snow. Feeble winter sun struggled through the clouds.

Clusters of tiny red-roofed houses hid in the mist

surrounded by leafless trees. At first, the farmhouses and villages appeared quaint and old, but up close, I could see that most were brand new. Many were still being built. Almost all were identical, with three stories of cement block walls, concrete balconies, red-tiled roofs and the same timber window and door configuration on each level. They looked as if they'd been built with a Lego set.

Between the dollhouse villages, however, were the remains of other houses—burnt-out shells, sometimes dozens of them together; the homes of people who hadn't yet come back to rebuild, or were not going to.

We were halfway to Pristina, and Erol and I were making stilted small talk when it became clear that he had no information about where to take me when we got there. My instructions had simply been to meet Erol. I'd assumed he would know everything else or would arrive with an envelope of information about the accommodation that had been booked for me and where I was to report for work. I started to worry.

'So who booked the taxi?' I asked.

'A lady in Washington call me on the phone,' he said.

'And how will they pay you?'

'You pay me.'

Now I knew what the supply of cash was for.

My first view of Pristina was a narrow main street lined with old apartment buildings glowing pink in a dusty sunset and a flock of blackbirds swirling noisily overhead. Erol suggested that perhaps I would be staying at the Grand Hotel. It was a reasonable guess.

The Grand turned out to be almost the only hotel in town. Everyone stayed there. Erol parked among all the other vehicles on the footpath in front of the building. It was now almost dark and getting cold, but the street outside the hotel was crowded with people walking briskly in both directions. The shops were open and lit up but there were no streetlights, just the glare of car headlights in the foggy air.

My impression of Pristina at that moment was that the population consisted almost entirely of olive-skinned nineteen-year-old men in black jackets with military haircuts. I saw almost no women and very few older men among the fast-moving crowd.

At first, there was no sign at the hotel reception desk that they were expecting me, but then a scruffy index card with my name scribbled on it turned up. At least someone in Kosovo knew I existed. I paid Erol the 150 Deutschmarks he wanted for the fare and he gave me a receipt written entirely in Cyrillic.

The Grand Hotel had awarded itself five stars but my room would barely meet the standards of a country motel. It had two narrow, rock-hard beds, a new phone with no dial tone, and a new TV with ten channels of static. In the bathroom, water seeped around the base of the toilet and the taps never produced anything hotter than lukewarm. By then I didn't care. I was exhausted.

•————•

THE NEXT MORNING, I contemplated the big questions. Did I really have a job here? And if so, how was I going to find it? Three credit card companies had jointly funded my trip and I was hoping I'd be reimbursed by my new employer before they wanted to be paid.

After a breakfast of tomato, cucumber and feta cheese in the cavernous subterranean dining hall, I sat in my room waiting for someone to come and find me.

Although there'd been a booking in my name there'd

been no message or instructions or contact information. The only phone numbers I had were Mike's office in Washington and the UN switchboard in New York, but the phone in the hotel room didn't work. Neither did my mobile phone and, of course, there was no internet connection.

I asked at the hotel reception desk about making a phone call but they claimed their line also wasn't working. So I sat in my room and waited. No one came.

After a while I moved to the hotel lobby and watched every new arrival closely, hoping it would be someone looking for me. The foyer of the Grand Hotel still retained faint elements of grandeur to justify its name, with green marble walls and rows of low leather armchairs.

That morning though it seemed more like the lobby of a ski lodge in mid-season than a luxury hotel. The milling and waiting groups of guests were dressed in anoraks, polar fleece jackets, jeans, fishing vests and hiking boots as if they were assembling for a day of bushwalking. I felt overdressed in my office suit. Across the lobby, the hotel's café was already busy serving short espressos and the air was dense with cigarette smoke.

After an hour of waiting with no result, I decided it was time to work out a plan B. I asked the smooth man with slicked-down hair behind the reception desk if he knew where the UN office was.

'Why, of course,' he said in fluent English, having just finished chatting to another guest in French, 'It's right behind this hotel.'

From then on, things started to slip into place. I had the names of some of the people I would be working with and the teenage receptionist behind the reinforced glass window at the UN office found them on her list. They would be in the 'government building', she said, back on the main street, four blocks to the left, next to the building with broken windows.

The building with broken windows was easy to find—a modern fifteen storey office block with every pane of glass missing. It had been collateral damage when a NATO bomb had destroyed the main telecommunications exchange next door. The reinforced glass of the entrance door was still standing, but the full-length windows on either side were gone.

At street level, the raked seats of a small theatrette remained intact but the walls around it had disappeared and the empty chairs looked out at the passing pedestrians. Scraps of torn curtain waved in the breeze.

The squat Government Building stood next to it, behind a stunted hedge and guarded by tall, good-looking young men in bright blue anoraks and matching baseball caps.

Another young receptionist behind a glass window made a phone call and, within a few minutes, I was led up a grand staircase to the second floor. The lino-floored corridor was an obstacle course of photocopiers, printers, computer racks and filing cabinets with thick bundles of cables hanging on hooks along either side. Every small office I passed was crammed with young people; three or four of them sitting around each desk.

I'd reached the heart of the chaos and excitement of Kosovo's post-war reconstruction. No one mentioned the fact that I was three hours late for work or asked where I'd been.

•———•

Until 1989, the Government Building, where I was now working, had been the headquarters of Kosovo's autonomous provincial administration. Its large auditorium, these days used for weekly movies for UN staff, was the former meeting chamber of the Kosovo Assembly.

In this part of the former Yugoslav Federation, Albanian speakers are the majority, and most of them are Muslims. During the communist era, they'd had their own local government and the provincial politicians had been fully committed apparatchiks of the Yugoslav bureaucracy. They'd spoken fluent Serbian, participated in national congresses and received generous grants from the central government for local development. They'd enjoyed almost the same powers as leaders in other republics of the Federation, including equal rights to, at times, misappropriate public funds or mismanage state-owned industries.

The autonomous government hadn't survived long after Slobodan Milošević became President of Serbia. The region was starved of government funds and Kosovo sank into poverty and a decade of conflict. The city of Pristina started falling apart.

By the time I arrived in early 2000, the roads were little more than joined together pot-holes and the public buildings were surrounded by weeds and discarded plastic bags. Water leaked into the street from broken sewerage pipes, and any open space had become a dumping ground for garbage.

At first, I'd assumed, like most people, that the devastation I saw around me was the result of NATO bombs. In fact, the war had done little damage to the city. What we found in Pristina after the conflict is what happens to a town when there's no money and no government, when roads are not repaired and rubbish is not collected, and desperate people steal manhole covers and electricity cables to sell for scrap.

Now, the war was over and the UN was in charge. Pristina had been transformed from a provincial backwater to the bustling capital city of a new country, and its tiny population had been enlarged by the arrival of several thousand foreigners.

The UN mission, officially known as 'UNMIK', brought in hundreds of staff and contractors. Foreign governments set up offices to coordinate their aid programs and the Red Cross and other humanitarian organisations arrived with fleets of vehicles and warehouses full of supplies. Entrepreneurs and adventurers flooded in to take advantage of the money to be made from imports, logistics and construction contracts.

The British, American, French, German and Italian soldiers who made up the 'Kosovo Force', KFOR, set up checkpoints and guard posts, and the international Civilian Police patrolled the streets in red wagons.

Between them, the foreigners took over every available office building and rented most of the vacant houses and apartments. Each UN member nation provided staff to the mission, so the foreigners represented every possible race and nationality. For many Kosovars, it was the first time they'd ever seen someone from Africa or Asia. They soon became commonplace.

●——————●

DURING THE NEXT two months, the main street of Pristina, between the Grand Hotel and the Government Building, became the centre of my world.

Every morning, after another breakfast of salad and cheese and thick black coffee in the unheated Grand Hotel restaurant, I walked the few blocks to our office, dodging puddles of mud, cars parked indiscriminately on the footpath, and sidewalk stalls selling sunglasses and flick knives. Large city buses, donated by foreign governments wooshed past, some still advertising their final destinations in their city of origin, apparently heading for Hauptbahnhof and Lyon Central.

It was the middle of winter and damp and cold. The air smelt like a gas leak. The six chimneys of the power station on the outskirts of town belched grey smoke, which drifted overhead, spreading ash and the smell of burning lignite, yet most of the time there was no electricity and, at night, the streets were dark.

In the 1970s, the Yugoslav government had poured money into the region to deal with rumblings of Albanian dissent and almost every major building, like the Grand Hotel, had been built during this time. The result was a town of brutalist concrete constructions and high-rise public housing.

The remains of the old Ottoman town of narrow cobbled lanes, stone mosques and courtyard gardens could still be found at one end of the main street, but most of the population lived in a huge housing complex at the other end of town—another legacy of the 1970s building boom.

The town planner's vision for this area had included underground shopping arcades, pedestrian plazas, grand stairways and green parks. Twenty years later, the underground passages were flooded and filled with rubbish, the pedestrian plazas were barren and windswept, the grand stairways went nowhere, and the lifts in the tall apartment blocks didn't work.

◆━━━◆

THE WORK I was to do in Pristina turned out to be not all that different from what I'd been doing before, I was just doing it in unusual surroundings. Steve, the fresh-faced young Canadian I was to report to, tried to explain it to me on my first day.

The peace agreement that had ended the conflict with

Yugoslavia had made the UN responsible for everything in Kosovo, from running the hospitals and getting kids to school to collecting the garbage and making sure the sewer system worked; all the routine things that governments do that we take for granted until they're not there.

I was part of a small team of experts, mostly former government officials from the US, whose job was to work out exactly what needed to be done, and how it would all be paid for. Millions of Deutschmarks had been promised to help Kosovo rebuild after the conflict, but little of it had yet been spent.

'What we're doing is a bit like a bridal registry,' Steve explained. 'We're making a shopping list of reconstruction projects that aid donors might like to spend their money on.'

Through the fog of jetlag and culture shock, a lot of this didn't make much sense to me at the time and only gradually became clearer over the next few days as I got to know my new colleagues.

Each of us had an area of expertise to contribute. There was a health expert, a transport engineer and an agriculture specialist.

'I see you've done some work on telecommunications policy,' Steve noted as he looked into the detail of my resume. 'Good. You can work on the telecommunications sector and the post office.'

I was also given a random selection of other topics to work on including mine clearance and cultural development, about which I knew very little. It seemed a casual way to organise things compared to the well-regulated bureaucracy I was used to, but I soon learned it was normal in this type of environment.

The situation within the UN bureaucracy seemed to be even more haphazard. While UNMIK was supposed to be creating a stable government and setting up a professional administration for Kosovo, the mission itself was struggling with a diverse hodgepodge of staff with no common philosophy, ideology or policy direction, a shortage of funds, and an archaic, exceedingly bureaucratic system of administration.

In each UNMIK department, staff from different countries, with different languages, worked with unclear terms of reference, and many seemed to have almost no relevant experience. The person managing electricity, water and sewerage, for example, was a social worker from a local council in Britain.

When we started collecting information on what needed to be done and how much it would cost, we found that many UN staff hadn't yet had a chance to work this out. They'd been too busy dealing with immediate, urgent problems, like the mounting piles of garbage and the almost total lack of electricity.

Amid this chaos, our little team soon became a tight-knit and rather smug group of experts. Every lunchtime, we were regulars at the snack bar across the road for more cucumber salad and feta cheese where we compared notes on the different UN offices we had met with that day.

Almost every night we ate together at one of the many restaurants that had sprung up to serve the well-paid foreigners. There were dozens to choose from, but apparently, only one menu—the same selection of pasta, pizza and schnitzel, washed down with freshly bottled wine from Kosovo's vineyards.

After dinner, I would stagger back to my room at the Grand Hotel, again dodging puddles and parked cars, but now in the dark. The city's power supply was on a rotating schedule, intentional 'load shedding' to ration the small amount of electricity produced by the derelict power station.

Despite this, the street was always lively and crowded. Street stalls selling pirated cassette tapes blasted loud samples of their music into the street, traditional wailing Albanian songs competing with modern techno-dance music.

The 'special representative' of the Secretary-General of the United Nations at that time was Bernard Kouchner, famous for being one of the founders of *Médecins Sans Frontières* and subsequently a minister in the French government. In Europe, he was a celebrity, but I'd never heard of him.

His office was on the floor below ours, and the landing outside was always full of people waiting for an audience. His security detail stood by the door, gripping their semi-automatic rifles.

Kouchner used the grand main staircase in the Government Building for his press conferences. He would stand on the stairs, a bright blue scarf wrapped stylishly around his neck in a very French manner, his head thrown back so that his voice carried over the crowd. With his full head of brown hair and a perpetual suntan, he looked nothing like his sixty years. Journalists and cameramen circled around him, all microphones and cameras pointing up in his direction, like iron filings around a magnet.

Kouchner was clearly popular with the Albanians in Kosovo who saw him somehow as their saviour. Along with Bill Clinton, Madeleine Albright and NATO, he'd been responsible, in their eyes, for driving out the hated Serb authorities and returning the refugees to their homes. He'd also restored many Albanians to the jobs and influence they'd enjoyed a decade ago before the Serb government had sacked them. In his travels around the country, he was always photographed surrounded by admiring crowds and happy children.

He was clearly good at negotiation and political deal-making. Some people I worked with, however, complained that he didn't pay enough attention to issues they thought were important—the nuts and bolts of government administration. In our private team meetings they dubbed him 'butterfly brain', or BB for short. Eventually though, they admitted that he could focus on these issues when he needed to.

Kouchner had a lot of things on his plate. After ten years of discrimination and abuse under Serbian rule, some Albanians were looking for revenge and the Serbs who still lived in Kosovo were the best available targets.

NATO peacekeepers who'd thought they were in Kosovo to protect Albanians from Serbs soon found themselves protecting Serbs from Albanians. Several Serbs were killed or assaulted every day during the first months of the international mission. Others were evicted from their houses and apartments so that Albanian families could move in. The violence soon convinced most Serbs who had thought of staying to sell up and leave.

The rest of the time the peacekeepers protected Albanians from other Albanians. When the conflict ended, at least two political groups claimed to be the legitimate government and had set up ministries and departments and started charging licence fees and collecting taxes.

The parallel government established by Ibrahim Rugova during the previous decade continued to operate and Rugova's political organisation, the Democratic League of Kosovo, the LDK, expected to assume power in an independent Kosovo. But the more militant supporters of the Kosovo Liberation Army, the KLA, claimed they were the ones who had defeated the Serbs and therefore deserved the spoils of victory in the new Kosovo. They quickly took charge of government facilities and local positions of authority.

It took many months for the UN to persuade these political groups to disband their alternative governments and join the new UN-led administration. Their leaders were appointed to senior positions, supposedly sharing responsibility with UN administrators.

Former KLA military leaders such as Hashim Thaci and Ramush Haradinaj now wore smart suits instead of uniforms and formed legitimate political parties. Some of their followers, however, thought the old methods of intimidation and violence would still work. Many of Rugova's LDK supporters seemed to think the same.

———

I BEGAN MY research into Kosovo's telecommunications straight away, but it took several meetings with the French post office executive and the Spanish engineer who'd been appointed by the UN to manage the Department of Telecommunications before I appreciated the depths of the problems they were facing.

Appropriately, their office looked out over the concrete rubble of what used to be the main telephone exchange, before NATO bombed it. As a result, only a few phone lines in the country worked. The UN had a car park full of satellite dishes behind its main building so we could easily phone New York, but we couldn't contact anyone in Kosovo.

Even before the conflict, Kosovo's phone system had been outdated, with equipment that was obsolete before most of the foreign technicians had started their training.

As a quick solution to the communications problem, the UN set up a new mobile phone network which had just started operating. Some Kosovars thought it was more than just a coincidence that the new network was installed by Alcatel, a

French company, at a time when both the head of UNMIK and the head of the Department of Telecommunications were French. They assumed there must be something dodgy about the deal.

The new mobile phone system operated only with prepaid accounts and it was almost certainly making lots of money which could perhaps be used to fund our list of reconstruction projects. The UN staff in the telecommunications department, however, seemed reluctant to tell me how much.

Kosovo's Post and Telecommunications company, PTK, like all Kosovo's government entities, had been effectively abolished in 1989 when it was merged with its Serbian equivalent. The Albanian staff had been dismissed and the whole operation was run from Belgrade for the next ten years.

As soon as the Yugoslav army left, however, thousands of former PTK managers, telephone technicians and post office clerks came straight back to their old offices and their old jobs and took up where they'd left off. The legal status of this resurrected organisation was unclear and the UN lawyers in New York were still trying to work it out.

In the meantime, the staff of PTK had started to pay themselves generous salaries, but were having difficulty getting their remaining customers to pay their outstanding phone bills due to the chaotic state of the billing records and the Kosovars' traditional reluctance to cooperate with any government instrumentality. One day the enterprise would need to be rationalised, downsized and commercialised, but that would have to wait a while.

FROM THE WINDOW of my room at the Grand Hotel,

I had a view of the building now occupied by the recently established Banking and Payments Authority of Kosovo. Every morning at 6.30 elderly people and women with small children gathered on the paved plaza at the back entrance to the building, waiting to collect the small social welfare allowance paid to the most vulnerable. They kept arriving until there were perhaps a hundred people milling around.

The temperature outside was below freezing and it would be several hours before the bank opened to let them claim their money. It was as if they were afraid the cash would run out before they got their share. From their previous experience of banks in this part of the world that wouldn't be an unreasonable expectation.

In fact, they were probably right to be worried—the UN was desperately short of hard cash. Although international donors had committed millions in contributions for the reconstruction effort, the money was simply accumulating in a bank account in Frankfurt. The problem was getting it into Kosovo in the form of real money that could be spent.

Similarly, my colleagues and I were receiving our salaries on a regular basis, paid into our bank accounts at home, but in the absence of any local banks it was impossible to access any of it; another reason I'd been told to bring lots of cash with me in small notes.

The morning queue outside the Banking and Payments Authority was almost the only place I saw old people in Pristina. I was getting used to the idea that almost everyone was young. It was no longer necessary to comment on the fresh-faced security guards, the teenage cleaners, the eighteen-year-old interpreters, or the twenty-something entrepreneurs running successful restaurants.

The average age in Kosovo at the time was believed to be about twenty-five. People have large families and life expectancy is low. The population in older age groups declines rapidly as emigration, hard work and poor health trim the numbers. Living to ninety gets your photo in the paper.

In Pristina, the average age must be even lower. Young people from rural towns and villages come to the city in thousands to find jobs or to study. The place sometimes felt like a university campus in the first weeks of term, the streets teeming with exuberant teenagers.

I found the young Kosovars very attractive. Some of the tall UN security guards with their light blue caps and twinkling eyes and the friendly English-speaking interpreters and secretaries in the office could have been models or actors. But perhaps the attractiveness I saw was just the inner beauty that comes from having a secure, well-paid job when everyone else was unemployed.

Unfortunately, the attractiveness of youth was short-lived. Anyone who'd passed the age of thirty-five looked old and worn out. The men were weather-beaten and gnarled as if they'd spent a lifetime ploughing fields or laying concrete, which they probably had. Their faces were furrowed and their expressions suspicious and insolent. They passed their days sitting in cafés and smoking and from their steely expressions and mumbled conversations, I could easily believe they were negotiating a narcotics deal or plotting an assassination.

The older women, too, were lined and worn for their age, with bad teeth and dry hair. The harshness of life in a poor country, the stress of caring for large families, a poor diet and the uncertainty in their lives during the past decades showed in every face.

OUR WORK ON the reconstruction strategy was part of a larger project funded by the US Agency for International Development as its contribution to the UN Mission in Kosovo. Every Friday morning, the whole project team met in the board room on the top floor of the Government Building to review progress, taking turns to recount the important events of the week.

The project had achieved a lot in the past few months. We'd set up a new customs service, a new tax system and a government treasury, devised an annual budget for the Kosovo administration and established a new central bank. Dozens of pieces of legislation had been drawn up and submitted to the UN for approval.

One group of experts had also been working out how to sell off or lease out hundreds of barely functioning socialist-era government-owned businesses ranging from cement plants to jewellery manufacturers.

The only real problem they seemed to have, judging by the comments at our weekly review meetings, was the UN itself. Important decisions about customs duties or tax rates were held up at UN headquarters in New York, legislation to regulate government finances sat indefinitely on the desks of senior UNMIK bureaucrats, and the constantly rotating UN staff and their extended holidays frustrated the short deadlines faced by consultants.

It seemed as if the whole exercise would run much better if the UN staff just did what the consultants told them to. I imagined, however, that similar meetings of UN staff would produce a parallel list of complaints about pushy consultants and their unrealistic expectations.

In late March, my team working on the reconstruction plan was summoned to a meeting with US officials at the USAID office to report on what we were doing with their money.

It had been raining all day and the power was off when our driver took the steep road up to the USAID building late in the afternoon. Their office had a generator, of course, but we were kept waiting in a cold, Spartan meeting room for an hour.

Paul, the USAID official responsible for our work, was very pale and very overweight. Like a cliché American, he drank can after can of Coca-Cola throughout the meeting, tossing the empties into the overflowing wastebasket in the corner.

The interrogation began with Dan, the health expert, who talked at length about hospital refurbishment, nurse retraining and purchasing pharmaceutical supplies for the government health system.

Paul's questions soon revealed his ideological leanings. 'What about user payment for medical care?' he asked. 'What about supporting private doctors?' 'What about privatising the hospitals?'

Dan struggled to provide diplomatic answers to deflect these enquiries. It seemed to me that these ideas were a long way from the immediate needs of post-war Kosovo, and certainly a long way from the political inclinations of either the Kosovars or most of the people who worked for the UN.

We moved on to talk about public utilities, then agriculture, and the same sort of questions were raised about the privatisation of government facilities, charging users for government services and other typical free market, 'neo-liberal' reforms. During the discussion on agriculture, Paul railed against a proposed program to provide free fertilizer to farmers to ensure there was enough food from the next harvest.

'We can't subsidise agriculture', he said emphatically.

There was silence in the room for a few seconds. He had apparently forgotten about the huge payments handed out by the US government to its own farmers.

It was eventually Jim, one of the Americans, who was brave enough to respond.

'So' he said, in his slow Southern drawl, 'it's OK to subsidise farmers in the US, but not in Kosovo?'

We quickly moved to the next topic.

I provided my information about the state of telephone services and infrastructure and Paul started talking about competition in the telecommunications market. He asked me to write a report for him on options for opening Kosovo's telecommunications to foreign investment. This wasn't part of my official job description, but I wrote it anyway, setting out the situation facing potential investors in the current environment.

A few weeks later an 'economic officer' from the US Office in Pristina came to talk to me about telecommunications. In my naivety, I'd thought the job of the economic officer was to help Kosovo develop its economy. He seemed impressed at my knowledge of the state of telecommunications in Kosovo and the related legal questions about ownership and licences, but I soon realised his real interest was in how US firms could make money in this market.

The discussion with USAID didn't finish until late at night. Our driver had given up waiting and gone home so we walked down the hill towards the centre of town.

The rain had stopped and left the air for once clear of coal dust. The power was back on and the city lights sparkled in the little valley below, pretty and comforting, like any normal town at night.

In April, Bernard Kouchner held another impromptu press conference on the staircase to announce that Kosovo Serbs had agreed to join the UNMIK administration. This appeared to be a big step forward in resolving relations between the two main ethnic groups in the territory.

That afternoon, the Government Building was swarming with UN security officials and armed soldiers while the Serb representatives attended their first Kosovo Transition Council meeting in the same top floor conference room we used for our project meetings.

A few nights later I was jolted awake by a loud noise somewhere nearby. I sat up in bed in the dark in my room in the Grand Hotel. It was close to midnight and everything seemed quiet. It didn't occur to me to be frightened.

I went to the window and peered around the curtain into the street. It all looked normal except for a barely discernible cloud of smoke drifting above the block of apartments across the road. But then sirens started wailing and soon there were police vans, military vehicles, ambulances with flashing blue lights and a growing crowd blocking the street. People in the apartments opposite looked down on the confusion from their balconies.

A British soldier with a loud voice announced, in polite, clearly articulated English, 'Ladies and Gentlemen. Please… move… back… down the street. Thank you.' The crowd understood the message even though most of them probably didn't understand the words and they started to shuffle away. The people on the balconies disappeared.

After straining my neck for more than an hour watching the flashing lights and trying to work out what was going on, there was nothing to do but to go back to bed.

It wasn't until the next day that I found out, from international news reports on the internet, that what had woken me had been a rocket grenade, fired from the footpath below my window, aimed at the home of one of the new Serb members of the Kosovo Transition Council.

The rocket, designed for piercing metal, had hit the wall of the apartment building and done little damage. No one was seriously hurt. From my window that afternoon, I could see a few chips in the concrete and scorch marks—nothing more.

My colleagues were remarkably uninterested in my first-hand account of the incident.

The experience made me realise how little I really knew about what was going on in Kosovo. I was living in the middle of Pristina, working in the centre of the government, right above Kouchner's office, but it was surprisingly hard to get news about anything that happened unless it was in a sanitised UNMIK press release.

So far I'd actually got to know very few Kosovars. Everyone I dealt with in the UN administration was another foreigner. Kosovars passed us in the street, worked in our office as translators and waited on us at restaurants, but apart from that I had little to do with them and knew almost nothing about them.

I hadn't realised, for example, that there were any Serbs still living in Pristina. The city seemed so mono-ethnically Albanian. Any evidence of the Serbian language in street signs had been removed or painted over. Even pork dishes had been crossed out on restaurant menus, although the Albanian Kosovars didn't appear to be particularly devout Muslims in any other respect. The Serb family from the building across the road had now been evacuated by the UN.

A few weeks later our team finally finished its report and I emailed it off to someone in Brussels. It was full of ambitious plans—new buildings, new roads, a better electricity supply, new phone lines, and new houses, sports centres, libraries and museums. Everything from the essential to the trivial. Every public building, every road and dam, every electricity line and telephone switch had been recorded, described and the cost of rehabilitating it estimated.

With our work done, our team were all leaving. I still had my job at home and they were expecting me back the following week.

I retrieved my supply of cash from the office safe and handed it to the cashier at the Grand Hotel to pay for my entire accommodation bill. This was one business that was in no danger of having a cash flow problem. With 360 rooms fully occupied at 150 Deutschmarks a night and payment in cash only it was more likely they had a cash storage problem.

Kosovo seemed a different place the day I left from what it had been when I'd arrived. It wasn't just that it was morning and sunny instead of late afternoon and grey and the countryside was now spring green.

The difference wasn't Kosovo, it was me. Two months earlier, everything had been strange and unknown and slightly threatening. Now in the light of day and the warmth of the spring sunshine, Pristina was a familiar, comfortable place.

I shared Erol's taxi to Skopje airport with colleagues who'd now become friends. Erol drove as fast and furiously as before and still dodged potholes, but we passed gangs of workers filling them with gravel and asphalt.

Skopje Airport was no longer the cold, empty building I remembered from February. That Saturday it was crowded with Macedonians meeting and farewelling relatives, the men still in black leather jackets, the young women with thick black eyeliner and bleached blonde hair towering over them in stiletto heels.

Vienna, on a Sunday morning, felt unnaturally clean and perfect and the next day, back in Canberra, the huge open spaces and vivid winter green grass seemed strange and alien.

GLOBAL VILLAGE
Kosovo, October 2000

In April 2000 I left Kosovo, apparently for good. I went back to work in my air-conditioned office cubicle and my old life in Canberra resumed. I was full of stories about my travels but I soon learned to restrain myself when I felt the urge to start another sentence with 'When I was in Kosovo…'

Then I received another email from Mike in Washington. The company was still looking for staff. Would I be interested in going back? Of course I was interested, but getting more time off work would be out of the question. I'd have to resign.

Some of my friends were horrified I would even consider giving up a nice, secure government job. I handed in my resignation, put all my things into storage, and by early October 2000 was on my way back to Kosovo.

While I was in the air, halfway between Sydney and Pristina, Yugoslav President Slobodan Milošević, the man who'd caused so much conflict and misery in the Balkans, was overthrown by the people of Serbia. Fed up with yet another manipulated election result, crowds of voters stormed the parliament building in Belgrade.

At first, however, it wasn't clear whether Milošević still had enough support from the police or the army to hang on. In Vienna at five am I was able to gather from the front page of *Le Monde* that Russia had given its support to opposition leader Vojislav Koštunica.

By the time I reached Kosovo, later that day, Koštunica was about to be sworn in as President of Yugoslavia. And just like that, a decade of evil came to an end.

Whether this would make any difference to Kosovo,

however, wasn't clear. Some Albanian Kosovars may have preferred it if Milošević was still in power. His bad reputation gave them the moral high ground and a strong case for not returning to Serb sovereignty.

It soon became clear, however, that the Serbian leaders who followed Milošević, and the Serbian public, were no more sympathetic to Kosovo than the previous regime had been. Non-cooperation between Serbia and the UN mission generally continued to be the order of the day.

The new political environment to the north did, however, mean that Serbia also became an object of interest to international organisations. The EU quickly set up an office there and many of the people who'd been working in Kosovo began spending at least part of their time in Belgrade. When they came back to Pristina, they gave glowing reports of the comfortable living conditions with reliable electricity and paved streets.

MY SECOND JOURNEY to Kosovo did not involve Skopje or Erol. The small military airport outside Pristina had been opened for commercial flights so international airlines now flew directly from other parts of Europe.

The crush of eager olive-skinned taxi drivers outside the arrivals area was just as aggressive as in Skopje, but this time the driver waiting to meet me with my name on a piece of card was called Yacob.

It was autumn but the weather was still hot. Along the road into town, the fields that had been grey when I'd arrived in February and green when I left in April were now yellow and dry.

I was much better prepared this time. I'd organised to stay at the Park Hotel, the smallest of the four available hotels in

Pristina. Before the foreigners arrived, it had apparently been a brothel, but there was more money in running a legitimate business now.

Reuters Television staff occupied several of the twelve rooms and their armour-plated broadcast vans were parked in the street outside. Each evening I would find out from their cameraman what the big story had been that day before I watched it on the television in the communal lounge.

Six months earlier the park across the road which gave the Park Hotel its name had been a rubbish tip, but there'd been a 'clean up Pristina' campaign, the rubbish had been removed and grass had started to grow. The hotel had set up a pleasant outdoor restaurant beneath the trees. The waiters dealt with the birds overhead by throwing firecrackers into the branches now and then.

Pristina was much more enjoyable at this time of year. The days were long, there were more people about, the streets were full of outdoor cafés and the atmosphere was relaxed. Most of the friends I'd made before were still around and a lot of the things I'd found difficult when I was there last time—the dirt and the rubbish, the pot-holed roads, the dust and the traffic chaos—now just seemed normal.

I was still working for the USAID project, compiling a new, improved and expanded report on what needed to be done to make Kosovo into a well-functioning, democratic country.

The European Union had stepped up its contribution to Kosovo since I'd left, bringing a dramatic change in the age profile of the international staff working on this exercise. Most of the team now seemed to be young graduates and junior EU officials.

Jordi, for example, was from Barcelona and refused to call himself Spanish, insisting he was Catalan. He was fluent in several European languages. Unfortunately, English didn't seem to be one of them. Another of the young staffers, had an Italian father and American mother who'd raised him in Morocco and sent him to school in France. His English was excellent.

The EU had recruited half a dozen local Albanian staff to work with us, but they didn't speak much English, and we didn't speak any Albanian, so a team of interpreters was also employed to translate every letter and report and provide an Albanian commentary for every meeting.

I had no idea what we were supposed to do with the Kosovar employees and I felt a bit sorry for them. They were given many lectures about what we were doing, but there were few practical tasks to keep them busy.

Most of our day seemed to be taken up with long, complex discussions about policy directions and funding priorities, sometimes arguing at length over the exact wording, in English, of a sentence in a policy statement. I doubted it made any sense at all to the young and inexperienced local staff.

Not surprisingly, most of the time they looked either bored or worried and spent their days sending emails and playing solitaire on the computers. It was initially a surprise to me that they all had Hotmail addresses, and that there were websites written in Albanian.

•———•

I'D COMMITTED MYSELF to living in Pristina for at least the next twelve months and decided I couldn't stay in a hotel for the whole year. USAID would provide up to $900 a month to reimburse rent costs for its consultants. Consequently, the standard rent for a furnished apartment in the city had shot up to $900 a month regardless of its size or condition.

Decent apartments were in short supply. Some families had hastily vacated their homes to capitalise on the rental boom. In a few cases, it was clear from the books in the bookcases and the Orthodox icons on the walls that the previous owners had been Serbs who'd left in a hurry.

I found a cosy one-bedroom flat on the third floor of an older apartment block, with sunlight on both sides and a tiny balcony looking out over a car park. The rent was within my budget, the owner spoke reasonable English, and his wife came and cleaned every Saturday. It would do.

The owner, Mark, his wife, Vera, and their thirteen-year-old son were still living there when I inspected it and were still there when I took the contract for them to sign a few days later. It was a standard document drawn up by the project which gave the tenant unlimited rights to pull out of the agreement at any time for any reason without notice and without penalty.

I was puzzled that there was no sign that the family were packing to move, even though I was due to take possession a few days later. When I moved in I understood. They hadn't taken their things with them. Some space had been made in the wardrobe and a few drawers were empty in the dressing table, but generally, everything was still exactly where it had been when I first saw the place. Their winter coats and shoes were in the cupboards and photographs of long-dead relatives were still hanging on the wall above the bed.

This family were from Kosovo's small Catholic community and the wall decorations included a crucifix and a garish three-dimensional picture of Jesus which turned into a lurid image of a bleeding heart when you looked at it on an angle. A long sofa that unfolded into a bed filled the small living room. This answered the question of where the teenage son had slept in this tiny flat.

Both Mark and Vera appeared to be quite old, rather mature to have a child of that age. Mark explained that during fourteen years of marriage, he and Vera had failed to produce children—a tragedy in a traditional place like this—but then they were blessed with a son. This sounded a little too miraculous for me and I surmised that the son was in fact adopted. He was certainly over-indulged and over-fed, a roly-poly boy who clung to his mother like a toddler.

Mark worked for the Mother Teresa Society, a local Catholic charity. It's not widely known that Mother Teresa, renowned for her charity work in India, was Albanian. She was born under Ottoman rule before the first world war in what is now Macedonia. Albanians make much of the connection, even though very few are actually Catholics.

Before the trouble started, Mark told me, he'd had a senior job in the press office of the Kosovo government, working in the very same Government Building where I still spent much of my time. They'd moved into this flat when they were married, in the days when accommodation had been distributed by the state. 'It was small', he said, 'but we were only two people. It was enough for us.'

I worried about where they were living while I was occupying their home and imagined them suffering in a distant relative's cramped attic. But a few weeks after I'd moved in, they invited me to visit them in their new house.

For the past eight years, they'd been slowly constructing a large brick and concrete home on a hillside not far from town. They'd bought the land and then, bit by bit, as they found the money, laid the foundations, built the walls, and finally, many years later, erected the roof. Meanwhile, the fruit trees and vegetable garden had been flourishing and the family had used the half-finished house for summer outings.

It had a good view of Pristina, so good that Serb snipers

had picked off unlucky Albanians from their second-floor balcony at the height of the conflict, according to their neighbours. At the time, Mark and his family had been driving to the Macedonian border, fleeing the Serb military in Pristina. The Macedonian authorities had let them cross into the refugee camp, but only after tearing up their passports.

Now, with some help from my advance rent payments, they'd been able to make the house habitable with windows and doors, and take up residence.

It seemed that most of the Albanian families living in socialist era apartments in Pristina also aspired to own a house on a block of land. There'd been an explosion of building activity since the UN had arrived. Brick and tile houses popped up like red-capped mushrooms on the hills around the city, on land that had previously been productive farms.

There was a building boom underway in central Pristina also. Every ground floor apartment with a street frontage had knocked out its front wall and replaced it with a shop window. Coffee bars, restaurants, boutiques and mini-markets now operated in what had been family lounge rooms.

Most apartment buildings had raised their roofs to create a new floor of apartments under a Cape Cod roofline. And in every suburb, old single-storey cottages were being demolished to make way for multi-storey mansions or shopping complexes, almost all without planning approval.

Many new houses imposed themselves aggressively on the small homes around them, but within months they, in turn, found the views from their windows blocked by the next new development.

The UN administration had put a local architect, Rexhep Luci, in charge of town planning and supported his attempts to enforce orderly development. In late 2000, he signed orders for the demolition of the most egregious illegal constructions and named the buildings that would go. One, for example, was being constructed on public land in a popular park.

A few days later he was dead—shot in the chest at close range with a semi-automatic. The police didn't seem to be able to identify the perpetrator. Shortly afterwards, however, KFOR secured all the construction sites he'd identified and guarded the workers while the buildings were demolished.

With unusual speed, UNMIK pushed a new city planning regulation through its convoluted legal system and Kouchner signed it with a fanfare of publicity, naming it in honour of Rexhep Luci. The previous frantic building activity in the centre of town came to a temporary halt, and a number of large, half-finished buildings stood empty and surrounded by barbed wire for a considerable time.

Incidents of criminal violence such as this were quite common in Pristina, but for foreigners, the city was very safe, in spite of the hazard pay most UN staff and consultants were entitled to. Both the Albanians and the Serbs seemed happy to have us there—the Albanians because they saw us as liberators and the Serbs because we were protecting them from the Albanians.

And Pristina was fun. It was full of people away from home and ready to party, suddenly free of spouses, children, parents, pets, gardens and other obligations, and with plenty of money. Our high salaries and generous allowances had created an economic boom for local restaurants and bars.

Within a few weeks, it seemed I'd met more people and made more new friends than I had since I left school. Everyone lived and worked within a few blocks in the centre of town between the various UN office buildings, an area small enough to walk around in one lunch hour.

It was impossible to go far without meeting someone familiar. In the corridors of the Government Building or the meeting rooms of the European Agency for Reconstruction or in the lunchtime cafés or the aisles of the supermarket, there was always someone to nod to, to stop and chat with, or to sit down and have coffee with.

There was a busy program of dinners at restaurants, happy hours on the top floor of the OSCE building, UN film nights in the Government Building auditorium, farewell parties for the constantly rotating population of short term advisers, and always copious amounts of Turkish beer at the popular expat bars on Friday nights.

If you were lucky enough to know someone with access to one of the big white UN vehicles there were also weekend excursions into the lush Kosovo countryside or sometimes trips across the border into Macedonia or, a few hours further on, to Greece.

There was always someone looking for company for lunch, for a drink or for dinner. Having always complained that my hometown was too small, I now found I was blissfully happy in a community the size of a country village.

In reality, of course, Pristina was not a village. It was a city and its real population was several hundred thousand Albanian Kosovars. But as far as most of the citizens of the international village were concerned, the Kosovars lived in a parallel universe, with their own social activities and networks, and their complex and sometimes dangerous politics, almost completely separate from ours.

A FEW MONTHS into my new contract I was re-assigned from the team working on reconstruction planning. My new task was monitoring the budgets of Kosovo's government-owned utilities. These included the telephone company that I was already familiar with, the electricity company, known as

KEK, and various irrigation companies, municipal water enterprises, district heating systems, a railway, an airport and some bus lines.

Most of these monopoly suppliers of public services, although designated as enterprises, received large amounts of public funding from the budget. The ones that didn't get money were presumably making a profit and should perhaps have been contributing to the budget, but unlike government-owned businesses in most other countries, they didn't have to provide financial statements to anyone so we didn't know.

The workers who'd come back to take possession of their jobs after ten years of exclusion from the workforce were mostly old-school socialists and it appears that the companies continued to be run by the workers largely for the benefit of the workers, rather than to provide services to their customers.

Staff in my local post office, for example, looked quite put out when I went there to buy a SIM card for the government-run mobile network. I was kept waiting at the counter while the female staff continued sitting at their desks, sipping coffee. The desks were empty apart from the coffee cups and their handbags.

Eventually, someone noticed my presence and managed to provide what I was after. Perhaps they were just surprised that someone would actually consider buying a SIM card from the official source when they were readily available on the black market from touts on every street corner at only a small markup. The post office was more efficient at selling stamps, but very few of the letters I posted ever arrived.

In the new capitalist Kosovo envisaged by international aid donors it would be necessary for organisations like these to shed staff, cut spending, collect revenue and provide better services. Over the next six months, I didn't make much progress in this direction, but I did compile some information on how many staff they had, how much revenue they earned and how much they spent. This was not as simple as it sounds, as accounting skills as we know them proved to be in short supply.

My new role meant I now worked at the other end of town, in the building occupied by the Central Fiscal Authority—a masterpiece of brutalist concrete at the intersection of Mother Teresa Street and Lenin Street that used to be a bank.

From my office window, I looked out over the busy intersection generally known as Suicide Junction and the traffic chaos that ensued every time the power went off and the recently installed traffic lights stopped working. Immediately, there was total gridlock. Drivers honked horns and swore at each other, giving way to no one. From their position at ground level, they couldn't see how truly hopeless the situation was. Eventually, the police arrived to untangle the mess.

Until recently, the international UNMIK 'Civ Pol' had been the only police service in Pristina, consisting of officers seconded from places as diverse as Pakistan, Nigeria, Italy, the US and other countries with equally high standards of policing. But the UN Police School, luckily run mainly by the British and Norwegian police, had created a new Kosovo Police Service and it was starting to make its presence felt around town.

When I had first seen the local police at work, nervously checking car registrations in Mother Teresa Street, there was always a team of armed and camouflaged British soldiers hiding discreetly behind trees, watching for any trouble. Now, there were dozens of Kosovo police on patrol and they didn't seem to need military backup. They looked professional in smart blue uniforms, driving around in little white Škodas painted with the emergency phone number to call to report incidents, if you could find a phone that worked.

About eighteen percent of the recruits were women; not a

bad number in a place like this. Some of them were tiny but full of confidence and authority.

The police recruits did their practical training in traffic control at Suicide Junction, taking turns to blow their whistles and make hand signals. UNMIK had enacted a new set of official traffic rules, replacing the Serb traffic ordinances which everyone seemed to think they were entitled to ignore.

Now the police were enforcing them. In just one day in the first week, they gave out 4,000 tickets and confiscated 400 unregistered cars.

Some people suggested that there might have been more important things for the police to do than giving out traffic tickets, but by doing it in the middle of town, where everyone could see them, they demonstrated that they were operating and might be prepared to enforce other laws also.

•———•

LIVING IN PRISTINA it was easy to forget that we were still, officially, in Serbia and that only a few months before, Serbs had controlled everything. But Serbian Kosovo was not far away, in the town of Gračanica, just a fifteen-minute drive from the city.

Historically, Gračanica, with its fourteenth-century monastery, had been the heartland of the Serbian Orthodox church. Now it was one of the larger Serb enclaves in UN-controlled Kosovo, a town of about 10,000 people.

A group of us drove out there on a Sunday. A Swedish army checkpoint inspected every vehicle entering the town. The small cottages spread out along the main road were surrounded by green gardens and fruit trees behind low fences, completely unlike the large, fortified, concrete-paved compounds built by Albanian families in Pristina.

Every house had a newly ploughed vegetable garden and pigs and chickens roaming the yard. There were also ancient stone barns, dilapidated wooden sheds and haystacks.

We walked around the town followed by large numbers of children. A few of the boys who tagged along behind us were strangely dark-skinned and it eventually dawned on me that that they were Roma who'd been driven from Kosovo's towns along with the Serbs.

We had lunch at the only restaurant in town, patriotically named '1389' after the battle of Kosovo Polje, which the Serbs had fought against the Turks in that year, just outside Pristina. They lost, but it is remembered as one of the most important events in Serb history.

The waiter brought huge platters of pork, ham, beef and chicken; a huge amount of food, except for the two vegetarians, who were left with cabbage salad. The wine was sweet Muscat from Germany, the beer was from Serbia, and the proprietor brought out his homemade plum brandy at the end of the meal. Paying for the meal was more difficult than we expected as, in this part of Kosovo, they still used Yugoslav dinars.

As we were getting into our white UN and OSCE vehicles to drive back to Pristina, I stood for a while watching the cars passing in front of the restaurant and realised that the road through the centre of town was also the main highway linking Pristina with regional towns. That Sunday afternoon, Albanian families were driving through the enclave, supervised by the watching military, but free to go anywhere in Kosovo. The people who lived in Gračanica could only watch them pass, their freedom of movement limited to the perimeter of their town.

Another smaller Serb enclave sat side by side with an Albanian settlement about twenty minutes on the other side of Pristina, down a narrow street off the road to the airport.

The houses were sturdy stuccoed cottages with neat vegetable gardens, wooden barns full of dry corn cobs and the remains of garlands of summer flowers arched over garden gates.

The village was like a museum of folklife in a different country and time. There were no satellite dishes and no rubbish. There didn't appear to be any significant economic activity in the town either, apart from three or four people standing at the muddy road junction selling petrol in large plastic drink bottles.

The few cars that drove past were tiny socialist era Yugos. They still had Yugoslav registration plates so it wasn't legal to drive them on the open road and they could only travel from one end of the sprawling settlement to the other.

A small shop in the heart of the village had faded Cyrillic advertising posters and a small display of dusty packets and cans in its windows. Inside it sold goods unobtainable in Pristina, such as pork salami and sausages from Serbia—one of the reasons for our visit. The shop was also the local café and restaurant and we found it full of people drinking coffee at plastic tables with red-checked tablecloths. It was old-fashioned and gloomy as if nothing had changed there since the 1950s.

A little further along the road, we came to a block of modern apartments and a green camouflaged KFOR guard post. This was the point where the Serb village met the Albanian town. Behind the apartment block, rows of damaged houses sat empty and derelict; a legacy of the recent conflict.

Some were in the process of being reconstructed but the new buildings were not just replacing the homes that had been burnt or looted. They were expanding and enlarging and modernising them into three-storey mansions with balconies and big windows.

We looked back from the Albanian houses across the

fields to the Serb village, no more than a few hundred metres away. The Serb and Albanian settlements were so close they could see and hear each other, yet they may as well have been on different continents.

●━━━●

THE FIRST MUNICIPAL elections under UN administration were held late in 2000. This was the first step in establishing a democratic government. Like a game of musical chairs, the music would stop and the UN would find out which of the local would-be political leaders actually had chairs to sit on.

Campaigning had been underway for almost two months. The city was awash with campaign posters showing pictures of children and ambulances, symbolising education and health care, even though these were two of the functions that were not, at that stage, responsibilities of municipal governments.

A rush of political rallies in Pristina involved impromptu marches by flag-waving teenagers up and down the main street. Cars drove around town tooting their horns with their passengers waving placards from the windows.

The election itself was a big success. There was no violence and seventy-nine percent of the electorate turned out to vote.

The results, declared by Kouchner a week later, showed that a majority of voters had supported Ibrahim Rugova's party, the LDK, the moderates who had led a Gandhi-style passive resistance during the decade of disenfranchisement. But the PDK and the AAK, parties formed by former commanders in the more militant Kosovo Liberation Army, had also won a good number of seats.

Christmas followed soon after the election. Most Kosovars are Muslims and some had been fasting for Ramadan that December, but that didn't stop them from enjoying

Christmas. Coloured lights were strung across the main street and flashed in shop windows and on balconies. Stalls selling tinsel, trinkets and plastic Christmas trees appeared on the footpaths. At the main supermarket, long queues of shoppers were loaded down with chips and pretzels and chocolates and other party food.

The Grand Hotel advertised its New Year's Eve function—dinner and a cabaret of popular local performers for DM 150 a ticket. That was more than half a month's salary for most government employees, but the hotel had booked out all three of its huge function rooms, not only for New Year's Eve but for the next two nights as well.

Most of the UN and EU staff and consultants had left for the holidays so the New Year's Eve party I went to was a quiet affair with a miscellaneous group of people who were too far away from home to get back for Christmas. They compared notes on the strange and exotic places they'd worked in before Kosovo. The food, the wine, the Scotch and the conversation continued into the night.

When midnight arrived, the town erupted in a frenzy of noise and explosions. The bangs of firecrackers were supplemented with the sounds of shotguns, pistols and assault rifles as people let off celebratory rounds. Red tracer bullets arced through the air from the windows of the apartment opposite. KFOR had tried to round up all the firearms in the country, but they had obviously missed some.

The next morning the footpaths in the centre of the city were littered with spent bullet casings.

THE NEXT WAR IN THE BALKANS
Kosovo, January 2001

The new year in Kosovo began with the departure of Bernard Kouchner, the Special Representative of the Secretary-General. Kouchner's final speech, in the sports centre across from the UN Headquarters building, was quite forthright, particularly when he addressed the local political leaders.

'You must stop the killing if you want the rest of the world to listen to you,' he told them. 'The rest of the world has already forgotten what happened before. All they remember now are the ethnic murders and the political assassinations.'

He was no doubt referring in particular to the killing of four men, members of the obscure Ashkali ethnic group, murdered a few weeks earlier on the day they returned to rebuild their homes. Or perhaps to the gunning down of Ibrahim Rugova's deputy shortly after the municipal elections the year before in which it became clear that Rugova's party had won the most votes.

Kouchner's replacement, the former Danish Minister for Defence, Hans Haekkerup, arrived a few days later. He was reported to be much more interested in economic matters and administrative details than Kouchner had been. The people I worked with in the CFA looked forward to getting more attention on the issues they thought were important.

At the same time, though, we would miss Kouchner's flamboyance and charisma. The first people who met Haekkerup said that charisma was definitely not a word they would use to describe him. He sat stony-faced and expressionless throughout their meetings with him.

The start of 2001 was also the beginning of the next crisis in the Balkans. Less than two years earlier, Serb police and civilians had forced hundreds of thousands of Albanian Kosovars to flee from Kosovo into neighbouring Macedonia.

On the weekend of Sunday the twenty-fifth of February, several hundred Albanian Macedonians fled across the border in the opposite direction, from Macedonia into Kosovo. This time they were escaping the Macedonian security forces. The Macedonian authorities said they were simply responding to attacks by 'armed men in black uniforms' from Kosovo.

The trouble had started in late January when a rocket attack on a Macedonian police post killed one policeman and injured three others. This was the type of tactic the Kosovo Liberation Army had used in its guerrilla war against the Serb authorities before 1999 and it had the predictable effect of provoking retaliation from the Macedonian police.

About a quarter of the population of the former Yugoslav Republic of Macedonia is ethnically Albanian. Most of them are concentrated near the Kosovo and Albanian borders.

The more militant Kosovo liberation groups argue that Kosovo's territory should extend from the Albanian populated areas in Montenegro in the west, all the way to Bitola to the south, deep inside Macedonia. In fact, some people support the concept of 'Greater Albania', which would unite all the Albanian-inhabited areas in a single state.

On our occasional weekend trips to Macedonia, the potential for trouble of this kind had been clear. Macedonia was a great place to visit. It has carefully preserved Roman and Byzantine archaeological sites, ancient Orthodox monasteries, popular lakeside holiday resorts and extensive ski fields. The capital, Skopje, is a modern city of wide boulevards and plentiful trees.

But when we left the main highway to drive through the Albanian-dominated town of Tetovo, it was as if we were already back in Pristina. It's hard to explain precisely what it was that made Tetovo so much like the towns across the border in Kosovo and so unlike the rest of Macedonia. Of course, the street signs and shop windows were all in Latin script, not Macedonian Cyrillic, and there were mosques and minarets instead of orthodox churches, but that was only part of it. There was something about the whole appearance and atmosphere of the place.

There was the amount of building work. The entire town seemed to be a permanent construction site, just like Pristina. And it was the style of the buildings, their size and the apparent lack of any kind of town planning. Large houses with high walls and big gates crowded in on each other with little consideration for the look of the street, the rights of neighbours or the safety of pedestrians. And just like in Pristina, there were large numbers of young people, more specifically young men, loitering everywhere.

We didn't stay long in Tetovo, but the difference in living standards between the two ethnic groups was clear. The Albanian minority believed they had legitimate grievances. Their language wasn't recognised and only a tiny percentage of the police, the military and other government employees were ethnic Albanians.

The Macedonians, for their part, feared that giving recognition and status to Albanians and their language would be the first step towards breaking up the country, as they had seen happen in Bosnia and Serbia. If conflict broke out between the Albanians and Macedonians, it could easily become yet another Balkan war.

Everyone in Kosovo hoped that the armed men in black uniforms were just a small misguided band of adventurers who did not have the support of the population on whose behalf they claimed to be fighting, and that the authorities in

Macedonia would exercise restraint when they dealt with the troublemakers, instead of simply giving the Albanian minority more reasons to support the rebels.

•———•

ON THE SAME weekend that the refugees started fleeing into Kosovo, the international donors who had supported Kosovo since it came under UN administration in 1999 gathered in Pristina to congratulate each other on the success of the reconstruction effort. They met in one of the recently renovated function rooms at the Grand Hotel, sitting on new yellow-upholstered dining chairs at tables with white tablecloths, looking more like a wedding party than a serious conference.

That Sunday was also the day winter finally arrived and it snowed all day. The visiting officials and diplomats, straight off the plane, wore their best business suits for the meeting. The local UN and EU representatives, who had to trudge through ice and snow to get there, arrived in unglamorous hiking boots and anoraks.

The donors heard positive reports about the amount of money spent so far, the number of houses built, the roads repaired, the improvements to the electricity supply, and the increased amount of tax revenue collected.

But there were also negative messages interspersed with the good news. It seemed that donors had been tripping over each other to provide money for 'media development', but reconstruction in agriculture and education had been significantly under-funded. There were hundreds of newly renovated schools, but not enough money to train teachers, and in a region with a long history of lawlessness, support for the justice system and the police had been less than was hoped for.

The generally positive message was also overshadowed

by a recent increase in violence against the remaining Serb population in Kosovo. Every day there were small incidents. Serb properties were destroyed, escorted convoys were stoned or shot at, and Serb Orthodox churches were blown up. The deaths of ten Serb civilians just a week before, when their bus was attacked while it was being escorted by the Swedish military, had been the most shocking incident for some time.

At the end of the conference, the representatives of the European Union and the United States made a joint statement for the benefit of the local television cameras condemning violence and subtly warning Kosovars that they and their political leaders must do more to stop it or risk losing international support.

Unfortunately, the armed men in the mountains probably weren't watching TV that night. Our hopes that the problems in Macedonia would settle down were not realised.

In March, more fighting broke out around Tetovo between the police and the Albanian rebels, forcing both Macedonian and Albanian civilians to flee to safety. Each night we watched reports of the fighting on the BBC, seeing plumes of smoke rise as rockets hit the hillsides around Tetovo, just an hour's drive down the road from Pristina.

Senior political envoys from the EU and NATO made frequent trips to the region to negotiate between the Macedonian government and the Albanian leaders in efforts to contain the conflict, but the fighting spread to other towns, more houses were burned down and the death toll rose.

The fighting had little impact on international workers in Pristina except that the road to Skopje was now out of bounds, along with the once safe weekend holiday destinations in Macedonia and Greece. Apart from that, life went on as normal, to the extent that any aspect of life in Pristina could be called normal.

I was still living in Mark and Vera's apartment, a short walk from my office at the CFA, and not too far from our favourite bars and restaurants. The weekly rounds of social events showed no sign of slowing.

At the CFA one of my tasks was to work out what to do with our new budget department staff. When I'd left the reconstruction planning team, the local staff had still been playing solitaire on their computers, waiting for someone to give them work to do.

Now the CFA had also recruited a group of people to be trained as budget analysts so they could take over when the UN left. Of course, if the Kosovars were suddenly left alone, they could certainly run things themselves; they'd done it in the past. The question was, would they do it the way the international advisers thought it should be done?

I met the new recruits a week after they'd started work. None of them spoke English so I took an interpreter with me to talk to them. Up to that point, they'd had nothing to do. They'd been given an office and desks and told to wait.

Their stories were similar. Many had degrees in 'economics' but they'd been educated under the socialist system and when I asked them what they'd actually studied the subjects all sounded like bookkeeping.

The older ones had had jobs as accountants or finance officers in government departments or in state-owned banks many years ago, but they'd all become unemployed in 1989 when the Milošević regime had dismissed all ethnic Albanian staff from the administration. The most interesting and energetic woman in the group had been a member of the Kosovo Assembly at the time it was dissolved by the Serb government. She'd then spent ten years in hiding in Croatia.

The younger ones had never been employed. This was their first real job and they were nervous and excited.

I hoped we wouldn't let them down, but I wasn't sure how we were going to educate them in the ways of western government administration and capitalist economic policy when we had no shared language and they had almost no relevant qualifications or experience.

One of the ways the CFA got around this problem was by transferring parts of the public service of the neighbouring country of Albania to Kosovo.

Petraq, the deputy budget director in the CFA, had, until recently, been the budget director in Albania. Florian, now working in Kosovo as a tax adviser, had been the director of taxation, and Fatos, now head of IT in the Kosovo tax office, had had the same job in Albania, working for Florian.

Albania was only a few years ahead of Kosovo in modernising its government after the fall of the dictator Enver Hoxha, but the demand for Albanian-speaking experts had worked out well for Petraq, Florian and Fatos, who were making much more money working in Kosovo as advisers to the Kosovars than they had while working for their own government. I wondered though how Albania, one of the poorest countries in Europe, was managing without them.

ON A WEDNESDAY in April, just before lunch, I was discussing a document with Vjollca, another translator, when we heard an explosion in the centre of town and saw a column of dirty brown smoke drift up from behind the buildings near the Grand Hotel.

'That's a bomb,' she said, with the certainty of someone who knows from experience.

We watched from the window as ambulances wailed up Mother Teresa Street and back again towards the hospital.

As usual, the only way I could find out what had happened was from international news websites. CNN had the story an hour later. One person had been killed and four seriously injured. They were all Serbs. Their car had been blown apart by a bomb as they were leaving their office in the badly misnamed 'Centre for Peace and Tolerance' which housed the Yugoslav government's representative office in Pristina.

It was not the first attack on the office. Its entrance, down a side street off Mother Teresa Street, was heavily sandbagged and guarded by KFOR soldiers. This explosion, however, had happened outside in a busy laneway where children played and people shopped. It was a miracle no bystanders had been hurt.

It was soon summer, which was wedding season. Each weekend the streets were full of processions of cars draped with Albanian flags and full of happy wedding guests.

An Albanian wedding is a multi-day event. It starts with separate parties for the bride's friends and the groom's friends, followed by a day of separate family celebrations.

On the third day, the groom's family all go together to collect the bride from her family. The lines of cars drive around town, honking horns, blaring music from stereos and blocking intersections. Young girls in glamorous party dresses lean dangerously out of windows or sunroofs, clapping and waving white handkerchiefs in time to the music. The bride would be somewhere near the back, wearing a white wedding dress, tiara and veil, wedged in between elderly female relatives.

The bridal cars were decorated with glitter and tinsel and plastic flowers, sometimes with a large plastic doll in a frilly dress on the bonnet. Every car had a multi-coloured hand towel wedged under the windscreen wipers.

My friends and I puzzled about this for quite some time. Jan, our project administrator, consulted the girls working in her office. The towels, they told her, are for the bride. 'This is her wedding night and if she's a virgin she'll need them to mop up the blood.'

I was aghast at this medieval concept. It seemed so out of step with the broadminded attitudes of the young people I knew in Pristina. Much later it occurred to me that, for people who lived in the city, it was probably meant to be a joke. Maybe not so much in some rural villages, though.

That summer, Albanian Kosovars also took holidays at the beaches in Montenegro, across Kosovo's western border. Several travel agents ran buses each weekend and offered packaged one-week tours.

Montenegro was still, for now, part of the Yugoslav Federation, but it was one of the few countries other than Albania which allowed cars with Kosovo number plates to cross the border. Albania itself, although sharing a language and a long border with Kosovo, was not a practical option at the time, as there were no safe roads across the mountains that separated them.

The drive through Montenegro was not that easy either, as I discovered when I made the trip on the UN charter bus one long weekend. The country consists almost entirely of rugged mountains and the journey involved steep hills, hairpin bends and unlit tunnels roughly hacked into the rock.

When we reached the Adriatic coast, our bus turned west and delivered us to the well-known beachside resort of Budva, popular with international tourists from Germany and Russia, as well as Serbs. The Kosovar tourists, on the other hand, generally stayed in the towns with large Albanian populations further to the east. A friend who'd been there described the area as 'Pristina by the sea'.

Back in Pristina, you could tell who'd been away and who hadn't. After their week in the sun, the young girls came home with suntans that were sometimes closer to second-degree burns, still wearing for a day or two the impractical beach dresses and shell necklaces they'd bought on their holiday. By mid-summer, it seemed as if the whole population of Pristina had made the trip to the coast.

•———•

IN LATE 2001, as summer came to an end, my one-year contract was about to expire. When I'd left home, twelve months had sounded like an eternity to put my 'normal' life on hold. But Kosovo had now become my normal life. Conditions were tough at times with the electricity blackouts, the dirt and every now and then a bomb or a riot, but I had friends, life was interesting, and the work seemed important.

I was still trying to regulate Kosovo's public monopolies and had organised an independent audit of the telecommunications company. The international accounting firm that had tendered for the job may not have realised what they were getting themselves into. The company didn't actually have a set of business accounts that could be audited so they'd had to construct the accounts themselves, gathering data from various ledgers and files kept by each branch office.

Not surprisingly, their final report was heavily qualified, but at least now we had some idea of what was going on in the company, what assets they had and what they were worth, and a financial baseline to measure them against in future. A new UNMIK regulation made financial reporting by public enterprises like this obligatory.

I was also on a task force preparing for the arrival of the Euro. At the end of the year, most members of the EU would replace their currencies with Euro notes and coins. As the German Deutschmark had been used as the currency in Kosovo since the UN had taken over, Kosovo would also have to change.

The task force included everyone in the interim administration who had an interest in money, from the UN lawyers who would need to revise legislation on fees and fines, to the economists concerned about the effect on inflation, and the police, who wanted to make sure the changeover wasn't used as an opportunity to launder profits from drug dealing, people smuggling or arms trading.

The meetings, which were held around the boardroom table in the central bank, were long and extraordinarily tedious. The IMF-appointed head of the bank, a small man from Tunisia, seemed to think his performance would be judged on the length and formality of the meetings he chaired.

The highlight each time was the arrival of coffee. A large woman with bleached blonde hair, masses of jangling jewellery and too much make-up arrived with a heavy brass tray arrayed with long-handled Turkish coffee pots, one for each person. She hoisted the tray around the room, stopping behind each chair to pour a long stream of black coffee into a disposable plastic cup. The coffee was sweet and flavoured with cardamom; a welcome change from the usual Nescafé and coffee whitener.

But the task force had to finish its work without me. I learned that the company had no plans to extend my contract. USAID's priorities had changed and consultants with other skills were joining the project, including a large contingent of experts to accelerate the privatisation of Kosovo's moribund socialist business enterprises.

I started thinking about going home and finding a new job. I wasn't looking forward to it. I couldn't think of anything at home that would be as interesting.

I wasn't unemployed for long, however. Something else turned up just in time. UNMIK had received a grant from the World Bank to reform the financial management of the education system. They needed someone who understood budgeting and I happened to be available.

One chapter of my life in Kosovo was finished, but another one was just beginning.

Return of the Apparatchiks
Kosovo, August 2001

On my last day of work at the CFA, I arrived during the morning electricity blackout and found that the office was in darkness. The generator had run out of fuel again. This was a constant problem. We regularly ran short of things like toilet paper, photocopier toner, printer paper and generator fuel that are used up at a fairly predictable rate. When they ran out, however, it seemed to come as a surprise to the staff in charge of the purchasing department.

On my first day at work at the Department of Education, the same thing happened. No power, because there was no fuel. The education project office was on the Pristina University campus and we were at the mercy of the university administration.

The electricity situation throughout Kosovo was particularly bad at the time. We were on a three-hours-on, three-hours-off schedule, and without power, there were no computers or printers or photocopiers and no electric kettle so no coffee. At home, there was no TV, no light, and no cooking. Without power, the water pumps that delivered water to the houses and apartments also stopped, making toilets un-flushable.

We were suddenly plunged into a primitive life of candles and torches and going to bed early because there was nothing else to do. And this was in summer. I dreaded winter when it would be dark and cold, and the added burden of electric heaters would make the blackouts even longer.

No one seemed quite sure why, after more than two years of UN administration and 600 million Euro of expenditure on repairs, the electricity supply was still not back to normal.

There were rumours about contractors taking money but not doing the work, and it seemed that just as one part of the generating equipment was repaired, something else developed a fault.

Apart from the lack of light and power, my first day in the new job was challenging in other ways. Education was one of the largest items in the Kosovo budget and my task would be to work out how to shift responsibility for managing schools and their funding from the central Department of Education to the municipal governments.

The predominant view among economists is that education should be run by local governments so schools can be responsive to the local community. This was what the World Bank's education adviser had recommended for Kosovo, and it was what I had been employed to implement.

On my first day on the job, however, I was surprised to be told by Alexis, the project manager, that the UN wasn't sure whether it would go ahead with the new school funding arrangement.

'Most likely we will do it,' he said, in his charming French accent. 'But we haven't made the final decision yet.'

It seemed there was a heated debate going on between various parts of the UN administration about whether it was a good idea. The people in the Department of Local Government, who seemed to be mostly Scandinavians, strongly believed that the more responsibilities transferred into the hands of local elected representatives the better. Others, however, were concerned about the risks involved in placing large amounts of public money in the hands of local officials who may be corrupt.

The World Bank's education adviser, on his short visits to Kosovo, was surprisingly ambivalent. He just made recommendations, he said. The final decision must be taken locally. All well and good, but in this case, the final decision was largely in the hands of foreign UN officials rather than local people.

At the end of the year, elections would be held to choose a new, independent government for Kosovo which would take responsibility for major policy issues like this. In the meantime, however, it was up to the UN to decide.

The UNMIK Department of Education was a multicultural outfit. The head of the department was a German professor, the department's budget was managed by a Pakistani called Aziz, and Alexis, the project manager, was a young Frenchman.

In addition, Canadians were organising teacher education, Germans were looking after vocational education, UNICEF was working on preschools, a Finnish team was improving education for disabled children, and some other Scandinavians were responsible for developing a new school curriculum.

There was a government primary school not far from our office. It was grimy and grey, the garden was overgrown, and some of the windows were broken, but it was considered to be one of the best schools in Pristina. All the well-off families in Kosovo sent their children there.

Like all schools in Kosovo, there were not enough classrooms to accommodate the number of enrolled students, so it operated several daily shifts from early morning until late in the afternoon. When one group of students finished, another started. This meant children were at home or in the streets for most of the day and only spent a few hours in the classroom.

But Pristina's students were much better off than those in rural villages where the schools were in disrepair and lacked basic supplies and facilities, including, in many cases, functioning toilets.

Kosovo's teachers were not well paid and often had second jobs. Although education was supposed to be free, they sometimes charged for the use of textbooks and for 'exam preparation' and 'extra tuition' to guarantee a pass.

It was also difficult for the Department of Education to be sure that every teacher on a school's pay list really existed, especially in remote schools, and even if they did exist it was difficult to be sure they were getting the correct salary. In many places, levies were 'voluntarily' paid to local political groups or skimmed off by the school principal before he handed the teachers their pay.

It was hoped that devolving education funding to the municipalities would make local people take more interest in who was and wasn't being paid out of their education budget, instead of seeing teachers' salaries as money from somewhere else and conniving in the scams.

•——•

WHEN MY CONTRACT at the CFA had been about to finish, I'd told Mark and Vera I was going home and cancelled the lease. They seemed very disappointed. They thought I was a wonderful tenant because I didn't rearrange the family photos and other personal objects they'd left behind.

They were also pessimistic about finding someone to replace me. They were probably right to be. Entrepreneurs were producing better quality rental properties and prices were coming down.

Now, even though I was staying, I decided it was time for a change. I moved into a shared house in the quieter district of 'Sunny Hill'. It was a bit like being a student again, although my housemates were, like me, well past their undergraduate days. They all worked for UNMIK in one way or another.

Patrick was trying to resurrect the Trepca industrial complex in the north of Kosovo, Charles was responsible for regulating Kosovo's small mining industry, and Amanda managed the accounts for the Department of Trade and Industry. We all worked such long hours, or in Amanda's case, had such busy social lives, that we rarely saw each other except briefly at breakfast.

The four-bedroom house was built above a hardware store a few blocks uphill from Mother Teresa Street. Like many Kosovar homes, the front of the building was just a brick wall and a gate but at the back, there was a balcony and a small garden.

The new house and my new job at the university gave me a different outlook on the city. Daily life was no longer focused on Mother Teresa Street, and the walk to work each morning now took me down streets of small old cottages built of timber, mud and straw.

But small houses with gardens were rapidly disappearing as Pristina's building boom continued. People were buying them up, bulldozing them and replacing them with cement and brick constructions, three or four stories high, extending to the edge of the block, or perhaps just a bit further. The houses were surrounded by high walls and metal gates and the upper stories and balconies overhung the street. Imitation Doric columns and concrete lions on guard at the front door were common and usually the only garden was what could be grown in concrete planter boxes.

AT WORK, THE long-running debate on municipal education funding continued for several weeks. In the meantime, I was paid to work on implementing the new policy, so I worked.

I started drafting legislation and instructions, held meetings with education officials and collected data on students and schools to calculate funding allocations.

Alexis had recruited several local staff to help. Avni was a tall streak who'd been lucky to get the job, which paid several times what he'd earned before, given that he hardly spoke English. I put him to work doing spreadsheets.

Mimoza was a different matter. She'd just finished her MBA in the US on a USAID scholarship and was significantly overqualified for this work. She was frank about how difficult she'd found returning to a place like Kosovo after a year in the US.

'When we started our course, the counsellors told us we would find it difficult and lonely at first, but by the end of the year, we would be happy and looking forward to going home. For me, it was the other way around. I was happy as soon as I got there. It was coming home that was difficult.' She looked despondent as she talked about it.

Unfortunately, there wasn't much I could give her to do that would challenge her. Given the impasse over the policy direction, I had trouble keeping myself fully occupied. But Mimosa spoke excellent English and was a useful source of local knowledge, so together we took one of the cars donated to the Department of Education by the Korean government and travelled around the country visiting municipal education offices. Kosovo is so small you can drive across it in a couple of hours so we covered a lot of ground in one day.

The Kosovo countryside in early summer was beautiful. Clear blue skies, rows of mountains, one behind the other, in the distance, rolling green fields and forests, freshly ploughed black soil and pretty red brick villages nestled in valleys. The roads had improved a lot in the last two years, but the other drivers were still dangerous.

Our first stop was the small town of Suha Reka, where we visited the municipal education director. He was one of the more competent local education staff, earnest and diligent, but he was apparently living under threat of assassination because he was in the wrong political party and a local powerbroker wanted to give his job to one of his supporters.

A computer sat on his desk, covered in a plastic dust protector. He said it was broken. It was one of the computers our project had recently given to municipal offices to collect student data.

I made a note to send someone from our IT team to find out whether it really was broken or whether perhaps he just didn't know how to use it. The two young computer geeks from our office visited a few days later and it turned out that the tender for the supply of the computers had, somehow, failed to specify that software should be included in the package.

This was a major problem and a subject of much discussion and handwringing in the project office for several weeks. The computers were not much use without software, but licenced application software would cost hundreds of dollars for each computer; money we hadn't budgeted for. Pirated versions were readily available in Pristina for a few dollars but using them would be illegal and it wouldn't do for UNMIK to be seen to be breaking the law.

In the end, we did nothing and let the municipalities make their own arrangements for installing software.

The next stop on our tour was a meeting with the UN's regional education office in the old town of Prizren. Prizren had once been Kosovo's capital, but President Tito had moved the provincial administration centre to Pristina because it was further from Albania and didn't have the historical significance of Prizren.

This was fortunate for Prizren, otherwise, it too would be full of ugly concrete buildings and high-rise apartments. Instead, it retains its reputation as the most beautiful town in Kosovo.

This is, of course, a relative concept.

The city straddles a narrow river which, at the time, was not much more than a thin stream running down the middle of a stone-walled drain. On one side of the river, the ground rises steeply to a stone fortification on top of a hill. The ancient fort has been used in the past by crusaders and Ottomans and every other invader and was now being used by KFOR.

The houses of the old town jumbled down the steep hillside from the fort to the river. Most were derelict. Many were burnt-out shells. This had been the old Serb quarter and the houses had been destroyed in the days after the end of the conflict. A large Orthodox church beside the river was surrounded by barbed wire to protect it from further damage.

A few blocks away, across the river, we visited the tiny old house where the Prizren League, the first movement for Albanian independence from the Ottomans, was formed in the late 1800s. The building had been blown up by the Serb military as they forced the Albanian population out of Kosovo in early 1999.

The house had now been rebuilt and the museum inside displayed historical documents in the ancient Turkish script, photographs of the leaders of the Prizren League, and maps of all the areas where Albanians live superimposed on the various political borders drawn at different times by different conquerors and different treaties. 'Real Albania' extended well into areas that are now Greece, Montenegro, Serbia and Macedonia.

The museum illustrated the many layers of history in Prizren—the Serbian Orthodox heartland, overlaid with centuries of Turkish administration, a few brief decades of socialism, and the recent history of interethnic conflict. Now the UN was putting its small touches on the town in the form of pale blue bollards around all their buildings, but it's unlikely they'll still be there for future tourists to wonder at.

We then moved on to Peje, near the mountain border with Montenegro. The Serbs regard this region, along with nearby Decani, as the cradle of their culture and some of the worst atrocities of the 1999 conflict took place there.

The UN office was in a former bank building, a multi-storey concrete construction in the style of a Chinese pagoda painted in 1970s brown and orange. A matching flying saucer-shaped auditorium sat on the ground beside it, but our meeting with local education officials was held in a room on the top floor with glass walls on three sides looking up to the mountains of Montenegro.

Late in the afternoon, as we listened to UN officials' complaints about corrupt local government leaders and UNMIK central office neglect and incompetence, flocks of Kosovo blackbirds swooped around the building, past the glass windows, seeming to fly right past our shoulders as the light started to fade behind the mountains.

●━━━●

Back in the office a few days later, we had just finished our weekly team meeting when Mimoza rushed into the room clutching her mobile phone.

'They're bombing the United States,' she said. 'Planes are dropping bombs on New York.'

Her sister, who worked in the USAID office, had just called her with this rather garbled account of what was happening in the US that day.

'Someone has flown to the US in a commercial aircraft and started dropping bombs on New York and Pittsburg.'

'Pittsburg?'

'Yes, Pittsburg.'

Avni turned on a radio and plugged it into his computer speakers. A local station was rebroadcasting CNN audio with a commentary in Albanian. They were reporting that two planes had flown into the World Trade Centre towers in New York. Another had crashed into the Pentagon in Washington, and a fourth had come down not on but near Pittsburg. At that point it was feared there were more attacks to come.

Mimoza's sister said the Americans in her office were hysterical.

For the first few minutes, I thought the whole story sounded preposterous. Surely it must be some out of season April Fool's joke or an elaborate hoax. Perhaps it was just a crazy misunderstanding. Wouldn't everyone be embarrassed when they realised it was just a big mistake?

But as the afternoon went on, it seemed less and less likely that so many journalists and politicians and commentators could be so thoroughly fooled. Work suddenly seemed irrelevant.

At home, the power was off again so Patrick, Charles and I watched the grainy news broadcast on a tiny television in the restaurant at the Park Hotel. For the first time, we saw the fiery explosions, the falling towers, the smoke drifting over New York City, pictures that would be replayed over and over again in the following hours and days and years.

President Bush made a speech. So did Tony Blair. The commentators speculated about which Middle Eastern terrorist group was responsible, and already CNBC was discussing the effect this would have on the stock market. Fairly obviously, insurance and airlines down, oil and gold up.

For days, there was no other possible topic of conversation and nothing else on any of the television stations. Soon the US Government was pointing the finger more firmly at

Osama bin Laden and his Al-Qaeda group, now based in Afghanistan. The US demanded that the Taliban government there give him up.

Reporters speculated about US plans to invade and there was talk of setting up an interim UN administration, like Kosovo, and extending the OSCE mandate to Central Asia, even bringing the former King of Afghanistan, now in his eighties, back from exile to rule the country again.

At the time I had no idea how significant these events would be for me personally.

•———•

IN OCTOBER 2001, after two years of UN administration, campaigning began for the election of the new Kosovo Assembly.

A few weeks before that, the people of Pristina had been bemused to see a team of workmen erecting huge advertising billboards all around the town. Huge steel structures were built on each corner of Suicide Junction, facing the oncoming traffic, and smaller upright billboards about the width of a phone booth appeared at regular intervals along the footpath in Mother Teresa Street. Each of them displayed an attractive young woman looking ecstatic as she sipped a cup of steaming black coffee.

The old concrete bus shelters were also removed and replaced with shiny stainless steel and glass constructions displaying more coffee posters. The high-tech billboards were lit up at night and against the scruffy Pristina streetscape, they looked as if they'd landed from Mars.

They were a topic of conversation for at least a week. The general conclusion was that the firm that had installed them had a wildly optimistic business plan. I wondered how long it would take for the new street furniture to become as grimy as its surroundings, how long before the glass bus shelters were covered with graffiti and the billboards coated with Pristina dust, and whether anyone other than the Turkish coffee company would be able to afford to advertise on them.

In fact, the billboards had been erected at just the right time. They were ready to capitalise on the advertising blitz brought on by the election.

For the next two months, as soon as the coffee campaign was over, they carried the glossy posters of the major political parties. The three main party leaders, Ibrahim Rugova, Hashim Thaci and Ramush Haradinaj, glared at each other across the snarled traffic from their respective corners of the intersection.

Rugova, with his scholarly glasses and eccentric paisley cravat, was shown looking out from his book-lined study. The other two leaders stood to attention, indicating their military background, but wearing dark suits and sober ties. The campaign posters were high quality, professionally-produced advertising material. A lot of money was clearly being spent on this election. Exactly whose money was another question.

Each of the leading political parties had produced a document setting out their policy platform. Rugova's had a position on almost everything, including a proposal to establish an institute for the study of crystals. It was possible that some of the other parties had bought their glossy campaign manifestos from a public relations firm, along with the posters and flags and give-away hats.

The major parties held their campaign rallies on successive days in the university hall next to our office. We had a good view as each party's supporters arrived.

Rugova's LDK party rally began with the arrival of several dozen security guards wearing black denim jeans and t-shirts and black baseball caps. They marched in two lines into the car park and stood at attention for a brief parade drill, before taking up their positions. The audience for this rally were mainly older people and school children who arrived in small groups.

Hashim Thaçi's PDK party event was quite different. Young people made up a large part of the audience. Groups of them came marching up the hill with banners and flags, chanting, 'Thaçi, Thaçi, Thaçi.'

The rallies generated discussion among the young people who worked in my office. It seemed they were all LDK supporters. They believed that the PDK used violence and was involved in illegal activities.

Then somehow the conversation turned to Marshall Tito, the former Yugoslav President. Both Avni and Mimoza could remember when Tito died, more than twenty years before, when they were both young children, and how upset they'd been about it. They were suddenly embarrassed at this admission and joked about it, chanting, 'Tito, Tito, Tito,' like the Thaci supporters outside.

They repeated what others had told me—that Tito was the only person who could hold the Yugoslav Federation together and that Yugoslavia had been the freest and most progressive of the Eastern European communist countries. Even these young people, with almost no experience of Tito or the communist era, were nostalgic for those days.

———•———

THE ELECTION TOOK place on the seventeenth of November, but it was some time before the results were announced. No single party was the clear winner. The electoral system, based on proportional representation in a single Kosovo electorate, was designed to produce this result. A coalition government would have to be formed.

An advertisement on local television urged people to 'Respect the results. It's the decision of the Kosovo people.' It was aimed at those who were already saying the vote was rigged. How else, they said, could the Serb minority, united behind one party, have managed to take third place, winning twenty seats in the Assembly?

There was an obvious increase in the police presence around town, but this could also have been because of Flag Day. The twenty-eighth of November is celebrated each year as the anniversary of an Albanian revolt against the Ottomans in 1443 led by Gjergj Kastrioti Skanderbeg. It's known locally as Flag Day.

Two years before, the first Flag Day after the conflict had been marked with violent riots. A year later, in 2000, Pristina celebrated by unveiling a statue of a man in a military uniform holding an assault rifle, a memorial to Zahir Pajaziti, a young man who had died during the guerrilla war against the Serbs.

This year, however, they would unveil a statue of Skanderbeg himself. The country was still in ruins and unemployment was at seventy percent, but the people of Pristina had raised funds to commission the world's largest statue of Skanderbeg on a horse. It was a replica of an existing statue in the Albanian capital, Tirana, but it was bigger!

It had been brought from Albania by road on the back of a truck and most of the population of Pristina came out to watch it arrive. Family groups streamed towards the centre of town, all dressed, in dark, dull colours, as usual in winter.

The event was broadcast live on local television. Skanderbeg looked like a Viking with flowing hair and goat horns on his pointy metal helmet. His horse reared up on its hind legs with veins standing out on its neck and its mane flying in the wind.

Lifting the statue from the truck and placing it correctly on its plinth was a delicate operation and there were moments when it appeared it might topple to the ground. But finally, it was securely in place, speeches were made, and the public milled around having their photos taken in front of the magnificent statue.

The monument was surprisingly tasteful by Kosovo standards and the sunken plaza built for it created a peaceful corner in the bustle of Mother Teresa Street.

THE NEW Kosovo Assembly finally met for the first time on the tenth of December in the auditorium in the government building where the UNMIK staff social club used to hold its movie nights. The room had been renovated and refurbished to make it into a suitable venue for the new Kosovo legislature but to me, it would always look like a picture theatre.

Kosovo now had an elected parliament, but it didn't yet have a government. The Assembly would need to appoint first the speaker, then the president, the prime minister and finally the ministers. Before this could be done, however, the parties had to work out between them who would get the jobs.

For those of us used to the Westminster system, where the composition of the new government is usually known almost as soon as the results are announced, this coalition-forming process was an incomprehensible mystery. The Europeans, however, found it perfectly normal.

The aim of the proportional representation system in Kosovo seemed to be to ensure that there were no losers, to convince as many contestants as possible that they had won something in the election lottery and therefore discourage any group from refusing to play the game.

The first session of the Assembly got as far as electing a speaker but no further. The PDK members walked out when the head of UNMIK, Hans Haekkerup, refused to allow a minute's silence for those killed in the conflict. In fact, he turned the microphones off to prevent the motion being proposed. The session was adjourned while negotiations continued.

A month later, in January, Haekerrup himself resigned, suddenly and unexpectedly, and Michael Steiner, a German diplomat, took over.

The change from the Deutschmark to the Euro also happened in January. As there were few private banks in Kosovo at that time, particularly outside the city, replacing the currency was a major exercise.

The new coins and notes had arrived in the middle of December, creating huge traffic jams as UNMIK police barricaded streets in the centre of town with armoured vehicles. A contingent of Indian police, wearing body armour and carrying assault rifles, patrolled one end of the city and the Italian Carabinieri guarded the other while a helicopter hovered overhead.

The arrangement was that, on the first of January 2002, all money held in bank accounts would be automatically converted to Euros. But most Kosovars had never learned to trust banks and people generally kept large amounts of cash hidden in their homes. They would have only two months to exchange their Deutschmarks for Euros and there was concern about how rural villagers would cope.

When January arrived, the public seemed to ignore the Euro completely. Shopkeepers still gave change in Deutschmarks if someone paid in Euros. I expected chaos in March when the old currency was taken out of circulation, but on the last day of February, the Deutschmark disappeared as if it had never existed. Shops and taxis simply started using the Euro.

Price tags on goods in the shops were changed, apparently overnight, although in many cases I suspect the prices were the same but were simply now called Euros instead of Deutschmarks; an instant 100% price increase.

People who had queued up before the changeover to deposit their old currency in newly-opened bank accounts started queuing up to take it all out again. The foreigners had underestimated the local population yet again.

Kosovars have had a lifetime of dealing with complex situations. Managing multiple currencies was no more challenging than coping with the multiple languages and shifting politics of their unstable homeland.

•———•

IN MARCH 2002, Kosovo finally had a real government. After months of haggling over the election results, the leader of the LDK, Ibrahim Rugova, was confirmed as the president of the Provisional Self-Government of Kosovo. The job of prime minister went to a member of the PDK, the other main party, and the agreed list of ministers represented all the major parties.

Thus, all the political factions were given a role to play in the new administration. It was a recipe for political peace, but not necessarily for effective government.

The new Minister for Education was Rexhep Osmani, who'd been responsible for running the parallel Albanian-language education system during the 1990s.

Over the next few weeks, it became obvious that life in the administration would be different with a real minister. Senior

UNMIK advisers found themselves spending large amounts of time in the minister's office listening to his ideas and trying to persuade him out of them. He wanted to be closely involved in the day-to-day management of his ministry, in particular, it seemed, in decisions on staff selection.

A few days after his appointment the new minister called a meeting to address the staff of the ministry, who all crammed into the university auditorium next to our office.

Osmani, a rotund, grey-haired man in a badly fitting suit, spoke in Albanian and his personal interpreter, a young woman, translated almost inaudibly. His speech contained all the usual statements about how pleased he was to be the minister, how he thanked the international staff for the work they'd done, and how he intended to continue to build on what they'd started. He also promised to reinvigorate several university faculties, in particular, the Institute of Albanology.

Then he got down to specific plans. The first was a review of all school staff, to get rid of 'parasites' and to make sure the payroll was correct. The criteria for identifying parasites was not explained.

Then he announced a new process for collecting information on teachers, students and schools. Our project had just completed gathering this information for the Education Management Information System, a hugely complicated process, but the minister wanted another set of figures and had developed his own forms to collect them.

Then he demanded reports on the use of official cars, how much they cost, and where they were parked at night. He harangued the audience, banging his fingers on the table, becoming more and more agitated, and spoke so fast that the interpreters didn't bother to keep up with him.

At the end of the meeting, the municipal education directors took the forms to fill in with information about their staff, their cars and their buildings and the minister went away satisfied.

By this time my work on the education finance project was almost finished. An agreement on school funding for municipalities had eventually been finalised and the annual budget reconfigured to allocate funds to each municipality according to a formula.

I spent my last few weeks delivering training on budget management to the staff of the newly created Kosovo Ministry of Education. Most of them were young and looked interested. They included two Serb women who'd married Albanian men back in the days when such things were possible. They tried hard to speak Albanian with their colleagues. Each day the Albanian trainees walked the few blocks from the ministry office to the training venue, but the Serb staff, to ensure their safety, made the same short trip by taxi, paid for by the ministry.

Once the training was finished, the project would be wound up. My contract would finish and so would the contracts of the half-dozen local staff we employed.

Mimoza was OK. She'd found a good job working on a private sector development project. The others were still looking. The World Bank had the idea they would move to jobs in the ministry to do the same work on a government salary, but the wages paid by the government were much less than what they'd been earning with the project. I couldn't see them being interested in that option.

As for me, I wasn't sorry to see the last of Alexis and Aziz and the Professor, but once again, I was facing unemployment.

Bringing Westminster to Kosovo
Kosovo, May 2002

When I'd first arrived in Pristina, the four-storey Germia department store had been one of the dreariest of the dreary socialist-era buildings in Mother Teresa Street. The business was clearly struggling to compete with the new boutiques and supermarkets of Pristina's booming private sector. Eventually, the building was taken over by UNMIK and, by the time the new government started work, it had been refurbished and converted into offices for the Ministry of Public Services.

The interview for my next job in Kosovo took place over coffee at the café in front of the newly refurbished building. It was now early spring in 2002 and the weather was just warm enough for us to sit outside.

Pristina had survived another winter of power cuts. Our household had debated the idea of buying a generator. It would be a major investment; a sunk cost that would be difficult to recover when we left. We were eventually persuaded against it by a young engineering consultant working with KEK who said a generator would be a waste of money. When the current repairs were finished, he assured us, there would be no more problems with electricity in Kosovo.

The people I met with in front of the Germia building were from a British government agency that had been contracted to develop a professional Kosovo civil service based on the British model. The London-based project manager needed someone who had experience in Kosovo and had worked with UNMIK to lead the project. I certainly met those criteria.

At that stage, however, my knowledge of issues affecting civil servants was based entirely on the fact that I'd been one for many years. I'd sat on recruitment panels, been involved in numerous annual performance reviews, and attended training in public service values and ethics. What more would I need to know?

I signed a two-year contract and turned up for work at an office in a recently built house a few blocks from the centre of Pristina.

A local office manager had already been appointed. Basri had spent most of the past decade working in Germany and, like many Kosovars, was fluent in at least four languages. He was now back in Kosovo to settle down with his young wife. She was only eighteen but their first baby was on the way.

A large team of civil service management experts and trainers from all over Europe would also be working on the project with me. I soon found out, however, that these other staff would not be based in Kosovo. They would just come for a week or two and then leave.

The rest of the time I'd be on my own with Basri and a handful of yet-to-be-hired local translators and administrators. I seemed to have missed this detail when I'd read the job description.

The Kosovo Civil Service was managed by another trio of German, French and sub-continental UN officials. Alain, an elderly Frenchman who chain-smoked Gauloises in his office, was charming but ultimately ineffective. Ashok, an Indian civil servant on long-term secondment, was also charming and friendly, and slightly less ineffective. Most of my day-to-day contact, however, was with Peter, the German director responsible for civil service policy.

After several months working with these men, I came to the conclusion that their governments had loaned them to Kosovo to prevent them from causing more havoc in their own countries.

One of the important things these three were supposed to do as a first step towards establishing a well-run civil service in Kosovo was to issue an 'Administrative Direction' setting out the rules for appointing and managing government staff. A draft of this document had been shuffling its way around the UNMIK bureaucracy for some time and my new job soon boiled down to visiting the Germia building every day and waiting for either Ashok or Peter to be free of their phone calls and meetings to find out whether some progress had been made.

Each time I met him, Peter delivered a portrayal of a competent-but-frustrated bureaucrat surrounded by incompetence and inefficiency. This was convincing the first few times, but eventually it became apparent that there was no one to blame for the delays except Peter himself.

Since the creation of the Kosovo government a few months earlier, there was now also a Kosovar Minister for Public Services. Jakup Krasniqi was a small, dignified man with long eyelashes and expressive eyes which made him look much younger than he probably was.

His office suite in the refurbished ministry building was impressive. The rooms had been designed by UNMIK to give the ministers and their staff an aura of importance and dignity commensurate with their new positions, with expensive, modern décor, timber furniture, recessed lighting and orange leather sofas. It was a stark contrast to the shambolic offices of many international staff.

Two neatly dressed young women at the reception desk sorted piles of correspondence into folders. Nearby, two young men in black suits and black turtlenecks lounged in the waiting room. Most likely they were the minister's security guards and the jackets probably hid guns.

We made a presentation to the minister on our plans for developing a professional and impartial civil service, the personnel management instructions we were developing, the huge training program we were organising, and the planned publicity campaign. He gave us his blessing.

But he had some issues of his own to raise. He was concerned about the civil service recruitment process being implemented by UNMIK. With the creation of a local government, the UN had suddenly realised it would need to recruit many more local staff to replace all the seconded UN bureaucrats who had been running the administration up until then.

'The problem,' he said, 'is that the UN says all new staff must have experience in public administration. This isn't fair. Only people who worked in the corrupt Yugoslav system will be selected.'

He had a point. Requiring government staff to have previous government experience would exclude younger people who hadn't had a chance to do this kind of work, or any work at all, in the difficult conditions of the past decade.

'And the civil service will be politically biased,' he added.

What I assumed he meant was that it would be biased towards a party other than his own. Krasniqi was a member of Hashim Thaçi's PDK party which had a large following among the young people who would be excluded by the UN's recruitment process. Government ministers had been appointed on the basis of party representation and they expected their staff to have similar allegiances. Krasniqi did not want to find himself with a ministry of LDK supporters.

An Independent Oversight Board was supposed to deal with this sort of problem, but its creation was one of the things that depended on finalising the Administrative Direction, which was still nowhere to be seen. By the time it was in place, he argued, it would be too late. The public service would be full of the wrong people.

Unfortunately, I didn't think that his proposed solution, to give him, the Minister for Public Services, the right to appoint all government staff, was the answer.

•———•

One of the challenging aspects of this job was that, for the first time, I had to recruit both Albanian and Serb staff. All our documents had to be translated into both languages and our training would be provided to both groups, so I had to hire Serb translators. This wasn't easy.

We found Vuk in Mitrovica. He was only about seventeen but was already an experienced translator for the UN and the military. With his chubby, freckled face and spiky blonde hair he looked remarkably like Bart Simpson and had the cheeky personality to match.

The second translator was referred to me by her friend who already worked for the UN. They shared a studio apartment in a guarded building on the outskirts of town.

It was almost midday when we arrived to meet her but Eva had just woken up. She stood in the doorway, bleary-eyed, in crumpled clothes she'd evidently slept in, her red dyed hair hanging over her face, tangled and matted, as she fumbled to light a cigarette. It was not a promising start for a job interview, especially as she'd known I was coming. I momentarily thought of turning around and cancelling the whole thing, but Serb translators were hard to find so I hired her on probation.

Security for our Serb staff was the next problem. Our office was on a side street away from the centre of town and it was probably not safe for them to work there. That was Vuk's opinion, anyway, and I think the Albanian staff were relieved when he decided it would be better to be based somewhere else. The Albanians might not be safe either if they were seen associating with Serbs.

The two Serb translators worked in their own temporary office in the ministry building. Under UNMIK's equal opportunity quotas, the civil service was now employing quite a number of Serb Kosovars and made special arrangements for their security. Buses brought them into the office each day from the protected enclaves where they lived and government buildings were surrounded by high metal fences and guarded by uniformed police. Once they were at work they were more or less imprisoned in the building, unable to go outside the compound without an international escort.

Eva was a bit different, though. She wasn't from Kosovo but from Nis, across the border in Serbia. She'd come to Pristina specifically to find work as a translator and was earning five times her previous salary.

She and her friends who were also from Serbia were much less frightened of moving around in Pristina. They left the government compounds and went to restaurants or coffee shops. Eva even talked to Albanians in Serbian, knowing that most of them were fluent in the language from when Kosovo was part of Yugoslavia.

I didn't like to tell her that just a few years earlier a UN employee had been shot dead in the street simply for using a few words of Serbian. In fact, she probably knew little about what had happened in Kosovo. In Serbia, under Milošević's regime, the media would have reported little of what was going on and, being quite young at the time, she might not have heard about massacres and rapes and people being forced from their homes. She talked naively about how everyone should learn to live together.

I tried to explain to her that some bad things had happened and people will take time to forget, but if her ignorance of the facts made it possible for her to feel safe, I didn't want to tell her too much of the truth.

•———•

AT THE BEGINNING of May, a small item in the daily news feed mentioned that a UN official had been arrested and charged with stealing more than four million Euros from the Kosovo electricity company.

Over beers after work that evening, everyone had a slightly different version of the story, but the general outline was the same. Jo Truschler, the former UN-appointed chairman of KEK, the electricity company, had been accused of siphoning huge amounts of the company's money into his personal bank account.

Like most foreigners, I found it hard to believe that an international official would be involved in corruption. Corruption was what the locals did. We were the good guys.

Even worse, I'd known Jo Truschler well. He'd been managing KEK when I'd been responsible for monitoring Kosovo's public enterprises. I'd like to be able to say that I'd always thought there was something dodgy about him, but I hadn't. He'd seemed charming and helpful and no different from any of the other slightly eccentric characters that found their way to Kosovo.

He'd told people he'd made a lot of money selling some software he'd developed and didn't really need to work so he was just doing this for the challenge. At that time, at the height of the 'dot com' boom, this actually sounded plausible, but it turned out that none of it was true, including his claimed university degrees and previous business experience.

KEK's finances were a mess but not so much of a mess that four million Euros would go missing for long, and with both the UN and EU auditors sniffing around he was soon found out, arrested and convicted. Most of the money was recovered. It confirmed for me that when it comes to corruption, no one is above suspicion.

Despite the absence of the long-awaited Administrative Direction, Basri, the visiting experts and I made progress in organising training courses, developing personnel procedures and formulating the publicity campaign.

We managed to get an invitation to talk to the Cabinet ministers about the civil service legislation. This meant returning to the Government Building where I'd started my work in Kosovo. It was now, once again, the headquarters of the Kosovo government and had been completely redecorated for this purpose.

The garlands of computer cables that had been strung along the corridors were gone, the walls had been painted a tasteful beige, and mushroom coloured carpet had replaced the muddy linoleum. In place of the foreign advisers, the staff were now all Kosovars, which also meant there was a lot more cigarette smoke.

By the time we were allowed into the cabinet meeting room, the government ministers, sitting on either side of a long table, had already started discussing the civil service issue. We put on our headphones and found ourselves listening to a heated debate.

The ministers themselves may even have forgotten that their every word was being diligently translated into English and Serbian by interpreters sitting behind a glass screen. Because it was a coalition government, they represented widely different political points of view and policy platforms. Indeed, some of them were sworn enemies.

But in this debate, they were all of the same opinion. They complained bitterly about the process imposed on them by UNMIK for appointing the 'permanent secretaries' in each ministry.

The ministers wanted to decide for themselves who got the top jobs in the areas they were responsible for. Instead, the law decreed that the decision would be made by a Senior Public Appointments Committee on which the relevant minister would be heavily outnumbered by UN officials and UN-appointed community representatives. The aim was to ensure that the appointments were made purely on merit, not ethnicity or political party membership.

Our British government-funded project was promoting a purist *Yes, Minister* concept of bureaucracy, in which the permanent secretary is a civil servant who works for any minister impartially, and ministers are prepared to work with whichever apolitical civil servant the system throws up. It's a noble concept, but difficult to achieve even in a stable democracy. In Kosovo, where every aspect of daily life is political, it was particularly unrealistic.

The ministers preferred the US system where senior officials are replaced with each change of government and are chosen as much for their political allegiance as for their expertise. Our brief presentation on the issue didn't convince them to change their views.

•———•

MY WORK AS manager of this project never seemed to end. Apart from daily meetings with Peter or Ashok, trying to coax them into doing something about the Administrative Direction, there were reports to write and documents to review. I was usually in the office on the weekend to catch up with it all.

One Saturday, I arrived at eight am to find the power was off. This wasn't unusual. But it was still off at ten am. That was unusual.

I phoned around to find out what was going on. It turned out there'd been a storm the previous night and power station B had been hit by lightning. The transformers, for some reason lacking an important piece of safety equipment, had surged power back into the generating unit, killing one worker and hospitalising a dozen others. The building had caught fire.

The generator, which had just been refurbished at huge expense to the European taxpayers, would be out of action for the next six months. The other one was already out of service for major repairs, so now there was no electricity at all being generated in Kosovo.

We would have to rely on imported power, load shedding and candles for the rest of the year. The engineer who'd assured us there would be no shortage of electricity after summer could not have been more wrong.

From Monday morning, life in the office became immensely difficult. The electricity blackouts now lasted for three or four hours at a time and, without electricity, our desktop computers were just plastic boxes.

The 'UPS' units attached to each computer had just enough power to keep the computers going while we saved what we'd been working on. These heavy batteries sitting under each desk were something I'd never heard of before, but they were essential items of office equipment here.

Needless to say, the printers, the photocopier, the internet connection, even the fan, were also useless without electricity. We had hundreds of pages of documents to translate in the next few weeks before the training course started and I couldn't see how we could do it without computers to work on.

It was clear we would have to buy a generator. It wasn't in the project's budget but the UK office approved and Basri and I went shopping.

Not surprisingly, there'd been a run on generators in Pristina in the past few days but plenty of suppliers were ready to import whatever we needed.

The question was, what did we need? Each supplier had a completely different suggestion about the size and power of generator we would require, possibly influenced by the size and power of the generators they were able to supply. My head was soon spinning with different power, size, quality, price and availability options. Finally, I took a stab and chose one somewhere in the middle of the range.

The generator still had to find its way to Kosovo by the circuitous mountain roads through Montenegro and every extra day without a reliable power supply put us further and further behind schedule.

The generator was bright yellow. The delivery driver wheeled it onto the front porch, next to the door. It was supposed to go down the steps into the basement, out of sight and hopefully out of hearing, but it was too big and heavy for us to move.

Basri went to find workmen to help. There was a section of the main street in Pristina where unemployed men stood on the footpath waiting for work as casual labourers. It was the Pristina equivalent of the job centre.

He came back with one of the bosses who controlled this informal labour market. The man looked at the generator, the basement and the stairs from every angle, rubbing his stubbly beard as he thought about the problem. Finally, he came to the conclusion that no matter how many men and pieces of equipment we used it couldn't be done.

So the generator stayed where it was on the front doorstep.

A workman came to bolt it to the concrete and the bolts were welded in place. It would take some fancy cutting equipment to move it, but Kosovo is full of resourceful thieves and I had nightmares every night about our expensive new generator vanishing.

At home, we regretted the decision not to invest in a generator for the house. We were without power almost every night and living on salads, biscuits and cheese for dinner.

In some ways, however, the hours without electricity were a peaceful relief from the stresses of the day. I read by candlelight and listened to the battery-powered radio until the whir of the fridge starting up and the click of the satellite television receiver coming to life indicated that the power supply had returned to our part of town.

In this way, we struggled on from month to month through summer and then autumn.

•———•

As WINTER ARRIVED, my glass box office started to feel chilly. The heating fuel we'd ordered some time ago still hadn't been delivered, but Basri somehow managed to start the central heating system.

I went down to the basement boiler room to congratulate him and found that instead of heating fuel, he was using diesel from the generator, which was being sucked straight from a plastic bucket sitting on the floor in front of the boiler. Every few hours he sloshed another few litres of fuel into the bucket to keep the heating going. I couldn't even begin to think about how dangerous this could be.

Upstairs in my office, I faced up to the fact that I was not enjoying this job. There was too much work and very little job satisfaction.

It was not just the drama of managing without electricity for months, the frustration of waiting for UNMIK officials to do their jobs or the stress of ensuring that our Serb staff were not assassinated on their way to work. I'd been unhappy from the start when I realised I would be, most of the time, more or less on my own. In other jobs, I'd always had the support of a team and professional interaction with colleagues. In this project, I felt alone and isolated in my clean empty office on the hill.

And the job, which from the advertisement had sounded like policy development with some negotiation and liaison with UNMIK, had turned out to involve an enormous amount of administration. Between recruiting staff, buying equipment, filing documents, writing reports and hiring training venues, I was working flat out just to get on top of the everyday chores.

My real interest was in the policy issues, the things that would affect the future of the people of Kosovo, not writing detailed job descriptions for staff and keeping the planning calendar on the wall up to date so that all four people in the office knew what the others were doing.

Every day there was a new problem to deal with. The UN had decided to limit the number of people who could have a UN ID card. Our staff no longer qualified and that meant our Serb employees couldn't use the UN buses to get safely to work.

Then the venue we'd planned to use for the next training course was suddenly unavailable—the Ministry of Public Services had reserved it for their own meetings. So I traipsed around Pristina all week inspecting dusty auditoriums and bleak meeting rooms looking for another option. None of them was suitable.

A week later, one of our training experts, a charming Danish man, was sick and needed a doctor. He was coughing badly and looking seriously unwell.

I phoned around and found a local clinic that had a good reputation and drove him there in the project's rattling Toyota, feeling annoyed and exasperated. This was not how I wanted to be spending my time, sitting in a doctor's waiting room at six o'clock on a Friday evening.

The Albanian doctor and the Danish patient managed to communicate with each other in German and the doctor diagnosed bronchitis and prescribed four different medications, all of which could be purchased at the pharmacy on the premises.

The Dane was much happier. He looked healthier already. Still, he decided to go home early, which meant my Saturday was spent on phone calls and emails to travel agents to get him on a plane out of the country.

Three weeks later, he was dead. The bronchitis turned out to be lung cancer. He'd been a heavy smoker, spending large amounts of time on the balcony outside my office chain-smoking. I wondered whether his nicotine-stained fingers and teeth had given the doctor a clue.

Perhaps it was a kindness to send him home to his family and his own doctor before he was given the bad news.

•———•

BY THIS POINT, I was thinking seriously about resigning. But how could I do that? How could I let everyone down? I was the only one here holding it all together while the rest of the team were off in other countries worrying about other problems.

I decided to tough it out a bit longer and, after a few weeks, things seemed to be improving. But I was certainly due for a holiday. I negotiated a visit home—the first for some time—got everything in the office in order, wrote detailed instructions for the staff, the other consultants and my temporary replacement, and flew to the other side of the world for a few weeks.

Holidays at home were not necessarily relaxing. There were always so many things to do. I visited the doctor, the dentist, the optometrist and the accountant, and travelled around the country catching up with friends and relatives.

I was therefore standing in a taxi queue at Sydney airport one evening when the project manager in London called on my mobile phone to tell me I'd been sacked! All my running around in circles hadn't been enough. As I inched my way to the top of the taxi queue he recited a list of things, most of them to my mind, trivial, that I apparently should have done but didn't.

I thought about how close I'd come to resigning during the preceding months. It was a lesson learned, a little too late. If you feel like resigning, you probably should. After the first shock, I felt a great sense of relief. I was more than happy for someone else to take over the worry and frustration.

But my life was still in Kosovo even if I didn't have a job. I came back from my holiday and served out my last weeks, packing up my office, writing my final report and briefing my successor. My friends commiserated over dinner at one of the better Italian restaurants in town.

'When something like this happens,' one of them said, 'it just means there's a mismatch between your expectations and theirs.' He pointed his left index finger to the right and his right index finger to the left, which seemed to pretty well sum up the situation.

We were on the footpath outside the restaurant, still discussing my career crisis, when there was a loud explosion. All the car alarms around us went off. Police sirens started wailing and blue lights flashed past.

I turned and saw billows of smoke rising into the air a few blocks behind us. We knew we should stay away but found an excuse to walk closer. From the top of Lenin Street I could see red flames and flashing lights and a gathering crowd of young men.

At home a short while later the local TV stations interrupted their usual quiz shows and variety acts to report the breaking news. It didn't take much linguistic ability to pick up the words 'car bomb', 'explosion' and 'hospital'.

Amazingly, no one was badly hurt. According to the rumours, the owner of the car had several reasons to be targeted. He was regarded as a former collaborator with the Serbs, was allegedly a drug dealer and, most importantly, had given evidence against the 'Dukadjin Five', former KLA members who'd recently been convicted and jailed for war crimes. The verdict had been handed down by a panel of international judges who'd all finished their terms of appointment and quietly left Kosovo as soon as the trial was over.

Popular opinion in Kosovo was strongly divided on the case. Some claimed the five were heroes of Kosovo's liberation. Others saw the trial as a test of the rule of law in Kosovo. If these men weren't convicted, no one would be prepared to give evidence against criminals.

The explosion happened in an area of town known for its association with crime, outside an illegal gambling club, and of the twenty or so people taken to hospital with injuries, around two-thirds had some kind of criminal record.

This was now the third time I'd been unemployed in Kosovo. I was learning not to panic. Something was sure to come up.

A few weeks later, there it was—another email from Mike

in Washington. I'd never met Mike, but he'd had a significant influence on the path my life had taken in the past few years.

He was looking for someone to work as a budget adviser on another large USAID project. It sounded exactly like the first project I'd worked on in Kosovo three years before and some of the same people, now old friends, would be working on it too.

Once again, we'd be reconstructing a government after a long war. We were going to Afghanistan!

Before I left, I had dinner with friends at Pristina's newest restaurant, *Pjata*, which means 'plate' in Albanian. From the large windows, I watched for the last time as the blackbirds flew overhead and whirled around the valley as the sun set behind the apartment blocks.

The modern restaurant was just one of the signs of progress in Kosovo. Based on the number of new cafés and boutiques that had opened recently, the economy was booming. The new shopping centres that had been empty and desolate for so long all now had tenants. In the city streets, the underground water pipes had been dug up and replaced with ones that didn't leak.

Lenin Street had been renamed 'Bill Clinton Boulevard' and a huge poster of President Clinton waved down from the side of an apartment building. And, after three and a half years standing empty and unused, Pristina's major landmark, the multi-storey tower in the main street with all the broken windows, was finally being draped in mesh and scaffolding in preparation for renovation.

On the day I flew out of Pristina for the last time the airport was busy. A crowd of elderly Kosovars were lining up for a charter flight. The men wore finely woven white hats and most of the women had their hair pulled back under white handkerchiefs. It wasn't until I was in Afghanistan that

I realised they were on their way to Mecca for the Haj.

While my flight was taxiing away from the terminal some strange ideas came into my head. Would Kosovo still exist when I wasn't there? For me, Kosovo was a reality that only came into existence the day I arrived. After I left it would be, for me, frozen in time somewhere in my past.

While I'd been living there, I'd sometimes been surprised to find evidence that, for the Kosovars, life today was simply a continuation of their life before. For them, the annual round of events would go on——mud and snow and cars sliding on the icy roads in winter, outdoor cafés, weddings and holidays in Montenegro in summer, and celebratory gunfire at midnight on New Year's Eve.

For three years their lives and mine had been travelling in parallel but that day, I veered off in a different direction and they sailed on into their own future. Even as my flight was leaving, other foreigners were arriving through the same airport to continue doing what I'd been doing and for them, Kosovo was created again on the day they arrived.

Afghanistan

Another War, Another Project
Kabul, Afghanistan, February 2003

At 4.30 am in the dimly lit lobby of my Dubai hotel, two young women, one a tall blonde, the other a petite Asian, clattered out of the lift in high heels and hotpants and headed towards the front door, their work finished for the night. They were followed at a discreet distance by their two minders, who emerged like ghosts from dark corners.

The girls were heading home. I was checking out and on my way to Dubai Airport's Terminal 2. Not the flashy new Dubai transit hub where international travellers strolled among luxury shops and fast food restaurants, but the small, old building used in those days by airlines that fly to obscure and possibly dangerous places, like Afghanistan.

The queue at the check-in desk comprised equal numbers of western men in suits and Afghan men in baggy pants and turbans. The Afghans looked like subjects from a *National Geographic Magazine* photo essay. Some dragged bundles wrapped in plastic bags and tied with rope and duct tape to the check-in. Others rolled out mats in the corners of the room for their dawn prayers.

I joined the line even though I didn't have a ticket. As usual, someone in Washington was making all the arrangements, but she'd assured me my flight had been booked.

The check-in clerk directed me to the airport's small snack bar where a young man sitting at a plastic table with an open briefcase was surrounded by a huddle of people who were also looking for their tickets. This was apparently the Ariana Afghan Airlines' Dubai office. The young man did indeed have my ticket and I handed over several hundred dollars from my cache of foreign currency.

Back at the check-in line, a tall American in a suit walked up to me. 'Mary Venner, I presume', he said, echoing Stanley's greeting to Dr Livingston in darkest Africa. It seemed appropriate in the circumstances.

His name was Bruce, and we were to be colleagues in Kabul. He'd identified me easily because I was almost the only woman in the queue; certainly the only western woman.

The Ariana flight attendants were also all male, except for a young woman dressed like a character from *The Arabian Nights* in a pink tunic and trousers with a pink pillbox hat and a pink gossamer scarf draped around her shoulders, held in place with a large safety pin. She walked slowly down the aisle pouring tea from a huge aluminium kettle into disposable plastic cups, finally reaching the last row of seats with cold tea as we were ready to land.

Meanwhile, the male flight attendants served up rubbery reheated breakfast omelettes from the grime-spattered aircraft galley, then lounged at the back of the plane smoking cigarettes under the illuminated 'no smoking' sign.

The landscape as we flew towards Kabul was stark and rugged. There wasn't a tree or a blade of grass on the brown mountains, just an icing sugar sprinkling of snow. Even the city of Kabul was the same brown as the soil and looked more like a geological formation than something built by humans.

At Kabul Airport, dozens of people swarmed the tarmac, greeting their friends who'd arrived on the flight. A line of sombre men in dark suits stood ready to greet a returning government official. Women in blue burqas looked down from the observation deck on top of the 1960s era terminal building.

Bruce and I were left to find our own way to the dark and crowded arrival hall. Immediately inside the door, before we reached passport control, we were met by our company representative—a dapper elderly gentleman with a neat white beard, a smart coat and a fur hat. He spoke impeccable English and introduced himself as Mr Nursat.

The airport was old and in disrepair but modern enough to have low ceilings and few windows. It had been built by people who'd assumed there would always be a good supply of electricity so we fumbled around in the dim light of a few underpowered light globes.

A baggage conveyor belt moved slowly along one side of the small room, carrying the bags and packages checked in at Dubai. Passengers from the flight crowded around it.

Suddenly, the belt stopped moving altogether. The crowd waited but it seemed it had broken irreparably and the luggage handlers started pushing bags through the hole in the wall and passengers frantically scrambled to retrieve them as they appeared. A dozen grizzled porters in grubby green overalls fought with each other for the right to carry each piece of luggage.

Through all this, Mr Nursat maintained his calm, dignified composure, standing quietly and patiently in the corner of the room. It took more than an hour to collect our luggage from the melee, but finally, Bruce and I and Mr Nursat and two porters passed through a cursory customs control to the exit.

Mr Nursat gave an elegant wave of his hand and our minivan appeared from among the mass of people and vehicles in front of the terminal.

My impression of Kabul as we left the airport was of poverty and destruction and dirt. The mudbrick houses spreading across flat fields on each side of the road appeared to be slowly crumbling back to mud.

We passed shops set up in rusty shipping containers, raw animal carcasses hanging in front of butcher's stalls, ancient overloaded buses and trucks and men slowly pedalling Chinese bicycles.

Suddenly, the van turned off the main road into an altogether different world, a tree-lined suburban street of modern houses behind high walls. The vehicle stopped outside one of the houses and the men started unloading the bags.

I was the last to get out of the car and as I turned, a blue shape leant in through the door towards me and extended a small dirty brown hand. The tiny woman in a grubby burqa had slipped quietly up to the car without anyone noticing. She whined at me. She was obviously asking for money. Her hand was delicate like a child's. I couldn't see her face, just the fine mesh screen that allowed her to see me.

I was trapped, frozen, as she leant closer and whined more insistently. After a few seconds, she gave up and turned to look for someone more responsive. She paused by the men but they didn't seem to notice her, as if she was a ghost. Then she walked away down the street. I felt guilty because I hadn't given her any money, but mainly, I was relieved that she'd gone.

The meeting with the burqa woman set the tone for the first few months of my life in Afghanistan. The feeling of unease she left behind compounded when I saw the armed police guards outside the house and read the long list of security rules and restrictions. We were told not to walk in the street, not to take local taxis or buses, to stay away from crowds and to avoid bazaars and markets.

A constant stream of alarming messages emailed each day warned us against engaging in almost every possible leisure time activity and would even have made going to work in our government ministry offices through the daily traffic jams impossible if we'd taken them literally. We were driven everywhere in radio-equipped vehicles and our guards and drivers kept logs of our movements and reported them to a central security office. It was not surprising that I started seeing all Afghans as potentially dangerous.

Living in Kabul was different from the relatively comfortable lifestyle I'd enjoyed in Kosovo for the previous three years but the political situation had some similarities. Both countries had just experienced a decade or more of conflict and disruption, and both were in the midst of an onslaught of foreign military assistance, donated money and thousands of foreign advisers.

Apart from that, however, the differences were immense. In Afghanistan, the poverty was much worse, the corruption more blatant, and the idea of getting hazard pay really meant something. The 700-year history of Kosovo was a blip compared to the 3000 or more years of conquests and empires in Afghanistan. The ancient Persians had once ruled here. Alexander the Great had married Roxanne in the ancient, still standing, city of Balkh. The town of Mazar had the oldest Islamic shrine in the world. Lapis lazuli from the mines in Badakshan adorned the robes of the pharaohs of Egypt, and there's a village where people claim direct descent from Roman soldiers.

Genghis Khan, the Moghuls, the British Empire, the Soviet Union and the Taliban had all imposed their vision on the place. Now the Americans and their allies were doing the same.

Once again, I was working with a large team of USAID consultants trying to modernise government finances. The terms of reference for my work, written by someone in the USAID office in Washington, were remarkably similar to the list of tasks USAID had set for us in Kosovo. It even talked at length about local government budgets, in spite of the fact that there was no such thing as local government in Afghanistan.

The document included all the terminology and jargon that went with public finance management in the western world, words like medium-term planning, government finance statistics, international accounting standards, program budgeting, outputs and outcomes and performance indicators. According to USAID, within twelve months the Afghan government would have all these things.

Many people I'd worked with in Kosovo turned up in Afghanistan. Even a number of Kosovars, on the basis of their experience with the UN and other foreign organisations, found jobs in Kabul.

But the UN wasn't as important here. Afghanistan already had a government, with Hamid Karzai as its interim president, and a collection of ministers who'd been appointed, it seemed, largely because they represented powerful warlords.

It also had a well-established government bureaucracy. The Afghan civil service had continued to operate during each successive regime change, from the monarchy of the 1970s, through the communist coup in 1978, the Soviet occupation in the 1980s, the civil war that erupted after the Russians left, and the rise of the fundamentalist Taliban.

Foreign advisers didn't have to start from scratch to set up an administration, as we'd done in Kosovo. In some ways, this was unfortunate.

•———•

THE MINISTRY OF Finance building in Kabul had been freshly painted a dusky pink. It was built around an asphalt courtyard which, on my first morning, as on every other morning, was crowded with Afghan men. Most were dressed in traditional clothes, their heads in turbans and homespun blankets across their shoulders, although some were wearing outdated suits or elaborate military uniforms with gold braiding on their sleeves and enormous hats. They were standing around, talking and waiting.

The main door into the building was so low everyone had to duck down to get inside, even me. It was curtained with a heavy quilt, shiny with dirt from the hands and heads of all the people who had pushed their way past it over the winter. The long wide corridor inside was also, like the courtyard, full of people, mostly men, standing or squatting on their haunches, talking and waiting.

The grey linoleum floor was filthy even though several cleaners were at work using small straw brooms to sweep dust into the air, where it floated in a haze then settled to the floor again. The cleaners swept small piles of dirt and debris into the corners and left a pattern of sweep marks after the brooms had moved on.

Along the corridor, scruffy attendants sat on rickety chairs guarding office doors. They paid no attention to the small group of foreigners as Bruce and I were led up two flights of marble stairs to our first meeting with the budget department.

The Afghan staff all jumped up and stood to attention behind their desks as if the president himself had arrived. Their desks were arranged around the edges of the room, facing into the empty centre.

The furniture would have been modern at one time, but that would have been around 1960. Now the desks were broken and crooked and barely provided a flat surface to write on. There was almost nothing left of the floor covering—just a few pieces of linoleum clinging to the less-used corners of the room, and even the concrete beneath was worn down in places to show gravel below the surface.

A pressure cooker hissed and steamed on an electric hotplate on the floor in one corner, a pile of onion peelings lying beside it. The room attendant was cooking lunch.

Although several tall, uncurtained windows looked out over the street, the room somehow seemed gloomy and it had a strong, rank smell like mouldy shoes and strong tobacco.

Against one wall there were several metal filing cabinets, chipped and rusty, with crooked drawers that no longer closed. An ancient typewriter sat on one desk. Another, even older, perched on top of a filing cabinet next to an antique electric fan. Dusty, tattered ring folders full of yellowing papers were piled on top of the cabinets. The one sign of modernity was a single computer standing on one of the rickety desks with a piece of its Styrofoam packaging perched on top to keep the dust off.

The men and women behind the desks all appeared to be middle-aged or even elderly but they may have been much younger. Given the life they have lived, many Afghans look much older than they really are.

Most of the men wore old suits but a few were in Afghan clothes, some with elaborate turbans with long tails hanging down to their shoulders. The women were swathed in layers of clothes—black trousers under long skirts under loose tunics, and white shawls like lace tablecloths wrapped around the top half of their bodies.

No one seemed busy. Most desks were bare except for a mug of tea. The interpreter introduced me to the group of people I would be working with for the next twelve months.

One man didn't leap from his seat when we entered. He stood slowly and moved from behind his huge ornate desk to meet us. The green marble desktop was cracked diagonally into two jagged pieces and, unlike the other desks, was piled with papers.

Mr Rafiq was a rat-faced old man with two prominent

teeth and small dark eyes. He was the head of this office and he'd been there a long time, probably at this very desk. He'd survived the Russians and the Mujahedeen and the Taliban. Although his formal greeting was polite, even obsequious, the expression on his face seemed to say he was ready to survive me.

•———•

AFTER OUR BRIEF meeting with the budget department staff, we were shown to the foreign advisers' office, an oasis of cleanliness and modern office furniture in the midst of the grime and decrepitude of the ministry. The walls smelt of fresh paint and there were new vinyl tiles on the floor.

Doug, another middle-aged American, had arrived a week before us, which made him, in relative terms, an expert on the situation in Afghanistan and what our work there would involve. It was clear from what he told us that the primitive working conditions in the building were the least of the obstacles facing the Ministry of Finance.

At that time the entire management of national revenue and expenditure was still being done on paper. Computers were almost unknown. Their version of a 'financial management information system' consisted of stacks of forms, gigantic ledger books, and rooms full of bookkeepers transcribing numbers from one piece of paper to another. It was Dickensian era bookkeeping with an overlay of socialist central planning.

In the late 1960s, a team of young advisers working for an American consulting firm, my equivalents on the US government payroll four decades before me, had created accounting rules and procedures for the Royal Government of Afghanistan. This had, of course, been in the time before computers and spreadsheets, even before faxes and photocopiers, when the typewriter and the Gestetner were the only ways to create documents and the post office or a telegram were the standard ways to transmit information. The system they'd set up had worked well in its day, and was, in theory, still in use, but it had fallen into serious disrepair during thirty years of war.

There were several other teams of foreign advisers also working in the ministry, each in their own foreign advisers' offices, providing expertise on all aspects of government finance, from tax collection and customs administration to central banking and auditing. There was even, as there had been in Kosovo a small team of USAID advisers busily trying to privatise some war-damaged and barely functioning government business enterprises.

In the treasury department, accounting experts had already set up a computer-based financial management system which would do, in a few minutes, the accounting work that currently took the ministry's bookkeepers most of the year.

Larry, another American, had been one of the first foreigners to arrive and had the best foreign advisers' office in the building, plus the only photocopier in the ministry. He also had access to the 'foreign adviser's bathroom', one of the few western-style toilets.

•———•

ACCOMMODATION FOR FOREIGNERS was in short supply in Kabul. The old Kabul Hotel in the centre of town had a large hole in its outside wall and was closed for renovations, which appeared to be going very slowly.

The former Intercontinental Hotel, perched on a hill to the west of the city, was no longer part of the Intercontinental chain and was still repairing bullet holes and leaking sewer pipes, but it charged Intercontinental room rates nevertheless.

Rents for decent apartments or houses were on par with London or New York. Almost all foreigners in Kabul, therefore, lived in housing compounds of various kinds. Our company had leased half a dozen houses in the general vicinity of the US Embassy and set them up as shared guesthouses. Six people lived in our house. Once again, it brought back memories of student accommodation, but my housemates this time were grey-haired, cantankerous old men who were not used to sharing and were too old to learn how.

We were located in the upmarket suburb of Wazir Akbar Khan, where the most important people have always lived. Eighteen months previously, these houses had been home to Taliban and Al-Qaeda leaders. Before them, the Mujahedeen commanders had lived here, and before them, the Russians. And before that, in the 1970s, when the houses had been new, it had been a luxury housing estate for wealthy Afghans.

The streets were laid out in a neat grid and consecutively numbered, and the houses were all more or less identical, Bauhaus inspired, two-storey buildings with terrazzo floors, large windows and timber feature walls. They were furnished with heavy, old-fashioned furniture from Pakistan and equipped with modern conveniences like fridges and freezers, microwaves and coffee makers. There was hot water and electricity, a fridge full of food we could help ourselves to, wireless internet, and a television attached to a satellite dish that delivered a remarkable number of obscure television channels, at least half of them porn.

The house staff included a 'house manager' who was about sixteen, two female cleaners, and a cook. There had to be two cleaners, as one woman could not possibly work on her own in a house full of foreign men.

A generator the size of a tool shed sat at the bottom of the garden. Like Kosovo, Kabul was short of electricity, but unlike Kosovo, the authorities were not in sufficient command of the situation to be able to ration power to different areas at different times. Instead, it was allowed to 'brown out' at peak times until even the brightest light globes merely glowed, and hair dryers, microwaves and network routers stopped.

A team of unarmed guards sat inside the front gate and a group of armed Afghan police lived permanently in a plywood hut on the footpath outside.

Every morning at about 7.30, our narrow street filled up with cars and drivers waiting for their passengers. The Ministry of Finance advisers from our house, the journalists from Agence France Press across the road, the Korean diplomats on the corner, and the interior minister and his entourage of armed police, who lived behind a boom gate at the far end of the street, all set off for work at about the same time.

Our driver, Emron, in his left-hand drive Corolla, imported from Pakistan, would drive us to the office through Kabul's right-hand drive traffic. On the map, our house was only a kilometre or so from the Ministry of Finance building; almost walking distance. But the main avenues of central Kabul had been blocked off around the homes of the president and the king, who'd now returned from exile, causing traffic chaos everywhere else.

Our journey to work thus involved a zigzag around the presidential zone, taking in the barbed-wire-topped walls of the International Security Assistance Force compound, the crowds forming at the Ariana Airlines office to buy tickets for flights to regional towns, the patient line of visa applicants outside the Pakistan Embassy, and streams of neatly dressed young children walking with backpacks to their crumbling primary school with its glassless windows.

The last part of the journey followed the banks of the dry, empty riverbed. At one time the Kabul River flowed all year, but now the dams that kept it full had been destroyed and it was little more than a trickle of smelly sewerage choked with discarded plastic bags.

The traffic snarled up here as buses taking government staff to their ministries competed for space with taxis and commercial vehicles on what was now the main route into town.

Finally, our cars lined up with all the other foreigners' vehicles for a cursory security check at the gate to the ministry building and another workday began.

1382
Kabul, Afghanistan, March 2003

On day two, Larry organised our first meeting with the Minister of Finance who, at that time, was Dr Ashraf Ghani. Many years later, he became Afghanistan's second post-conflict president.

Dr Ghani was a western-educated Afghan who'd come back to Kabul after the Taliban had left. He'd worked for the World Bank in Washington so he knew how to talk to donors and had been put in charge of coordinating foreign funding for reconstruction. Now, he'd also been appointed as the Minister of Finance.

The four of us walked to his office past an unattended metal detector and a security guard who took little notice of us. Like all politicians in Afghanistan, the minister was always surrounded by heavily-armed guards, but foreigners were never seen as a security risk. We were apparently exempt from the rules and restrictions that applied to Afghans. As a woman, for example, I wasn't expected to wear a headscarf as Afghan women were, and simply having blonde hair gave me the right to go almost anywhere without an identity card or security screening.

The minister's office was full of brown velour sofas and low coffee tables arranged around a square of carpet. A photograph of President Karzai hung on the far wall.

Dr Ghani, a small man with a balding head, was dressed in Afghan clothes and reclined on one of the sofas. A circle of other advisers and staff, all foreigners, sat on the other sofas. Two young men had laptop computers open in front of them and worked on them intently. A young woman was taking a call on her mobile phone.

Larry introduced Doug and Bruce and me to the minister. The other foreigners ignored us and continued what they were doing. Ghani apologised for his reclining position on the sofa, explaining that he was recovering from surgery. Others later told me he was in fact seriously ill, frequently travelling abroad for treatment.

We took our places on the sofas. Ghani pushed an electric doorbell on his coffee table and an elderly attendant came rushing into the room to stand rock-still and ramrod straight in front of him, with his hand over his heart, waiting for instructions. He returned a few minutes later with cups of weak green tea, bowls of sugar cubes and plates of toffees.

Larry had a long list of budget issues to discuss, but reconstruction projects, funded by donors, were clearly still the minister's main interest. He talked passionately and at length about what needed to be done, how much money he was requesting from donors, and what he would spend it on. He issued instructions to his other advisers, the ones with the laptops and mobile phones, about arranging meetings or writing letters.

Larry managed to draw his attention briefly back to ordinary budget issues, such as the salaries of civil servants and expenditure in the provinces, and Dr Ghani made a few pronouncements.

There was, for example, a proposal from the Ministry of Borders and Tribes for money to set up an armed border patrol. It was not clear to me what the Ministry of Borders and Tribes did but it apparently had nothing to do with controlling the national borders, for which there was already a separate border police in the Ministry of Interior. Dr Ghani thought the Minister for Borders was simply planning a private militia and the proposal was rejected.

Little else was resolved, however, and after half an hour he dismissed us and we gathered our papers and left. The meeting had been little more than a formality. We returned to our foreign advisers' office with a better understanding of where our budget reform project stood in the minister's priorities, and where we ranked in the hierarchy of ministerial advisers.

•———•

I RARELY MET Dr Ghani again. This was partly because he was seldom in the ministry building and worked mainly from a more secure office in a walled compound a few kilometres away.

The Ministry of Finance was on a busy corner of Pashtunistan Square in the centre of the city. It could easily be flattened by a well-placed bomb or invaded by a rioting mob. The reluctance of the Afghan minister to work in the building didn't give us foreigners a great sense of confidence.

Ghani also didn't appear, in my experience, to be particularly interested in the ministry's routine work of raising tax revenue and paying the government's bills. His passion for big, donor-funded projects took up most of his time and attention. On other issues he generally let the foreign consultants get on with whatever we were doing.

There was no doubt, however, about his commitment to his country. He worked long hours, holding meetings from early morning until late at night. His position as minister brought him no apparent financial gain. He didn't have the trappings of power, the expensive car and the lavish office. His position did, however, give him ample opportunity to exercise his ego.

My few meetings with him were a one-way conversation. He spoke, we listened. He would hold forth for hours on his ideas, his plans for the future of the country, his views on every topic, and his criticisms of the rest of the Afghan government.

On a day to day basis I mainly worked with the Deputy Minister for Finance, Mr Rahimi. Rahimi was quite different from Dr Ghani; a thoughtful man who spoke quietly and infrequently. The only similarity with the minister was his obvious commitment to Afghanistan and his concern for its future. Nevertheless, his family lived in Dubai where he went to visit them every few months.

There were several other deputy ministers, each with their own sphere of activities. In the Afghan political system, neither the minister nor the deputy ministers are elected politicians. In reality, they are merely superior civil servants, appointed by the president, but they were given all the status of royalty. Ordinary ministry staff stood to attention when they entered a room. Even the third-ranked 'president' of the budget department was treated with formal deference.

We shared our foreign advisers' office in the ministry with three Afghan staff who turned up each day in neat suits and sometimes ties, and spent most of their time translating documents from Dari, the official local language, into English, or from English into Dari. They'd picked up their English and computer skills in Pakistan while they were refugees and were fluent in the two official Afghan languages, Dari and Pashto, and no doubt also Pakistani Urdu.

Wajid was tall, skinny and always meticulously well-dressed. Noori was a suave, good-looking young man with cocker spaniel eyes and long eyelashes whose entire family seemed to be working for one international organisation or another.

Yunus was a little older. He'd once worked for an American project across the border in Pakistan, which he said supplied donkeys to Afghanistan. Eventually, it dawned on me that the donkeys would have been used to carry weapons such as Stinger missiles across the mountains to the Mujahedeen to help them fight the Soviets. The same weapons would later be used by the Mujahedeen to fight each other during the civil war and then by the Taliban against the Americans.

Yunus was old enough to recall a much freer life in Kabul when he'd been a university student and had had a girlfriend. By the time he was ready to marry, however, the Taliban were in control. His marriage was arranged by his family and he had seen his wife's face under the burqa for the first time on the day of the wedding.

He now had four children, all girls, and another was on the way. This turned out to also be a girl. Yunus claimed he didn't mind, but he told me his wife was in tears when she found out she had another daughter.

I'D ARRIVED IN Kabul while the Ministry of Finance was in the midst of preparing the national budget for 2003, although in Afghan terms it was the budget for 1382, measured in solar years from the birth of Mohammad. It was a suitably mediaeval date for a place which was, in many ways, still in the dark ages.

Preparing the national budget is a difficult process in any country. The amount of money available from taxes is almost always less than the amount that needs to be spent to do all the things people want the government to do.

There are several options for dealing with this situation. The government can reduce what it plans to spend, it can raise more taxes, it can go further into debt to cover the shortfall, or it can just print more money. Governments in Afghanistan had been opting to print money regularly over previous decades and, as any first-year economics student should be able to tell you, printing money eventually wrecks the economy.

I had a chance to explore these concepts, through an interpreter, with the deputy president of the budget department, Mr Amir Gul, shortly after I arrived. Mr Amir was a good-humoured man, rotund and round-faced, with strands of greasy black hair combed forward over his balding head. He explained the Afghan approach to the budget.

'We have a tradition,' he said, 'A good leader must provide for his people. Somehow, he must find the money.'

It was not the advice I'd expected from a senior official in the budget department.

The next day I sat in on discussions with a group of officials from one of the forty-two government entities funded by the budget. The meeting was held in the office of the budget 'president'.

The position of budget president, at that time, appeared to be largely ceremonial. The current incumbent, when he was there, never spoke and his main function appeared to be to sign whatever paper was put in front of him, usually without reading it. Consequently, although the meeting was in his office, he wasn't actually there.

The room had a large desk on a raised platform in one corner and, as usual, brown sofas around the walls. Sofas are an essential item of office furniture in Afghanistan and they were always brown. The more sofas, the more important the person who owned the office.

The furniture, like everything else in the building, was old and dusty. The worn carpet was badly laid and thick brocade curtains kept the room dark.

The meeting was conducted by Mr Rafiq, the head of the budget department, who I'd met on my first day. He sat at the big desk looking down at the representatives of the Ministry of Public Works who were perched on the edge of one of the sofas with their papers on their laps.

Bruce, Larry and I sat on another sofa, like the three wise monkeys, while an interpreter whispered a translation of the proceedings. Mr Amir was also there, lounging on yet another sofa. As soon as the meeting started a servant arrived with mugs of green tea and placed one in front of each person.

I was impressed that both the Ministry of Finance staff and the officials from the Ministry of Public Works seemed quite numerate. When it came to analysing the numbers and calculations in the budget forms they all seemed to understand what they were talking about. My local staff in Kosovo, even the ones who claimed to have economics degrees, had usually looked at me blankly when I started talking about numbers.

This discussion, however, was entirely about numbers and nothing else. Mr Rafiq went through them with a fine-tooth comb. He picked up his calculator, which was wrapped in plastic to keep out the dust, and checked that the projected salary budget matched the authorised staff numbers.

He then calculated how much overtime, travel allowance, hazard pay, qualification allowance and so on should be added, based on 'norms' established at some time in the past and presumably written down somewhere, but I could never find out where. Fifteen percent of the salary budget was added for overtime, for example, and ten percent of the staff were assumed to require hardship pay for working in remote areas. The requests for increases in budget funding were calculated on a similar basis.

Most of the requests seemed to be for things that were already being paid for but were somehow not covered by the existing budget. For example, the ministry had started hiring buses to get their staff to work. They'd decided to do this of their own accord and had been paying for the buses for some time, but it was agreed that they needed extra money for it and the cost was calculated.

New offices had been opened and the lease documents were produced to verify the extra rent required. The rate of some allowances had been increased by decree of the president, so the amount needed for that was also added.

For each item, Mr Rafiq punched numbers into his calculator and announced the result. If the ministry officials were content with the answer, he wrote it down on a scrap of paper. If they queried it, he went back to the calculator, entered more numbers and came up with a different result.

At the end of the meeting, he pulled out a blank sheet of paper and wrote down the sum of all the calculations. He announced the grand total like a judge reading out a verdict.

The final number was somewhat less than the ministry had asked for. The ministry officials muttered complaints, looked crestfallen, but accepted the defeat with dignity. They had no doubt padded their budget calculations in expectation of such an outcome. Mr Rafiq signed the paper with a flourish. The ministry officials also signed and Mr Rafiq stamped it.

The meeting was over. As far as Mr Rafiq and the other officials were concerned, the budget for the Ministry of Public Works had been decided. All that was required now was for the president to sign a decree to make it official.

I could see that Afghanistan could easily get itself into financial difficulties this way. It was traditional, incremental budgeting, based on automatic adjustments to last year's budget in accordance with rules and 'norms', rather than a decision-making process based on economic reality and government policy.

In this system, the budget can only go up. It was exactly like bargaining over a carpet in the bazaar. No detailed records were kept of what had been decided and why, except in Mr Rafiq's head or perhaps on the scraps of paper he kept in his bottom drawer.

During my time in the budget department, I sat through five rounds of discussions about the budget and it seemed that the same calculations were done again and again. I felt certain some ministries had been given a 'correction' to the same items in their budget three years in a row.

The process was entirely in the hands of Mr Rafiq. There was little opportunity for scrutiny by anyone else, even his superiors, and I more than half suspected that some of the more surprising results he produced from his calculator may have been arranged outside the office long before the meeting started.

There was also no reference in the discussions to what the ministries were going to do with their budget. This would have seemed to Mr Rafiq a stupid question. Obviously, the Ministry of Education operates schools, the Ministry of Health runs clinics and hospitals, and the Ministry of Public Works builds things. There was no discussion, however, about how they were doing it, whether they were doing it well, or whether they needed to do it at all.

I soon found out, however, that all these long discussions about the budget, in reality, had little to do with how government funds were actually distributed. Decisions to spend money were largely made on the run during the year, as ministers got their chance to lobby the president, usually without any involvement from the Ministry of Finance.

The president would sign a presidential decree, known locally as a 'hokum', to authorise extra spending on things that hadn't been included in the budget, and money would be found from copious 'reserve funds' and 'emergency funds'. Under previous regimes, these reserve funds had constituted as much as eighty percent of the annual budget. In fact, during the Taliban era, their leader Mullah Omar had apparently kept his government's money in a trunk under his bed, to be handed out as required. It seemed the current president hadn't moved far from this model.

President Karzai signed dozens of hokums every week, even though he himself had approved the carefully calculated, fiercely argued annual budget. The budget process was merely the stage at which the Ministry of Finance caught up with what was already a *fait accompli*.

So the ministers who had the best relationship with the president, or the most political clout, were the ones who had the best chance of getting their budget proposals approved, rather than those who could really do something useful with the funds.

Dr Ghani understood that this was not the best way to manage things. He'd ensured that the most recent budget decree included a clause that set strict limits on what hokums could be used for and how much the president could authorise from reserve funds.

Nevertheless, Deputy Minister Rahimi received a new hokum just a few days after the budget was signed, a request for $50,000 to pay for the destruction of opium poppy crops. It was no doubt a worthwhile activity, but I wondered why such a large project hadn't been mentioned by anyone during the long and convoluted process of preparing the budget.

'What can I do?' Rahimi lamented. 'He's the president. It's impossible to refuse.'

●━━━●

JUST A FEW weeks after I arrived in Afghanistan, the US government decided to start another war. George Bush issued an ultimatum to Saddam Hussain, the President of Iraq. If he didn't give up his 'weapons of mass destruction' the US would invade.

In Kabul, thousands of miles from Washington but not that far from Baghdad, hundreds of experienced aid workers and foreign relations experts, watching the diplomatic confrontation unfold on the satellite news channels, were all thinking the same thing. 'Please no! Don't do it!'

Surrounded by the devastation and trauma caused by years of conflict in this country, we couldn't understand why political leaders in Washington seemed hellbent on embroiling themselves in more trouble. From our vantage point, it sounded very ill-advised.

The war was due to start at eight pm US time, prime time viewing for Americans. In Kabul, it was early morning. On the television in our living room excited BBC, Euronews, Fox and CNN commentators interviewed each other, crossing from reporters in their studios to reporters at the UN Security Council, and to US and British troops waiting in Kuwait or Saudi Arabia for their orders.

Just as we were about to leave for the office they reported that missiles had been launched at Baghdad and we received the order to stay at home until further notice. In Kabul, as war was being fought just one time zone away, it was a sunny early spring day and we organised a barbeque in the back garden.

Like most of the world, we followed the war on television every evening. Within a few days, US Army tanks were racing across the desert towards Baghdad with cameras and journalists on board sending live pictures by satellite.

When it became clear that the people in Kabul weren't going to rise up against foreigners in sympathy with the Iraqi government we were allowed to go back to work. The very idea that they might have done so perhaps shows how badly some people misunderstood the situation in that part of the world.

A few weeks later, US forces finally reached Baghdad and the Iraqi Army melted into the desert. We watched on TV as people in Baghdad tried to pull down a statue of Saddam Hussein. Even when the US army brought in its heavy equipment the old man was hard to shift. His legs were reinforced with metal rods. Instead of the quick, decisive toppling of the hated oppressor that the Americans had expected, it was a slow, messy and unsatisfying affair, as was the whole Iraq adventure, in the end.

In retrospect, it's clear that the invasion of Iraq was a turning point for Afghanistan. The US government and other donors started shifting their resources to Baghdad and news reporters were only interested in Iraq.

Some of my colleagues from Kosovo and Kabul also got sucked into the Iraq vortex. At first, their reports of life in Baghdad were positive, even amusing. They described their accommodation in rows of demountable cabins set up in an underground car park, and posed for photos sitting on Saddam's gold throne in the palace they now used as their office.

Then the kidnappings and beheadings started and life there became progressively more dangerous. Simply travelling to and from the airport in the UN's armour-plated truck was a life-threatening undertaking. One friend went home with post-traumatic stress.

But others loved the excitement. One woman who worked with us in Kabul found Afghanistan too dull and couldn't wait to go back to Baghdad. A few weeks later she was dead, killed by a car bomb as her vehicle waited in line for a security check at the entrance to the green zone.

In Kabul, the effect of the new war in Iraq wasn't immediately perceptible; just a gradual decline in interest and effort. It's impossible to know how things might have been different if Iraq had never happened. Afghanistan may still have become the intractable mess it is today. But it might also have been a lot better.

BIBI MARU
Kabul, Afghanistan, Summer 2003

In late March, with the annual budget finalised, Bruce and Doug went home to Washington.

Before they left, we organised a company car and driver to take us on a sightseeing tour of the city beyond the normal routine of the office and the house. As our guidebook, we used a recently reprinted edition of a 1972 *Historical Guide to Kabul* which was being sold on street corners by young hawkers.

We tried to direct the driver along its suggested tour routes, but it was difficult to match the grand palaces and modern public buildings described in the book thirty years before with the rubble and dereliction that now stood in their place. New roads had been built, new suburbs of Soviet-era public housing had been constructed, and the grand avenues were now blocked by military checkpoints.

Across the Kabul River, we passed kilometre after kilometre of bombed and burned buildings. The walls around a high school were perforated by rockets. A large apartment building had collapsed into rubble at one end, but people still lived and businesses still traded in what was left standing.

It was Friday, a religious day for Muslims but not a day of rest, and the streets were crowded with people buying meat, fruit, hardware, clothes and jewellery from open-fronted shops.

At the end of a long wide road on the southern outskirts of the city, we came to the shell of the building now known as the King's Palace. In the guidebook, it was described as an impressive castle in the grounds of a luxurious park.

In 2003, however, the walls were crumbling from the impacts of shellfire and the former domed roof was a post-apocalyptic metal skeleton. We could see where the ornamental gardens and hedges had once been, but now they were scattered with empty missile casings, spent bullets and abandoned military equipment.

It was vivid evidence of the destruction rained on Kabul during the years of civil war, when opposing mujahedeen factions controlled positions on the hills around the city and smashed everything between them to smithereens.

A small herd of goats chewed on the weeds, led by two young boys who were keen to have their picture taken, even though they would never see the photo.

AFTER BRUCE AND Doug departed, their places in the shared house were soon taken by other middle-aged men including a tall, lanky American media adviser whose job was to give the Afghans helpful messages about the benefits of paying taxes, and a grumpy Australian farmer who was promoting private sector development.

Larry and I were now left with the task of improving Afghanistan's convoluted budget implementation processes. The official system of financial management, such as it was, broke down almost entirely anywhere outside Kabul, making it difficult for the government to actually spend the money allocated in the budget.

There was almost no communication between the central government and most other parts of the country. There were no phones, no reliable postal service, and travel on the bad roads was slow and dangerous. As a result, the government in Kabul didn't know what was happening in the regions, and the people in the regions didn't know, or possibly care much, what was happening in Kabul.

If taxes were collected by regional government offices they were often kept by the local governor or warlord and used to buy support or to fund his personal army. In many other provinces, civil servants received salaries intermittently and there was never money for things like schoolbooks or road repairs.

Getting this rusty old machinery of budget implementation working effectively again was now my main challenge. But first I had to understand it.

The Afghan staff in the Ministry of Finance said they knew how it all worked, but the more I investigated and questioned them, the more I realised that they didn't fully comprehend it. They knew the rules, they knew which forms must be filled in, which columns should be added up, and who should sign at the bottom. But they couldn't explain why it had to be done this way.

There was a thirty-year-old Xeroxed document setting out the official procedures, but most of the current practices were not written down and this provided scope for subtle modifications that served somebody's interest, not necessarily the government's.

Wajid soon became my principal assistant in the quest to understand the budget management process and we spent large amounts of time engaged in intense and convoluted discussions with Mr Rafiq and Mr Amir about the functions of B20 and B27 forms, later moving on to explore the intricacies of B4s and B6s.

Mr Rafiq, at his marble desk in the budget office, was clearly exasperated by my constant questions. He probably thought I was a little slow. He'd told me many times already how things were done. First, you fill in this form, then it is approved, then this form and afterwards that one. What else could I possibly want to know?

IN A COUNTRY where most people can't tell the time there's no point changing the clocks with the seasons so when summer arrived, the sun rose very early. This was a good time of day to walk around the streets of our quiet neighbourhood in the cool morning air, ignoring the strict security rules about leaving the house.

Men on bicycles and a few horse-drawn carts were almost the only traffic on the roads. A few women, hidden under burqas, walked to their jobs in the rich foreigners' houses.

Two blocks away from the house we reached Bibi Maru Hill, the steep pile of dirt and rocks that rose like an industrial slag heap in the middle of our suburb. Other foreigners from the neighbourhood also used the hill for their early morning exercise, running up the winding road to the top or toiling up the steep gravel sides, hoping that if they stuck to the well-used paths they would avoid the landmines that might still be buried there.

Every morning the local soccer team and their coach jogged up the road in their bright baggy track pants. Itinerant beekeepers pitched tents and spread their wooden beehives out on the hillside. All the Afghans we met were friendly and the world seemed like a good place.

From the top we had a view over most of the sprawling city of Kabul, from the few tall buildings in the city centre, the suburbs crawling around the steep hills, and the shanty towns climbing their slopes. When a windy day blew away the city dust, the Hindu Kush mountains, still topped with snow, seemed crisp and close enough to touch.

On the top of the hill, hidden from sight until you reached it, was an empty swimming pool—a concrete-lined pit with the shattered remains of a diving tower at one end. It was a relic of a previous era when life in Kabul must have been unbelievably different.

Near it was a huge metal advertising billboard, as unexpected as the swimming pool. When I'd arrived in Kabul it had displayed a gigantic portrait of Ahmad Shah Massoud, the leader of the Northern Alliance, who'd been assassinated by Al-Qaeda in 2001, just a few days before the 9/11 attacks on the World Trade Centre in New York. His face had gazed across the houses of Kabul in the direction of the presidential compound.

A few weeks later we looked up at the hill one morning and Massoud was gone. The billboard stood rusty and bare. The Afghans told us the poster had 'blown away' during the night. It was never replaced.

I EXPECTED TO be staying in Afghanistan a while so I decided I should try to learn the local language. In Kosovo, I'd started Albanian lessons but the Kosovars had proved to be far better at learning English than I was at learning their language and it soon seemed a pointless exercise. I was hoping I'd be more successful here.

I asked around if anyone knew someone who could teach Dari. Bill, the media adviser, referred me to his teacher, Marya. Her main job was with an NGO, teaching reading and writing to young women who'd never had a chance to go to school, but she was happy to spend an hour a week with me for an extra ten dollars.

Then Mr Haqiqi, an Afghan American accounting adviser from New York, introduced me to his wife's cousin, Zeba, a young primary school teacher. I didn't have the heart to tell her I'd already found someone, so I ended up with two Dari teachers and lived in dread that either one would find out about the other.

Marya came to the house at lunchtime and her lessons were an unstructured excursion through Dari phrases and vocabulary. There was no textbook or lesson plan and I was usually the one who decided what topic we would explore that day—perhaps the names of fruits and vegetables, telling the time, or buying things in the market. None of it seemed relevant to work, and the phrases I wrote down in my notebook in phonetic English never seemed to stick in my head. Nevertheless, my vocabulary gradually expanded.

I met with Zeba in the office. She brought the official grade one primary school reader as her textbook and we worked our way through simple sentences about a young boy and his goat and donkey. Dari is a dialect of Farsi, the language spoken in Iran. Its text, like Arabic, runs from right to left, and is devoid of vowels but with apparently several different symbols for each consonant. Zeba patiently explained to me, again and again, the difference in sound between the symbol for 'koff' and the symbol for 'koff'. No, I couldn't hear a difference either.

Learning the alphabet had its uses, though. I was soon able to work out which column of numbers was the budget and which was the spending or the balance, and which table was for which ministry. But I never became either fluent or literate in Dari. Most of my tentative efforts to make conversation with the house staff or the guards were greeted with either blank confusion or guffaws of laughter.

But I did learn a lot about Afghan people and history from my two teachers. They both provided titbits of information, scraps of gossip and stories from the past that I would not have got from anyone else. Marya had been a young woman when the communists were in power and Dr Najibullah, who she clearly admired, had been president. She told me about going to a summer pop concert in a park at night with her friends only a decade earlier, wearing a miniskirt and high heels and no scarf.

Zeba told me about the shopkeeper who chastised her for wearing nail polish and about the high cost of getting a taxi in Kabul. When I realised, after several months, that she spent most of the money I paid her simply getting to and from our lessons, I arranged for Emron, the driver, to pick her up and take her home each week.

•———•

IN THE BUDGET department, I rarely dealt with anyone other than Mr Rafiq and Mr Amir. Delegation was not a feature of their management style and most of their staff seemed to have little to do. I decided to organise a training program for them, to explain some of the concepts of modern government financial management.

The ministry didn't have any dedicated training facilities at that time so we did all our classes in the large former 'mosque' on the top floor. In July, it was stiflingly hot. The windows were left open to catch any small breeze, but they also let in the dust and the insects. Two large electric fans circulated the dust evenly around the room.

One side of the space had been partitioned into offices, so staff and their visitors came and went throughout the lessons. Another corner of the room was still used as a prayer space by ministry staff and, from lunchtime onwards, men arrived with freshly washed feet and hands to face the glass-brick wall which indicated the direction of Mecca.

The ministry's childcare centre was on the other side of the glass bricks and the shouts and cries of playing children and the sounds of organised singing and banging on drums and tambourines filtered into the training room.

Delivering training in these conditions was hard. It was difficult for the students to hear either the lecturer or the interpreters and in the heat, they soon started to lose concentration. The women in particular sat and endured stoically, swathed in layers of cloth from their feet to the tops of their heads, delicately mopping the sweat flowing from their faces.

For a whole week in this environment, the students learned about the economic role of government and the importance of setting economic and social policy goals, and about technical issues like expenditure classification and cost-benefit analysis. At the end of the course all participants duly reported they'd found it interesting and useful and would recommend the training to others.

Then they went back to their offices where they had almost no meaningful work to do because it was all done either by their bosses, like Rafiq and Amir, or by advisers like myself, who could use the computer and talk to the other foreign advisers in English.

•———•

SUMMER IN KABUL, just as in Kosovo, was wedding season, and Noori invited me to his wife's younger brother's wedding party. He'd been appointed by his in-laws to organise the event and he was keen for me to go.

I'd heard that being a foreign visitor at an Afghan wedding was more an ordeal than a good night out, but Noori assured me that his family all spoke English and that he would look after me.

Rob, an American lawyer who lived in the house next door, agreed to come too. He spoke fluent Dari and I thought it would be good to have his company. I didn't realise I wouldn't see him all night.

Noori's brother-in-law and his fiancée had come from London for the wedding. In the UK, they may well have been just another modern young couple doing what young people in London do, but they'd come home to Kabul to get married in the Afghan style as if they had never met before.

The wedding was held on a Friday evening in an outlying suburb of Kabul in one of the many brightly lit, multi-storey 'wedding halls' in this part of the city. Each wedding hall was surrounded with parked cars and looked more or less like a suburban shopping mall.

Noori was outside waiting for us when we arrived. As soon as we left the car, Rob and I had to part, as all the men went into one room and the women into another. Even the door to the women's room was hidden behind a wooden screen.

Inside it was packed with people. At one end a live band was playing deafening pop music and a group of teenage girls in sequinned dresses were dancing energetically on the dance floor.

Noori came with me into the women's room. As a close relative of the groom, he was allowed to be there. So were his father-in-law and various uncles, cousins and teenage boys, and, of course, the male musicians and waiters.

A couple danced together *Saturday Night Fever* style, wiggling their shoulders and pointing at the ceiling. At the end of their dance, someone threw a handful of one Afghani notes, worth about two cents each, in the air above their heads, which were immediately scooped up by the children.

Noori introduced me to his wife. I should have known she would be beautiful—a tall woman in a spectacular cream satin dress and masses of gold jewellery. She carried a small child who was crying loudly. It was way past his bedtime and there was far too much noise.

I also met Noori's many younger sisters, all wearing bright coloured outfits, and his father-in-law, a grey-bearded man who worked for the UN. They all spoke English, but the music was so loud that it was almost impossible to have any kind of conversation. I tried practising my Dari with some of the children but, as usual, they reacted with howls of laughter.

I sat with the sisters and cousins watching the dancing and admiring the women's clothes. In the street or at work, Afghan women, if not completely covered in a burqa, wore sensible clothes in sombre colours, but here they were dressed in a fascinating variety of fashions from sequined ball gowns and smartly tailored western-style suits, to colourful Pakistani shalwar kameez, sequined trouser suits, black beaded abayas, even a purple and gold Indian sari, accessorised with elaborate gold necklaces, bracelets and ornaments. Their hair was teased, curled and sprayed into complicated styles and decorated with glitter.

In all the noise and movement, it took me a while to notice that the bride and groom were in the room, sitting on large chairs on a raised platform decorated with white ruffles of fabric and garish plastic flowers. He wore a turban and she was in a brightly coloured traditional tunic with a gold embroidered vest. They both looked very glum.

After a while, during a break in the music, they stood up and paraded once around the room and out the door, with a video cameraman walking backwards in front of them, his floodlights glaring in their eyes. It was the signal for dinner to be served.

Until then, the tables had been bare, with no food or refreshment of any kind. Now waiters brought out piles of plates and cutlery and glasses and dumped them in the middle of each table. The young men who'd been dancing with the girls were scolded out of the room by the older women. Platters of food were delivered unceremoniously to each table in quick succession.

It was the usual Afghan banquet meal—several kinds of rice, overcooked chicken and a plate of salad, plus a huge platter of fresh peaches and large bottles of Pepsi. Now that the music had stopped I was able to talk to Noori's sisters, who seemed exactly like teenage girls anywhere in the world.

When the meal was finished, which was quite soon because the food was gobbled down quickly, the waiters came back and bundled everything, all the used plates and cutlery, the glasses, and the unfinished platters of food, into the tablecloth and carried it away. The band returned and the dancing started again with even more noise and energy.

Suddenly, the musicians broke into a solemn tune as the bride and groom re-entered. He was now in a suit and she wore a white bridal gown and was clutching a posy of plastic flowers. They looked as downcast as before. Apparently, this is intended to indicate their sadness at leaving their families.

Several solemn rituals were performed, photographed and recorded from every angle. One of Noori's sisters tried to explain them to me. First, they lit two candles. This had some symbolic significance to do with the flame of undying love but unfortunately, on this hot night, the overhead fans blew the candles out as soon as they were lit. After a few tries, they gave up.

Then the young couple were photographed jointly reading the Qur'an and then looking at their reflections in a mirror. They shared a plate of sweet dessert—he fed her and then she fed him—and finally, they cut the lime green and white cake, repeating the spoon-feeding. Most of the people in the room paid no attention to any of this and were either dancing, gossiping or getting ready to leave.

There were probably more rituals to be performed, but Noori came with a message from Rob. He was ready to go. It seemed to me the party was just beginning. The dance floor was still full, the band seemed set to play on and I could have stayed much longer.

On the way out, I stopped to peer into the men's party on the other side of the foyer. It was a much larger room but dark and almost empty. Another band was playing and four men danced a slow traditional dance together. It looked excruciatingly dull. No wonder Rob wanted to leave.

As we left the wedding hall, my thanks to Noori for inviting me were genuine. We found our patiently waiting driver and headed back into town.

'It wasn't too bad,' Rob said once we were in the car. 'I met some useful contacts.' He'd been to Afghan weddings before so he'd known what to expect. Nevertheless, he decided we'd call in at the bar at the Mustapha Hotel for a drink on the way home.

•———•

Marriage was a fraught issue for all the young Afghans I worked with.

Shahzia, a tall, self-assured young woman with excellent English, who seemed to have a promising future, came to my office one day looking downcast. She'd come to say goodbye. She was going to visit her parents in Quetta, across the border in Pakistan, and they wanted her to get married. She was clearly not keen on the idea. She told me she would prefer to keep her job.

I told her she should find a husband who would let her work. 'That's the problem,' she said, with a sigh of resignation. 'There aren't any.'

Some families were more enlightened. Nasir's parents had announced one day that it was time he married, but they gave him an opportunity to find his own bride.

He was studying at university part-time, as most of our staff seemed to be, and was friends with a fellow student. His parents contacted her parents and they came to an agreement. They were lucky. He assured me that his fiancée wouldn't be staying home to look after him and getting pregnant as soon as possible.

But Naim, one of the many doctors working as interpreters in the Ministry of Finance, had said exactly the same thing. He was in his thirties when he'd married a seventeen-year-old. She was still a high school student when I attended their engagement party. It was more or less a smaller version of the wedding I'd been to a few months earlier, held in a similar gigantic wedding hall.

Naim's young fiancée arrived in a car decorated with bows and streamers and plastic flowers, not unlike the wedding cars that paraded through Pristina every summer. She was dressed in a brocade gown with flimsy sleeves that daringly revealed glimpses of her pudgy young arms. Her hair was piled up and rock-hard with hairspray and her eyelids were weighed down with bright blue glitter and thick false eyelashes. She looked like a kewpie doll.

While the guests gorged on platters of rice and chicken, washed down with Pepsi, the engaged couple stood on the stage for an hour or more, patiently posing for photographs with every possible combination of relatives.

After they married, she sat the university entrance exam but was soon pregnant, which meant the end of her university studies. I was continually disappointed when men in their thirties who I'd come to have a high opinion of announced they were getting married and I found out that their bride was only fifteen or sixteen.

Most of the marriages I knew of were between cousins. Some of my western colleagues were appalled at the popularity of cousin marriage in Afghanistan, seeing it as something close to incest and likely to lead to genetic abnormalities. But I could see the logic of it.

Afghan families are large, and the definition of 'cousin' is broad. Many couples have ten or more children, so some people could have up to 100 first cousins on each side to choose from when they look for a spouse, and that doesn't take into account second cousins, cousins by marriage, and more distant relatives, who are also counted as cousins.

The major advantage of marrying someone who is already part of the family is that there is a chance the young couple have actually met each other at some time at weddings, engagements or other family celebrations. Certainly, their parents probably know each other, and the whole extended family will have an interest in making the relationship work.

In particular, cousin marriages help to protect the girl from the risk of ending up with a violent husband or abusive in-laws. In times of insecurity and uncertainty, and given the lack of legal protections for women, or for anyone really, it's the safest option.

GHANI'S TANTRUM
Kabul, September 2003

During one of his frequent temper tantrums, Dr Ghani sacked the budget president. The minister was renowned for his temper and the shock waves from each outburst would ripple through the ministry, radiating from his office down through the ranks of officials, finally dissipating as increased grumpiness at the level of the lowest staff.

On this occasion, he'd been studying the payroll figures for all the ministries, looking for cabinet colleagues to castigate over their ballooning staff numbers, when he noticed the 2200 new people who had somehow been recruited by his own ministry without his knowledge.

The budget president was immediately summoned to explain his failure to adequately control the ministry budget and disappeared from the building a few days later. The position remained vacant for several months. The work of the budget department seemed to proceed quite well without him as he'd never been much more than a figurehead.

Then, in October, Ghani appointed a new budget president who could not have been more different from the previous one. For one thing, she was a woman. In her dress and demeanour, Seema appeared to me to be every inch an independent young western woman, apart from the flimsy headscarf she draped loosely over her hair. She'd left Afghanistan in the early 90s and had spent the next decade studying and working in the UK. She was now in her early thirties and had come back to help her country rebuild.

On her first day at work in the ministry, she chose to sit in the foreign advisers' office, rather than the budget president's official room down the corridor. She finally went to meet her

Afghan staff in the budget department several days later and I had the impression that, in those early days in the job, she found the grizzled old guys in the ministry almost as challenging and intimidating as I did.

Seema was just one of many strong, independent and competent Afghan women I worked with during my time in Kabul, despite the country's reputation for gender inequality.

At the time she arrived, the foreign adviser team in the budget and treasury departments were in the process of formulating plans for fixing the convoluted and corruption-prone system for managing the government's spending. We were going to rationalise and streamline the form filling and reporting required to implement the budget, transform the accounting procedures and reorganise the chart of accounts.

Now that the advisers had all agreed between them on the essential changes, all we had to do was to persuade the Afghans. There was almost universal resistance among Afghan civil servants to any change in the existing administrative processes. The smallest amendment to accounting codes or our attempts to speed up communications with provinces, whatever we proposed, required hours of discussion and explanation and still our Afghan counterparts claimed it would be the end of civilisation as they knew it and on our heads be it.

Their stubbornness was perhaps not such a bad thing. I was constantly amazed at the resilience of the system they already had. In spite of coups, revolutions, civil war and neglect, it just kept on going, with all its flaws and inefficiencies. That's the great strength of bureaucracy, and also its weakness.

So it was perhaps not surprising that government officials in the regions weren't prepared to accept a single memorandum from Kabul, signed by some young woman who claimed to be the new director-general of budget, as sufficient authority to change the established practices of decades.

Meanwhile, I finally felt I'd achieved something through my work in the budget department, although it was a rather small achievement. Jabar and Touryalai, two of the middle-aged Afghan civil servants in the department, had prepared an Excel spreadsheet for a meeting of the Council of Ministers.

They'd needed a little help from Wajid on Excel formatting and formulas, but basically, the spreadsheet was all their own work. They'd found the data, designed the table, and entered it into the computer.

They were delighted with it and so was I. Before we'd arrived six months earlier they had, quite possibly, never seen a computer. Almost certainly, they'd never used one for their work in the ministry. Our project had provided the computers, taught them how to use them, and suggested they could transfer all their data from hand-written forms into a spreadsheet. The rest had been up to them.

I WAS NEVER entirely sure whether Seema and the many other English-speaking returnee Afghans employed by the ministry should be regarded as locals who happened to speak good English or as expat consultants who happened to speak Dari. They could play either role, depending on the context. How other ministry staff, the 'real' civil servants, saw them I had no idea.

Nevertheless, Seema did get things done. Over the next twelve months, we wrote and enacted a new public finance law and restructured the budget department. The restructuring was a consequence of the mammoth priority reform and restructuring program being implemented by the Civil Service Commission, which involved developing a new organisational structure, writing new job descriptions for all positions, and interviewing all the staff to place them in the new positions, after which increased salaries would be available.

The review was, of course, supposed to be done by Afghan officials in the ministry, but in most ministries, including finance, it was actually done by advisers. In the case of the budget department that meant me.

There was a massive amount of paperwork required, which I diligently prepared and had translated into Dari. The actual decisions on staffing, however, had to be taken by someone in a position of authority.

My initial proposal had been to keep all the current staff, although not necessarily in the jobs they'd been doing. There were new functions to incorporate now that we were computerised and a greater need for analytical skills rather than just form filling.

Seema, however, took a more radical view. She decided to axe half the positions in the department. She conducted one-on-one interviews with each person to decide who would go and who would stay; not an ideal HR practice and, in the end, many of her decisions seemed to have been made on compassionate grounds, based on people's family circumstances, as much as on their suitability for the job.

The redundant staff apparently accepted their dismissal without complaint. They would not be without an income. They would be placed on the Civil Service Commission's list of surplus staff and continue to be paid for several years until they were found a new job. They were, however, off our books.

RAMADAN ARRIVED IN October; a day later than expected. The mullahs failed to see the new moon so everyone had one more day of eating and drinking before the month of fasting began.

The indecision about the date of the holiday caused havoc in the office. People arrived late for work and many didn't come in at all.

For the rest of the month, normal life in Kabul was more or less turned upside down. Government work hours were reduced. Everyone went home at one pm to rest and wait for sundown. In the office, people seemed either more light-hearted or more angry than usual. There was no enthusiasm for work and meetings were easily cancelled.

Previously, I'd never seen the point of Ramadan, but now I thought I understood. When it's celebrated by everyone, as it is in places like Afghanistan, it creates a strong sense of shared community. Everyone endures the same discomfort and hardship and looks forward to the end of the day and ultimately, the end of the ordeal.

The people of Kabul woke at three am to eat before the mullah called the prayer at the first sign of daylight. From then on there was, officially, no food or drink until the mullah called the evening prayer, at about five pm. During the day, restaurants were boarded closed. At sundown, the streets were suddenly deserted. Everyone was at home eating and drinking for the first time in twelve hours.

It was not only food and drink that had to be foregone. Makeup, perfume, even deodorant and toothpaste seemed to be forbidden. I'm sure one of the men in the budget department had decided to give up washing completely for the month, as he smelled so much worse than usual.

During the last week of the fasting month, the city streets were even more jammed with traffic as crowds of people prepared for the Eid celebrations at the end of Ramadan, carrying parcels and bags and boxes, just like pre-Christmas shoppers. Aziz, one of the Afghan American advisers on our team, bought two sheep to sacrifice and kept them tied up in the front garden of his house in anticipation.

As at the start, the exact day Ramadan would finish and the Eid holiday would begin wasn't certain. We'd been told it would be on Wednesday, but on Tuesday morning, I looked out of my bedroom window and saw that the street was completely deserted. The usual morning rush hour traffic was missing and there were no pedestrians. The start of the holiday had been announced sometime the previous evening.

The city began to stir around mid-morning. Two men walked down the street selling bright coloured helium-filled balloons on strings and blow-up toys that made squeaking noises. One of the policemen who was permanently posted outside the house bought a balloon for his little boy who was apparently visiting Dad at work that day.

The office was closed for the next few days but, in fact, not much work had been done for the past week because many people, including our minister and deputy minister, had already left town for the holiday. Aziz's sheep disappeared from his front garden, one after the other.

A week later Zeba, my second Dari teacher, invited me to her house for tea and 'Eid food' which meant biscuits, pistachios and what she called chocolate but was really butter toffees.

We sat on cushions made of carpet in the small front room of her parents' house, around the woodstove. The room also seemed to be where she and her parents slept. Her mother's long hair was dyed bright ginger under her scarf.

Zeba showed me photographs of her uncles in the US, with their American girlfriends, and other relatives in Canada and Germany. It seemed that everyone I knew in Kabul had relatives in the west. Her mother cried melodramatically when we talked about her absent family.

Zeba's older brother came in from having his bath at the local bathhouse. He and another brother were musicians who performed at weddings. There was no shortage of weddings in Kabul, and every wedding required two bands, so they probably made quite a good living from it. Of course, during the Taliban days, when all music and dancing had been banned, things were not quite as good. 'We had to go and live in Pakistan', Zeba explained.

One brother was married and the other was engaged. Zeba, who was about twenty-seven, was still single. I asked if she wanted to get married. 'My mother likes me too much to let me go,' she told me.

I was taken on a tour of the house. It was very old and hadn't been painted for a long time so the outside was the colour of its mud bricks, but it was quite a substantial residence with a huge overgrown back garden hidden behind the high outside walls.

The married brother and his wife lived in a large room with rugs and cushions arranged around a TV set and an ornate double bed in one corner. The other brother, the one who was engaged, had the largest room—a man cave annex attached to the back of the house, with a huge TV, stereo, DVD player, more carpets and cushions, and another elaborate double bed. It seemed that the two sons lived like kings while Zeba and her mother and father slept on the floor in the living room.

•———•

WHEN WINTER ARRIVED, Kabul looked like a Christmas card. The snow that topped the mountains for most of the year came to the city. It pulled branches from trees and brought illegally connected phone lines and power cables down across the roads. None of the cars had chains on their tyres and they slid into each other, causing worse-than-usual traffic jams.

Working conditions in the Ministry of Finance hadn't improved much since I'd arrived and winter made it much worse. The building was very cold. The central heating, which was only turned on when people arrived at work and turned off again when they left, barely took the chill off the air and all the electric heaters had been confiscated because they overloaded the wiring. Our office, with its big, badly sealed windows, was freezing.

The local staff in the budget department were worse off. When Seema asked them what heating they had in their room they all replied in unison, 'Heech!' None!

Then, on a Friday, when the office was empty, the central heating pipes burst, flooding most of our floor. The carpet squelched under my feet when I got to work on Saturday morning. Workmen took it away, revealing the green marbled linoleum of decades before, now coated with mud.

A few weeks later the building's water pump broke down so there was no water in the taps for two days. The toilets were all locked to stop the staff from using them. I had no idea what they were supposed to do instead. The reserve water supply in the foreign advisers' bathroom—a big plastic rubbish bin—was soon used up so our 'chowkidor' hauled buckets of water up two flights of stairs to replenish it.

Every room in the ministry had a chowkidor, who was supposed to look after the office. The chowkidor generally didn't do anything particularly essential or useful. Most of the day he simply, in keeping with the name, sat on a chair—a chowki—in the cold corridor, doing nothing. Every now and then he made tea or ran an errand, but his main role was just being at the beck and call of his superiors.

Something similar applied to cleaners—the women who splashed water around in the bathrooms and the men who pushed brooms and mops around on the floors. They went through the motions of cleaning but they didn't make anything cleaner. The dirt remained, perhaps redistributed, and the water splashed on the bathroom tiles simply nourished the mould and added to the multiple layers of grime.

At the other end of the hierarchy, it seemed that the traditional role of a senior official in the civil service was simply to be important, to have a large office with many sofas and many visitors, to preside at formal meetings and to sign documents that the lesser-ranked staff put in front of them. That was certainly the role played by the officials in the Ministry of Finance before Dr Ghani shook them out of their comfortable niches.

Perhaps this was also the way President Karzai saw his job, as simply a matter of travelling to important summits and conferences, receiving high-level visitors and delegations, and signing apparently any piece of paper his staff put on his desk.

•—•

IN THE DEPTH of winter in December 2003, 500 Afghan dignitaries, representing all of Afghanistan's various tribes and factions, assembled in a large tent on the outskirts of Kabul under international military guard to convene a 'Loya Jirga' to agree on a new constitution.

Dr Ghani was heavily involved in the discussions so he had even less time to deal with questions about the budget for the coming year. It seemed difficult for some of the foreign consultants I worked with to understand that the issues that were important to them, because they were being paid to deal with them, may not be the most important items on the government's agenda. Negotiating a constitution that kept the peace between different factions and ethnic groups might perhaps take precedence.

The process took almost a month but eventually, the Loya Jirga ended with agreement on a new constitution. Karzai seemed to have won his bid for more power for the president, possibly at the expense of more concessions to Islamic fundamentalists.

The new constitution would lead to the next stage of the process of bringing democracy to Afghanistan—the election of a national parliament and a president who would have a stronger claim to legitimacy than one chosen by foreigners.

DynCorp
Kabul, February 2004

February 2004 was the anniversary of my arrival in Kabul and supposedly marked the end of my twelve-month contract. No one in the company I worked for brought this up. I continued to go to work and they continued to pay me.

By now, strangely enough, Kabul felt like home, almost as much as Pristina had felt like home. I'd become accustomed to the unusual way of life, made some friends and discovered that, given enough time, it's possible to get used to sharing a house with even the most difficult residents.

Life in Kabul more generally also seemed to be improving. The city was in the middle of a construction boom. Every day another old, damaged building was demolished and another new, modern shop selling computers or sequined Pakistani clothing opened in its place.

The post office building across Pashtunistan Square was painted and renovated. The Hotel Kabul site started to look as if it could emerge as the luxury hotel it was supposed to be. An impressive western-style shopping mall with an escalator and shops selling electronic goods and expensive sportswear had just opened, and President Karzai himself had formally launched the construction of an international luxury hotel on land opposite the US Embassy.

Big, shiny new Japanese buses with huge clean glass windows now swished through the streets of Kabul, replacing the heavy, battered and rusty old Indian buses that had travelled around with people hanging from the doors. The new buses looked completely out of place surrounded by mule carts, bicycles, herds of goats and painted lorries.

The buses had been donated by the Japanese government,

along with light blue bus stop signs decorated with the red and white Japanese flag and little ticket booths placed along the main roads.

Minister Ghani was furious about the buses. He was usually furious about most things. He would have preferred the Japanese to simply donate money. For the price of one modern Japanese bus, designed for the streets of Tokyo, the government could have bought ten rugged Indian buses, built for Indian conditions, without delicate computer-controlled engines and air conditioning.

It seemed to me the burqa count was down too. A year before, there'd been dozens of blue shapes floating down the streets, but now I only saw one or two as I watched the flow of daily life in Kabul from my office window.

On the dirt footpath immediately below our window, two little boys sat begging every day. The oldest may have been eight or nine. The younger one couldn't have been more than five. They were dressed in rags and sat forlornly in the dust as passers-by dropped tattered Afghani notes in front of them.

An older boy came past every few hours to collect the money. If it rained, they would sit in a puddle of water, looking even more pitiable. The younger child had a talent for producing five or so minutes of heart-rending crying and wailing from time to time, with tears streaming down his face. He sounded genuinely distressed. It was very effective. The boys would be showered with money by women in burqas and men in dirty clothes who probably had little to spare themselves.

Across the road, several old men sat on folding chairs with their backs against a wall offering their services to the public as freelance letter writers. They were former government employees who gave advice on how to deal with the different ministries to get your problem solved. They worked using the surface of their briefcase as a desk, composing impressive-looking hand-written correspondence for illiterate supplicants.

From this vantage point, I could also see, or at least hear, the many gatherings that took place in Pashtunistan Square, just next to the ministry, where people congregated to publicise their grievances. At various times there were meetings of dismissed military officers wanting their salaries, devout Muslims angry because women singers had been broadcast on national television, or street vendors upset at new restrictions on where they could take their carts, a policy aimed at improving Kabul's congested traffic.

The street vendors were still plying their trade in the less busy areas and they trundled their rickety barrows past the ministry each day laden with peanuts or cucumbers, fresh fish or used clothing. One barrow sold goldfish, swimming in clear plastic bags of water hanging from rails.

The most poignant was always the cart of second-hand soft toys with its collection of floppy bunnies and careworn teddy bears, outgrown and discarded by their first owners, sitting hopefully, waiting for a new life in a new family.

One afternoon the street outside seemed ominously empty. Then a dozen aggressive men on crutches lurched down the road, clearing bystanders away to make a path for hundreds of wheelchairs and various kinds of homemade wheeled contraptions, some propelled with hand-powered bicycle pedals or levers that were pushed backwards and forwards. Behind them came hundreds more disabled war veterans on crutches or walking sticks or just limping on artificial legs. It was a ghoulish and depressing sight—a deserted, rainy street filled with the maimed and impaired from two decades of war.

The parade was a protest about the pitiful amount of their pensions. They received 300 Afghanis a month—about six dollars—but payments were erratic. I knew that the Ministry of Finance had allocated money for their pensions in the budget, but somehow the Ministry for Martyrs and the Disabled had so far failed to spend any of it.

•———•

THE NEW FINANCIAL year started in March. It was now 1383. Another annual budget had been approved by the Council of Ministers and was signed into law by the president a few days later.

However, despite my efforts at improvement, the process for spending the money was still complicated and time-consuming. Each ministry had to divide its budget into quarterly amounts for each office across the country and each category of spending. Until all the forms had been approved by the Ministry of Finance and recorded in their ledgers, nothing could be spent. In the meantime, a succession of emergency payment orders were processed every day to ensure that the important activities of government continued.

In the distant past, this process may have achieved what it was supposed to achieve, although I was never sure exactly what that was. Its main purpose now, I suspected, was to generate a little extra income for civil servants in the form of 'facilitation payments' or 'tips' in exchange for expediting their signatures on the multitude of forms and emergency payment orders.

At first, I couldn't understand how or why an underpaid civil servant would bribe another civil servant, but then I realised why so many members of the general public seemed to have business in the corridors of the Ministry of Finance. If you were a building contractor, a fuel importer, a stationery supplier, or any other businessman who dealt with the government, you had an interest in getting your account paid so you took the official forms to the Ministry of Finance yourself and paid the 'tip' to the official who had the power to release your money.

The newly installed, reform-minded leaders in the Ministry of Finance, such as Mr Rahimi, had tried to limit the number of people with access to the building to prevent this practice, but it never seemed to work. Guards forgot to check IDs and locked doors were mysteriously left open.

In the meantime, teachers in Helmand and hospital workers in Mazar, without any hope of paying 'tips' in Kabul, waited patiently for the central administration to get around to approving the forms that would allow their salaries to be paid. The year could be half over before that happened.

The arrival of an army of highly paid and therefore mostly incorruptible foreign consultants and their computerised financial management system only changed this a little. Now all the data from the forms was in the computer and there was, supposedly, no scope for special circumstances or special favours for special friends.

This just made government officials more ingenious. They started putting pressure on my IT staff to make exceptions, or waited until the foreign advisers were at lunch so they could harass the computer operators, or slipped their forms into the piles of documents that went to the deputy minister each day, hoping he would sign them without checking, which he sometimes did.

On the other hand, the slow start to spending the new budget had one advantage. It prevented the government from running out of cash. When the Council of Ministers had deliberated on the budget, they'd found that the estimated revenue for the year was less than the total amount the various ministries planned to spend. Instead of telling the ministries to spend less, they'd decided to assume that the country would receive an extra fifty million dollars from foreign donors. These hypothetical donor grants had yet to materialise in the form of genuine funding, however, so the government's cash position was tight.

The budget of the Afghan Ministry of Defence was a particularly large black hole. Immediately after the attack on the World Trade Towers in 2001, just before the US invasion, American intelligence services had estimated that there were only a few thousand armed Afghan militia actively fighting the Taliban. Somehow, in the two years since then, the number of men supposedly bearing arms to fight against the Taliban on behalf of the new government had ballooned. Ismail Khan, the Governor in Herat, for example, claimed to control 300,000 military personnel and expected all of them to be on the government payroll.

A young German from the UN came to our office to talk about plans to disarm and demobilise all these militias. The US military was in the process of recruiting and training a new Afghan National Army which would report only to the central government, and the UN was offering generous cash payments and other benefits to members of the old military forces who agreed to hand in their weapons.

The German's name was Eckert and he looked the least likely person to be dealing with military matters with his floppy mane of hair and a satin cravat tucked into his open-necked shirt. The demobilisation was not going at all well, he admitted. He showed us his lists with large blocks of red shading indicating the groups that refused to cooperate, yellow for those that had shown some interest and, rarely, green for the ones that were fully complying.

He'd come to the budget department to find out how much government money had been going to the Afghan militia forces and where it had been going. This made it clear why many militia commanders had been resisting the demobilisation program. Whenever the UN had turned up to disarm and pay off the thousands of men each commander claimed to have under his authority, the actual numbers of fighters who'd presented had been much smaller, sometimes only one-tenth of the expected number. Yet for the past two years, the commanders had been claiming and receiving government funds to pay salaries to these men and to provide food, uniforms and housing for them.

In the budget department, we'd always suspected that a portion of the soldiers being funded by the budget might not exist. Unlike other government organisations, the military hadn't been required to submit detailed payroll reports with individual names. The money was just paid to the commanders to pass on to the troops. At the very least, we'd expected them to be taking a cut of the payroll, but now we knew they'd probably been pocketing most of it. This significant source of income was about to cease.

———•———

SOON IT WAS summer again. The snow on the mountains melted and the city briefly turned green, the round of expat social activities accelerated and the popular restaurants re-established their outdoor bars.

My social life became almost as busy as it had been in Pristina, despite the difficult logistics of getting around the dark and deserted streets of Kabul at night There were plenty of eating, drinking and socialising options in Kabul. The Mustafa Hotel was legendary as one of the first establishments to cater to the foreigners who flooded into the city after the departure of the Taliban. All the celebrity journalists seemed to have stayed there or drunk in its bar.

Other new restaurants were opening all the time, aiming to capture the excess expat dollar. They seemed to have no problems providing beer, wine and spirits at not completely unreasonable prices, given the context.

The Taverne du Liban served Lebanese food in the front lounge of one of the houses in Wazir Akbar Khan. Zadar, a Croatian restaurant, had walls painted a sunny light blue and decorated with touristic posters of Adriatic seaside resorts, red-tiled roofed villages and medieval churches. The menu included all the Balkan staples of grilled meat, stuffed cabbage leaves and cucumber salad and made me homesick for Kosovo.

A French restaurant called L'Atmosphere was popular mainly with the younger UN crowd. Late at night, the narrow street outside was usually crowded with UN and NGO vehicles and their patiently waiting drivers while the young passengers partied to the small hours.

Many of my evenings that summer were spent on the rooftop of a friend's house in the Shahr-e Naw district, looking out over the city as the sun set behind the mountains. Steve was a friend from Pristina; a British police officer who'd been training police recruits in Kosovo. Now he was in Kabul training the Afghan police.

The police training program was run by DynCorp, an American military contractor that also provided security for President Karzai. Their main office was a huge corrugated iron and barbed wire construction in the centre of town, near the palace, but Steve lived at 'DynCorp Site 2', a sprawling house run more or less like a military barracks with Gurkha guards on duty at the front gate.

According to the neighbours, the house had been rented by Osama bin Laden during his years in Afghanistan and he was apparently responsible for the interior decoration, including the ceiling of geometrical black and white shapes and matching glass light fittings.

On Thursday nights, the last day of the working week in Kabul, the rooftop terrace was open to visitors and the company provided free beer and wine and generous quantities of barbequed meat and prawns to anyone who turned up. The objective was presumably to attract women to the compound but I'm not sure my friends and I were the types the American men behind the bar had in mind. The young Filipinas who also turned up were probably more their target.

The Americans played endless albums of John Cougar Mellencamp and Bruce Springsteen singing about mid-western towns and working-class boys. In the dark, several floors above the city, you could forget that the pretty lights on the Kabul hillsides were the run-down shanties of Kabul's slums and imagine you were somewhere nice.

The shopping options in Kabul were quite good too. Although all daily needs, from food to soap, toilet paper and office supplies, were provided by the project, there were plenty of other things to buy, especially in the Chicken Street area of Kabul. Chicken Street was where tourists used to congregate when Afghanistan still had tourists.

In the 1970s Kabul had been one of the stop-off points on the hippie trail from Europe to Asia. That was a long time ago, but Chicken Street was still lined with shops selling local handcrafts and souvenirs. There were embroidered scarves, racks of handmade dresses, carved Nuristani furniture, Turkmen jewellery, blue glass from Herat and pottery from Istalif, antique rifles and sabres and armour, and artefacts from the Russian occupation. You could buy rough Mujahideen wool pakols and the finest karakul hats, gold-embroidered Afghan dresses and waistcoats, or a Karzai style green and purple chapan. Other stores were stacked with dusty piles of handmade Afghan carpets.

Business in Chicken Street was better than it had been for years. Aid workers and consultants with their big dollar salaries came to pick up souvenirs for their friends and to buy antique furniture and carpets to ship home and resell. In their dusty dark little shops, the traders offered glasses of sugary tea and then charged foreigners double or triple the price that would be paid by a local.

I didn't mind. I understood that it wasn't just the lapis lazuli earrings or the carved wooden chest I was buying. It was being able to say, 'I bought that when I was in Afghanistan.' And in any case, the price of that carpet that may have taken a rural family six months to make was just two days' pay for a foreign consultant.

Not far from Chicken Street, Flower Street was full of small supermarkets and DVD stores and, surprisingly enough, flower shops, although these mainly sold elaborate arrangements of artificial flowers for weddings.

One of the surprising things about Kabul was that it seemed possible to find almost anything you wanted in the supermarkets. Traders imported goods from every corner of the world; exotic tinned foods, herbs and spices for any cuisine, American ice cream, even Australian vegemite, were easy to find.

One Sunday, a normal working day in Kabul, I asked my driver, Emron, to take a detour to Flower Street on the way home. There were few foreigners around. Young boys with dirty faces insistently asked for 'one dollar, one dollar, one dollar,' grabbing my elbow, but the swarms of beggars with amputated limbs and disfiguring diseases who usually turned out on Fridays had gone to beg somewhere else.

I bought some recent release movies on DVD to watch on my computer on boring evenings, hoping they were the good quality kind of pirated movie, the ones taken from reviewers' preview copies, rather than the kind filmed in the cinema on a home video camera while the audience rustles their chip packets and shuffles to their seats in front of the screen. At two dollars a movie, though, if some were duds it didn't really matter.

I felt a slight twinge of guilt about buying pirated movies, but legitimate copies weren't available in Kabul at any price so there was no other option.

My shopping didn't take long and Emron and I were soon on our way back to the house. As the car drove slowly down Chicken Street, I looked at the exotic displays in the small shops and tried to imagine what it would look like to me if I really was a tourist. What it would have been like if I'd been one of the travellers who'd been here years before on their way overland through Asia, instead of being a stressed and nervous consultant sitting behind the driver in my air-conditioned car with the windows wound up so that no one could throw a grenade inside, and the doors locked so that I wouldn't be kidnapped or my expensive laptop computer stolen.

Back in those days, I could have driven around in a taxi and eaten at local food stalls, slept in a dormitory at a cheap guesthouse, and travelled from one part of the country to another by public bus. I imagined myself doing these things and thought that if I could keep that image in my mind, I could feel as relaxed and happy as those travellers probably had and I could make Kabul into that sort of place again, in my mind, at least.

But as we drove towards home, I heard a muffled explosion. 'It's a bomb,' Emron said.

'No it isn't,' I told him. 'I think it's just a truck going over a bump.'

When we turned into our street a few minutes later, however, our guards were standing outside pointing over the tops of the houses towards a plume of smoke in the distance. A man with a camera rushed out of the journalists' house across the road and jumped into his car.

Something had happened. I still hoped it would turn out to be a gas bottle explosion or something similarly unfortunate but unimportant, but the internet news services were already reporting that there'd been an explosion at a house in Shahr-e Naw, only a few blocks from Chicken Street where I'd just been. The building was still on fire and there were bodies lying in the street.

I suddenly realised that I knew the house. It was the DynCorp house where Steve lived. Given DynCorp's activities in Afghanistan, it was perhaps not surprising one of their buildings had been targeted by the Taliban. The bomb had been hidden in a donkey cart and had gone off in the street outside. The Ghurkha guards out the front would have had no chance.

A few anguished hours later, I had a call from one of Steve's close friends. He gave me more details about the explosion but was slow to get around to the important part. I held my breath.

'Steve's OK,' he finally said. 'I just spoke to him.'

Steve had been in the gym when the bomb had gone off. A piece of Osama bin Laden's elaborate tiled ceiling had fallen on his head. A few minutes earlier, he'd been outside in the street trying to get a mobile signal. It would have been a different story if he'd managed to make his phone call. Others weren't so lucky. Some of his police school colleagues were killed.

From then on, our daily security restrictions became progressively more restrictive and our suburb of Wazir Akbar Khan became more and more like a fortress. Four-metre-high fences were built around many of the houses and more roads were blocked off with concrete barriers or gravel-filled Hesco walls.

The US Embassy was no longer satisfied with just taking large chunks out of the main road and surrounding itself with three concrete walls. It closed the road completely and stacked cargo containers around the half-built new embassy building.

The walls of the ISAF compound, home to the Italian, French and German NATO troops, were reinforced. The supermarket frequented by expats tightened its security, searching cars and demanding IDs from customers. Some streets were now floodlit at night and everywhere there were more guards with guns.

It all seemed to me to be a bit excessive. The DynCorp attack had been serious, but the level of violence in Kabul was still considerably less than in Baghdad, where life had become extremely dangerous. I still received regular reports from former colleagues who were now working there. Suicide bombs, which were at that time rare in Afghanistan, had become common, and foreign workers were still being kidnapped. So far, Afghanistan was nothing like that.

It seemed that the type of security precautions now being introduced in Afghanistan were largely the backwash from Iraq. Security advisers simply transferred everything they did there to Kabul, despite the difference in the threat level.

But the new precautions just created their own problems. Closing off streets caused traffic jams, making us perfect targets for an attack, and stirred resentment among the local population, while restrictions on our movements cut us off from the very people we were meant to be helping.

Democracy
Kabul, Autumn 2004

In late 2004, the Ministry of Finance was already planning the budget for another year. We were now up to 1384 in Afghan time.

The annual ritual of checking, calculating and trimming the ministry bids for fuel and rent continued. That year, even Dr Ghani joined the meetings now and then to grill officials from other ministries about their excessive staff numbers and their unspent allocations, and to harangue them about corruption and mismanagement.

Nevertheless, we were already about seventy-two million dollars over the pre-agreed spending limit, in spite of my daily scoresheet tracking how far away from the target we'd drifted, and we hadn't yet started dealing with the large ministries like education and defence.

An IMF mission from Washington arrived to discuss the fiscal outlook. The three smart young men of different nationalities but in identical blue suits asked difficult questions about the revenue estimates for the following year and how the government planned to fund all its expenditure.

Meanwhile, the budget committee kept approving even more big-ticket items, including a whole raft of new government agencies such as the Disaster Management Organisation, the Human Rights Commission and an Enterprises Commission. International advisers regarded these bodies as indispensable components of effective modern governance and the resources had to be found to pay for them.

Afghanistan's first democratic election was now only a few weeks away. The Constitution prepared by the Loya Jirga had been agreed and enacted and the next step was to choose a president.

Our project leader called a meeting a week before the election to explain the security preparations being made. Our group of well-travelled consultants sat around the dining table in our shared house wondering what the fuss was about.

He told us we would have armed guards in patrol vehicles in the street outside the house, snipers on the roof, and an evacuation plan had been drawn up which involved a US military escort to the airport and a US military flight out of Afghanistan to an unspecified location. It sounded as if we were preparing for war.

We now also had an eight pm curfew, and all restaurants were out of bounds.

A few days later, in the dead of night, a truck loaded with huge concrete blocks pulled up in our street and a crane unloaded them onto the footpath under the glare of portable floodlights, building a barrier that blocked part of the street. The crane was noisy and its exhaust fumes filled the house.

Then the truck moved around the corner and unloaded more blocks in front of other houses. It seemed we now needed more protection than even the despised Russians had when they were there.

There were a total of eighteen candidates for president. Each of them had campaign posters stuck on walls and power poles around town. The posters were all the same size and similar in style as if they'd all been designed by the same graphic designer, which is quite possible, as they were probably part of some donor's democracy support project. Each had a photo, a short slogan, and a recognisable symbol such as an ear of wheat, an eagle or a dove so that illiterate voters would know who was who.

On local television, which consisted of one government station broadcasting for five hours a night, the program was a monotonous parade of candidates reading their election manifestos with, in most cases, a notable lack of charisma.

Karzai's campaign announcements had slightly higher production values than the rest. He wore his colourful signature Afghan cape of purple and green and addressed the camera, alternating between the two official languages of Pashto and Dari, interspersed with video of the interim president himself opening reconstructed schools and meeting villagers.

We were well aware, though, that campaign speeches on TV wouldn't count for much on election day in a place where some people had only a vague idea about how the election process was supposed to work. Tribal or ethnic loyalties would decide many people's votes rather than policies.

Two days before the election, our bullet-proof vests were delivered. The project's security director arrived at the house with a rifle slung across his shoulder and half a dozen sand-coloured, metal-reinforced vests on his arm.

I left mine sitting neatly beside my bed. It was far too big for me. When I tried it on I looked like a tortoise.

On the morning of the election, our American guards climbed onto the roof of the house and set up a machine gun on a tripod facing out over the street. As it happened, our Washington office chose that day to email a memo about hazard pay.

While we were locked in our houses with our bullet-proof vests at the ready and armed men on the roof, we learned that the US government auditors had decided that we were not entitled to hazard pay on a Saturday. It seemed that Kabul is only hazardous six days a week and that the terrorists go home on the weekend.

As I'd expected, there were no major security incidents on election day. There were no bombs, no explosions, no attacks on polling stations and no riots. Not in Kabul, anyway. We didn't need our bullet-proof vests and the sniper on the roof had a boring afternoon.

Counting the votes took weeks but, eventually, it was clear that Hamid Karzai had won and would remain president. His inauguration was a few weeks later, in early December.

Kabul was in a festive state for the event. The streets were decorated with strings of coloured lights, the national flag hung from light poles, and banners were strung across the main roads beside miscellaneous flags in every colour, including pink and lilac.

Frantic roadworks were underway to prepare the main routes for the important international visitors. We were stunned to see, among the workers, a solidly built woman driving a huge piece of road building machinery; a novelty in a place where very few women even drove a car.

It hadn't been officially announced who would be coming for the event. Maybe Kofi Annan, or Condi Rice. There was even a rumour that George Bush might visit. Our housemaids were delighted. 'I hope he comes', one of them told me, using the house manager as an interpreter. 'I want to thank him. I'll go myself and throw flowers at him.'

The VIPs turned out to be Vice President Dick Cheney and Donald Rumsfeld, the Secretary of Defence, and their wives.

Security was about as tight as it could be. In the streets around the palace, there was a foreign soldier of some type— German, Italian, American or British—every few metres. Armoured personnel carriers and small tanks patrolled the suburbs. Elsewhere, Afghan National Army soldiers in their clean new uniforms and bright green berets lined the roads.

For once there was no traffic congestion.

We were, of course, confined to our houses for the ceremony. I watched it all on Afghan state TV. The broadcast started at eight am with a program of old footage of famous Afghan performers of the 1970s. Young men with shaggy hair and sideburns and women with centre parts and black eyeliner sang folksy songs in grainy black and white, and young girls in Afghan costumes danced and sang. This in itself was shocking, as there are many in Afghanistan who believe that women shouldn't appear on TV, let alone sing or dance. More surprisingly, the program also included modern pop videos of Indian girls in midriff-revealing saris, Egyptian women with wild windblown hair and plunging necklines, and Britney Spears wearing almost nothing at all.

Live pictures of dignitaries arriving at the palace started at eleven am. Karzai wore his purple and green cape and held hands with the elderly king. After the recitation from the Qur'an, cute little children in various Afghan costumes sang patriotic songs.

A group of judges in identical black and gold robes, white turbans and grey beards paraded onto the dais and Karzai recited the oath of office with his hand on the Qur'an. I could see Dick Cheney and his wife sitting on uncomfortable looking wooden chairs in the front row.

The ceremony, taking place only a few blocks away from where we were, lasted barely an hour. Almost as soon as it finished, two large green transport helicopters with twin rotors rose into the air from the direction of the palace and began to make slow, noisy circles over the neighbourhood.

One flew so low over our house that it blew leaves from the tree outside my window and appeared to be about to crash into the garden next door. I thought for a moment I was about to witness the Vice President of the United

States immolated in a ball of flaming helicopter, but the machine rose slowly into the air again and flew off in the direction of the airport.

THE DAY AFTER the inauguration, Dr Ghani summoned several advisers to meet him at his house late in the evening. Now that Karzai was officially, finally and securely president, he was expected to announce new appointments to all the government ministries. We hoped he would now have the authority to appoint technocrats who knew what they were doing, rather than warlords.

The expat community in Kabul was abuzz with rumours about who would get the jobs and there was a feeling that the unpopular and short-tempered Dr Ghani would not be Minister for Finance for much longer.

Ghani's house was not far away from where we lived but our security director felt he needed to escort us armed with his rifle. When we arrived, we were greeted by Ghani's wife, who played the genteel hostess while we waited for our turn to see him.

We looked around for any suggestion of extravagance or luxury. We found none. The house was plain and functional. Dr Ghani received us in his lounge room, which was much like his office—full of sofas—with the minister reclining and holding court on one of them.

We had many issues to discuss about the budget, but we never really got to them. Most of the meeting was taken up by a lengthy dissertation from Dr Ghani on his views about development priorities; another rambling, stream-of-consciousness oration much like others I'd heard from him.

Some of it made sense. A network of new roads connecting Afghanistan with its neighbours and a reliable national electricity supply, certainly. But then he set out his plans to improve Kabul with new housing developments, public parks, commercial zones, cultural precincts and 'world-class architecture'.

One day, perhaps, that all might happen. But it was a long way from the current grubby, unsewered city and, just getting a president elected and safely inaugurated had been a major achievement. His ever more fanciful proposals that evening started to sound like the rantings of someone who has completely lost touch with reality.

Karzai spent weeks negotiating the composition of his new ministry. During this time, the fate of all the staff Dr Ghani had brought to the ministry, such as Seema and Rahimi, was up in the air. They had all made it clear they would only work for Ghani.

The frantic budget activity that we'd expected at this time of the year suddenly disappeared. It was almost Christmas and many of the advisers had also disappeared, leaving for the holiday season. I was one of the few international staff still at work.

The new ministers were announced on television on Christmas Eve. Dr Anwar Ahadi, who had been Governor of the Afghanistan Central Bank, was appointed the new Minister for Finance. Ahadi, like Dr Ghani, was another returnee from the United States. In fact, he'd been a university lecturer in Washington at the same time Ghani had been at the World Bank.

Dr Ghani was appointed to the role of vice-chancellor at Kabul University, which he apparently told people was what he'd really wanted, although it looked like a demotion. At our last meeting with him, I remembered this was one of a number of possible appointments and ambassadorships he had mentioned, ensuring that almost whatever he got would appear to be what he'd hoped for.

Christmas Day was a normal working day in Kabul and the first day of work for all the new ministers. Dr Ahadi made a ceremonial procession across Pashtunistan Square from his Central Bank office to the Ministry of Finance, where Dr Ghani formally introduced him to his new staff.

The corridors of the building were crowded with people who didn't appear to belong to the ministry. Wajid joked that they must have come from the Ministry of Tribes and Frontiers, the ministry responsible for the more exotic minor ethnic groups from remote rural areas of Afghanistan. They certainly seemed to fit this classification—the swarthy, sun-browned men all wore turbans and traditional clothes, and the women were loud and pushy.

A group of drummers had set up in the car park and men in traditional dress danced in a circle around them. The men stepped, clapped, swirled, jumped, tossed their longish hair and clapped a few more times before starting again. They were apparently from Ahadi's tribal homeland and had come to celebrate the achievement of their countryman.

The budget department team was due to be presented to the new minister at 11.10 am precisely, but when we got to the conference room it was already crowded with people we didn't recognise. Dr Ahadi stood at the head of the conference table while the visitors filed around in a circle, congratulating him.

He was surrounded by large, elaborate displays of artificial flowers which had been presented by previous well-wishers. The thing that struck me most was the pale pastiness of his skin, made even more so by the blackness of his slicked-down hair. It looked like a wig. It was certainly not its natural colour.

Finally, it was the turn of the budget department team to be introduced. Wajid and Noori had gone out during the morning and bought an arrangement of green and white plastic roses surrounded by gilded oak leaves on a wooden stand. They thought it was beautiful. We presented it to the minister as a gift from our project. Rafiq and Amir were also there to introduce their staff.

As we filed out of the room after our brief, two-minute audience, we passed through another crush of people waiting for their turn to congratulate the minister, carrying their floral tributes. Some had even brought real flowers. Similar scenes were repeated that day all over Kabul as the newly appointed ministers were welcomed by their new staff; an economic boom for florists, if nothing else.

Things settled down over the next few days and we soon decided we liked Dr Ahadi. Even some advisers who'd been staunch supporters of Dr Ghani, who'd thought they couldn't work for anyone else, admitted that the new minister's work style was more productive. He listened, made decisions, and managed his time effectively. Meetings now started on time and finished on time.

At our first real meeting with him, we spent almost an hour discussing all the high-priority issues. He looked at us through his smart gold-rimmed glasses, like a hawk, listened to what we said and asked short, direct questions. Several times he even asked the Afghan staff of the ministry for their suggestions.

In contrast to meetings with Dr Ghani, he didn't use the occasion as an opportunity to expand at length on his proposals for solving the problems of the world. He gave clear instructions to Rafiq and Amir about reducing expenditure and in particular, controlling the 'contingency funds' that they'd been relying on to pay for the president's hokums.

A few weeks later, however, the new minister and the deputy ministers he'd appointed, started expanding their office accommodation. Dr Ghani and his deputies had always been satisfied with simple, modestly furnished offices. The new leaders, however, seemed disappointed with the standard of accommodation they'd inherited.

The minister decided to create a new ministerial suite and planned to convert a room which was currently an office for seventeen staff into a formal dining room. His wife came one afternoon to advise him on colour schemes and furnishings.

One of the new deputy ministers decided he also needed more space and took over rooms that had been part of our budget office. We all had to move, taking with us our three sets of computer cables, installed by our various donors at some expense less than six months before. My high opinion of the new minister sank a little.

●———●

IN JANUARY, THE Afghan Haj pilgrims, supposedly selected by lottery, left on their journey to Mecca, despite the mismanagement and outright corruption of the Ministry for Haj.

One of our local IT staff had organised for his mother to make her once-in-a-lifetime pilgrimage. Several days before she was due to leave on the chartered Ariana Airlines flight, the Ministry of Haj 'mislaid' her passport. Only a generous payment helped them to find it again.

In Kabul, herds of sheep, goats and even camels were led through the streets for sale to households as their Eid sacrifice and dinner. In front of each butcher's shop on Jalalabad Road, a dozen or more animals waited their turn to be slaughtered.

Then it was spring again. As the snow disappeared from the mountains, the water level in the Kabul River rose. From a green pond of sewerage and floating garbage, it started to become a flowing river again. Water gushed over the small weir that we passed on our way to work.

Fruit tree saplings were for sale along the banks of the river, their roots planted temporarily in the damp mud of the riverbed and their leafless branches sprouting above the river wall. There were more trees this spring than there had been the year before. Tall deciduous trees, lengths of grapevine, small pencil pines, rose bushes and other plants were arrayed in the temporary nursery. Cars pulled up beside the river and buyers drove off with trees tied to the roof or protruding from the boot.

It was now more than two years since I'd started my one-year contract. The company still showed no interest in winding up my assignment and the money kept rolling into my bank account. In fact, I had the impression I could stay there indefinitely.

Part of me thought that sounded like a good idea. The work I was doing was stimulating, challenging, even rewarding. I felt I was making a useful contribution. I had a few good friends and a fairly busy social life, and Kabul had turned out to be a surprisingly convenient departure point for seeing the rest of the world. During the past year, I'd been to Europe several times on the ridiculously cheap Azerbaijan Airlines flight to Paris via Baku, flown to Istanbul to meet up with friends from Australia, and spent shopping weekends in Dubai and Islamabad. There were a few good reasons for staying a bit longer.

But there were also a lot of reasons to leave. The working environment was confronting. The dirty building, the women in burqas and the obnoxious toilets never seemed to get easier. I started to feel that I'd had enough of swarthy men with scruffy beards and baggy clothes, muddy floors and dusty furniture, smeary windows and trying to follow what was happening in a language I didn't understand. Then there was the boarding house lifestyle and the necessity of tolerating whoever I happened to be assigned to live with for however long they were there.

I started to yearn for a more normal life and a place that I could call home. There had to be an end sometime to this strange life.

I debated with myself for several months and eventually decided I didn't want to do another Afghan budget and I didn't want to survive another Ramadan.

The continually worsening security situation wasn't a big factor in my decision; the annual toll of road deaths back home far exceeded the number of foreign civilians who'd been killed in Afghanistan. But the occasional explosion or kidnapping meant that more and more restrictions were placed on our daily lives, limiting our freedom of movement and creating the feeling that it wasn't safe to even leave the house. Higher walls, more lockdowns, and larger and more fortified housing compounds kept reminding me how bad things had become.

By then, it was clear to everyone that the removal of the Taliban had not brought stable government to Afghanistan. It had simply restarted the civil war, re-empowered the warlords, reinvigorated the criminals and drug dealers, and stirred up the fundamentalists. We had gone back a decade or more to the early 1990s, to the days when lawlessness and crime made people welcome the Taliban because at least they brought stability and security.

In their efforts to defeat Al-Qaeda, the foreign military had allied themselves with local strongmen and their private militias, but these warlords owed allegiance to no one but themselves. They weren't seriously committed to the current government and would change sides as soon as there was an advantage to be gained, as they had done many times before.

Some of them were the same people who'd destroyed Afghanistan during the four years of civil war before the Taliban came to power, and their militia fighters used the weapons and the power they'd been given by the foreign forces to terrorise and exploit the local population.

•━━━•

My last day in the Ministry of Finance was more stressful than any during the previous two years. I was excited to be leaving and impatient to be home, but at the same time I had a huge amount of last-minute work to do, and I had to say goodbye to people I'd come to know well.

Noori and Wajid and Yunus gave me a going-away present, which, luckily, was beautiful lapis lazuli jewellery rather than the heavy hand-carved marble chess set they'd expected one of my colleagues to fit into his hand luggage at the last minute.

After a few hours of broken sleep, I was up and ready to leave before dawn. As usual, the route to the airport at that time of day was crowded with girls on their way to school in the dark. There were hundreds of them, all in the same uniform of black tunic and pants and a white headscarf. Some were tiny, surely much younger than the official school starting age of seven. Others were big, maybe seventeen or eighteen, but they were on their way to primary school to make up for the education they'd missed during the Taliban years.

My flight was delayed by a Kabul dust storm. All planes were grounded. The small departure lounge kept filling up with people arriving for local and international flights but no one was departing. Afghan families, already dressed up for some family celebration in a regional city, squatted in the corners of the room. The snack bar ran out of chocolate and Pringles, and the smokers decided that the 'no smoking' sign didn't apply in these circumstances.

Then at eleven am there was a sudden rush of activity outside on the tarmac. German ISAF soldiers took up positions around the building, two huge six-wheeled armoured vehicles drove onto the parking apron, and fire trucks and ambulances with lights flashing raced to one end of the runway, then raced back again. The waiting travellers pressed towards the big windows to see what was going on.

Then I recalled that President Karzai had announced he would go to Rome for Pope John Paul II's funeral. Why the recently elected president of an unstable and poverty-stricken Muslim country needed to attend the funeral of a Catholic pope was a mystery to me.

Ariana's best plane, the Airbus, was dragged across from its parking place to stand in front of the terminal and two motorised staircases were driven up to the side. The red carpet—a handmade Afghan Bokhara—was rolled out on the front stairs.

The audience in the departure lounge waited expectantly for the president, but Karzai was notoriously bad at time management. One of my colleagues who'd been engaged to provide advice to the president's office had made three appointments to talk to him about his diary management, but they'd all been cancelled at the last minute.

The urgency of the preparations died down. The German soldiers drifted away and were replaced by Karzai's private American security guards, distinctive for their lack of uniforms, impressive weaponry and back-to-front baseball caps.

They were joined by a group of young Afghan security guards, or it could have been the Italian mafia—good-looking young men with long hair, sharp suits, black shirts, sunglasses and semi-automatics. They stood at the four corners of the plane with their backs to each other and their guns pointing outwards, much like a scene from a Tarantino movie.

Unfortunately, I never saw the president depart. After six hours of waiting, my flight to Dubai was finally ready to board.

As we taxied past the terminal, I looked back to see that the observation deck, where women in blue burqas had stood when I first arrived, was now bristling with armed men.

Bizarre, Tragic, Hopeful

CITY OF WHITE DEATH
Astana, Kazakhstan, June 2005

Another job, another country, another airport. There were no rugged mountains to look down on during the flight across Kazakhstan. The country is mostly a vast expanse of flatness, from the Volga River on one side, across to Siberia and China on the other. The windows of the modern airport in the capital, Astana, looked out across a flat green plain all the way to the horizon.

Only a month earlier I'd still been in Afghanistan. An urgent invitation to spend six weeks in Kazakhstan on another American project had arrived by email soon after I'd returned home. I'd barely had time to find somewhere to live and get my furniture out of storage.

The company in Washington needed someone in Astana as soon as possible and I had the impression that my main qualification for the job was simply my willingness once again to get on a plane at short notice and travel halfway around the world to a place I knew nothing about.

Astana had become the capital of Kazakhstan only a few years earlier, in 1998, so almost everything was new. The wide highway from the airport was lined with modern buildings, fountains and abstract sculptures, looking as if they'd come out of a self-assembly kit from the same firm that designs casinos in Las Vegas. The glare of the sun and the huge blue sky reflected off mirrored glass windows. Closer to the centre of town the buildings were older, but not much older. Most wouldn't have been there ten years before.

It was a strange place to choose for a national capital. Out there on the Central Asian steppes, the winters are bitterly cold with temperatures below thirty-five Celsius for six months of the year. But it was summer and the weather was, for a few brief months, oppressively hot and humid. Every evening the sun shone through the thin brown curtains of my bedroom window and I tossed and turned in the heat on the king-size mattress, waking in the morning tangled up in the queen-size sheets that didn't quite cover the bed.

The town has had several names in the last fifty years, reflecting its changing political circumstances. The old Kazakh name was Aqmola, which can be translated as 'white mausoleum' or 'white grave' but some people I met said it meant 'white death'. Its new name, Astana, simply meant 'capital city'. The government had moved the capital there because of its strategic location in the empty north of the country, near the border with Russia; a 'keep out' sign to their powerful northern neighbour.

Thousands of government workers had been moved there. In only a few years the town's population had grown from almost nothing to half a million. But businesses and embassies, and indeed the president himself, were still based in lush, leafy Almaty in the south.

The office I'd be working from was in one of the 'older' Astana buildings, probably built five years before. We occupied a large open space scattered with modern desks, chairs and filing cabinets.

It was a much smaller team than I was used to. In Kabul, there'd been several dozen foreigners working together in our group. In Kazakhstan, Peter, the team leader—a fifty-something ginger-haired Canadian—was the only one. Now that I'd arrived, we were a team of two, plus the local staff, who outnumbered us three to one.

At the end of my first day, I walked to the banks of the river that winds in large arcs through the city and marvelled at the futuristic landscape of glass and granite buildings, all elaborately decorated with columns, cupolas and other post-modernist flourishes. It looked like a film set, or perhaps the cover illustration of a science fantasy novel. I half expected an interplanetary spaceship to descend from the sky at any minute. It was late in the evening, but the sun on this strange planet still hung high and bright in the sky.

This didn't look in any way like a place in need of foreign aid. The river was clean and free-flowing, and the families and young people strolling along the embankment were dressed in western fashions and looked well-fed and prosperous. On the other side of the river, a noisy funfair was hidden in the trees and further upstream children paddled in brightly coloured plastic boats and fat matrons waded in the water by a gravel river beach.

Kazakhstan was once part of the Soviet Union. It became an independent nation when all the former Soviet states in Central Asia went their own ways in the early nineties. It's a huge country, as big as Argentina, but with just eighteen million people.

Only a small fraction of the land is arable but it's what's under the land that makes the country so interesting. Every item of the table of elements is found and mined here. Large amounts of oil and gas are produced in the west, by the Caspian Sea, but there's also uranium, chromium, lead, zinc, manganese, copper, coal, iron, gold and diamonds. Kazakhstan's economy was booming.

The country was regarded as a success story of post-socialist development. It had done all the right things by the IMF and the US, and had 'transitioned' to free-market capitalism with minimal fuss. Its economy was growing at nine percent a year, it had an elected government—in theory at any rate—and its citizens were mostly well-educated, well-dressed, well-housed and apparently happy.

The new electoral democracy did not, however, seem to include the right to change the president. Nursultan Nazarbayev had now been in power for almost fifteen years, the opposition party was carefully controlled, the parliament had limited power, and the press were free only as long as they didn't criticise the ruling regime.

On my second day, I had my first meeting with Dina, the Director of 'Budget Process Methodology' in the Kazakhstan Ministry of Economy and Budget Planning.

We walked on wide uncluttered footpaths the few blocks to the ministry building—another modern structure of glass and steel. In the busy foyer, a high-tech security system beeped staff in through automatic doors but kept us out while the security guards looked for the low-tech piece of paper that authorised us to go inside.

On the way to Dina's office, along a curved corridor, we passed room after room of young men and women working at computers. Dina also seemed young but was probably in her forties. She obviously understood almost everything I said in English but answered my questions in Russian, which Azhar, our interpreter, did her best to translate.

Dina knew what she was talking about. She explained that the Minister of Finance was keen to adopt modern budget practices, in particular, the idea of 'program budgeting'. Program budgeting means preparing the budget according to objectives and performance targets rather than items of expenditure and it has been used in many western countries for a long time. Its proponents say it makes government expenditure more effective and the budget process more logical.

I knew a lot about program budgeting from my previous career, but I didn't yet know whether they were ready for it in Kazakhstan or had the capacity to implement it. It was quite possible that the minister was going down this path mainly because that's what modern successful countries do, not because the government saw a need to change anything about their current system.

•———•

SHAIZADA, THE OFFICE manager, had organised an apartment for me on the top floor of one of the elaborate new buildings near the river, a modern flat with polished floorboards and wide windows looking out over the city. The rooms were enormous but sparsely furnished—just the huge bed in the bedroom and a beige modular lounge suite in the middle of the living room. A mini-supermarket on the ground floor sold canned food from Russia, black rye bread, wine from Moldova, and infinite varieties of vodka.

Similar buildings on each side were separated from each other by expanses of bare dirt ready for the next construction project. Large cranes dipped and swung around the metal skeletons of new buildings to the north and west, welding torches sparkled at twilight, and a pile driver pounded until late into the night.

Up close, however, I could see that many of the pretentious new buildings that looked so impressive from a distance were shoddily constructed. Paving tiles were starting to come loose, weeds grew in the playgrounds and car parks, and the foyers and stairways were grubby and graffitied.

In the evening, after work, it was hotter than it had been at midday. The air conditioning unit in the bedroom, if I turned it on, made a noise like the jet I'd just arrived on, which is why I spent so many nights tossing in the heat.

The sun didn't finally set until late at night and it hovered over the flat horizon for hours—a large red ball, somehow getting hotter and brighter, forming a red backdrop to the still pounding pile driver and the forest of cranes.

•———•

On day three I tried to organise another meeting with Dina. Azhar made a phone call to her office but it seemed she was too busy to see me. She'd be tied up all that day, and the next. Sometime next week might be possible.

I wasn't used to this. Until then, I'd always worked directly with government staff, sitting in the same office, talking to them day to day, finding out what they did and just walking in to see senior officials without an appointment. Here, each time I wanted to visit the ministry, Azhar needed to make a formal appointment for me, and Dina's assistant had to write an official letter to the security guards at the door authorising them to let me in.

In the meantime, there wasn't much work I could do. I found myself spending large amounts of time staring through the window at the flashes of acetylene torches on the construction site next door and the onion-shaped minaret across the road, a replica of an identical structure in Kuwait City, donated by the Kuwaiti government. This was another piece of interesting information provided by Azhar, who was becoming my guide to the culture and history of Astana.

She explained, for example, that there are two major ethnic groups in Kazakhstan—the Kazakhs and the Russians. She drew a circle with her finger around her attractive almond-shaped face and her brown almond-shaped eyes to explain what Kazakhs look like. They were the Asiatic descendants of nomadic tribes that had lived on the Central Asian Steppe before the Russian Empire had engulfed them during the eighteenth and nineteenth centuries.

The European-looking segment of the population is mostly Russians, although, during the Soviet era, large numbers of Germans, Ukrainians, Georgians and other nationalities also settled there, many unwillingly during Stalin's purges. About half the population are Muslim and the other half Russian Orthodox. Azhar assured me that all the different cultural and religious groups got along wonderfully together, but I remembered that people used to say the same thing about Bosnia.

Eventually, I managed to get another meeting with Dina. We were five women around a table—Dina, her deputy, my interpreter, our economist, and me.

Most of the other staff in her office were also women. On my first visit, I'd assumed they were assistants and secretaries. Later, I was embarrassed by my own prejudice. This was something else that was different from my recent experience. Even in Australia, most staff working on the budget had been men. In Astana, almost all government employees were women, even the uniformed security guards at the front door.

Dina gave me a list of issues to research and asked me to prepare some training material. It seemed that on this project, unlike the others I'd worked on, the consultants did what the local counterparts told them to do, rather than the other way around.

I spent my days from then on trawling internet sites for information and writing lesson plans and lectures. Although it was refreshing to work with someone who understood the issues and knew what she wanted, I sometimes felt like an over-paid research assistant.

My days fell into a relentless routine of office, home, another walk by the riverbank, and home again. On Friday nights, the weekend stretched ahead of me like a prison sentence. I visited different supermarkets to buy food, walked in different directions from the apartment to see what was there, and looked in vain for shops with anything of interest to buy.

After the restrictions of life in Afghanistan, it was peculiar to be able to walk wherever I wanted to, on my own, and to wear normal clothes. Everyone in Astana dressed more or less like people in any western country. Although more than half of them are supposedly Muslim, there were no women wearing headscarves.

I didn't look different from any of the Russian women, so no one knew that I didn't speak a word of Russian until I stared blankly at them when they talked to me. Almost no one spoke English, and all the signs were in Cyrillic letters. Occasionally, I found an out-of-date *Herald Tribune* for sale in a shop but generally, there was nothing to read in English.

I rattled around in the huge empty apartment. On television, only the BBC news ran its endless hourly cycles in English and my internet connection was a slow dial-up arrangement, useless for anything but basic email.

After Peter and I had spent the whole week together in the office, spending more time together at the weekend felt strangely uncomfortable. There were no young UN or NGO humanitarian workers with their wild parties, as there had been in Kabul, and most western expats were still based in

Almaty. The largest group of foreigners in Astana were immigrant labourers from Kyrgystan and Uzbekistan. The local staff had their own families, their own language, and their own lives to lead when they weren't in the office.

Eventually, another adviser arrived. David, an American, came for a few days to work on macroeconomic analysis. As there were now three foreigners in the office there was sufficient critical mass to go out to dinner.

We went to an Uzbek restaurant in the park across the river—a temporary establishment set up for the summer under a colourful canopy. The young staff wore traditional Uzbek costumes, the girls in headdresses decorated with gold coins dangling around their faces. The menu included fermented horse milk and horse sausage but I settled for the standard meat-on-sticks option, similar to the cuisine found everywhere from Turkey to Afghanistan.

Inevitably, it became more or less a working dinner as the conversation always came back to Kazakhstan. Both Peter and David had been observing the situation there for some time.

They described Kazakhstan ten years ago as a completely different place—poor, backward-looking, isolated from the west, with almost no modern technology or automation and no enthusiasm for modernising. Things had certainly improved since then.

They were reluctant, however, to talk in public about the president, Nursultan Nazarbayev, as they found little to say about him that was positive. We started to talk in code and decided that around our dinner table we would refer to him simply as 'Mr Brown'.

At the last election, Mr Brown had won eighty-one percent of the vote, compared to his nearest rival's twelve percent. His relatives all held influential positions in public life. In fact, his daughter was the leader of the opposition, which might indicate how vigorously the opposition party had campaigned against him.

Every evening on the local language TV channels, the first three or four stories of the news bulletin always featured Mr Brown in some capacity. That day, for example, he'd been holding a press conference in Astana with the President of China and then somehow found time to dash off to another major Kazakhstan city to inspect the laying of a new gas pipeline.

The World Bank keeps a database of 'governance' indicators which gives scores to countries on things like government performance and political transparency. I looked it up during my days of filling in time in the office. Although the economy was doing well under Mr Brown's supervision, Kazakhstan's governance scores were going in the opposite direction. It was ranked in the lower percentiles, below many much less developed countries, and its scores had been getting lower each year. Even measures such as 'government effectiveness' and 'quality of regulations' were going down fast, in spite of all the excellent advice provided on these matters by people like me. The corruption index was heading straight for the floor.

Most of the population, however, seemed to respect Mr Brown for holding them together and delivering prosperity and stability. He had certainly achieved something remarkable in a country with so many different ethnic groups, languages and religions.

•———•

DAVID'S BRIEF VISIT was soon over and Peter and I were again a team of two. One evening, Peter suggested we go to the Windsor Room at the Intercontinental Hotel for dinner.

The Windsor Room was the nearest thing to an expat

meeting place in the city. It was a plush, windowless, club-style bar air-conditioned to the temperature of a cold storage facility. A handful of customers, all men, sat on stools at the bar, shovelling down food from the buffet. The waiters were obsequious and tried their best to speak English.

Peter had been working in Astana for several years and said he liked it there. Most of the men I knew who'd worked in Kazakhstan or other parts of the former Soviet Union had come home with attractive young Russian wives so I assumed he had a local girlfriend to sustain his interest in the place. If he had, he kept her well-hidden. Over several beers and an unappetising, overpriced meal, he talked about his wife and his grown children at home in Canada and his pastimes in Astana, which seemed to consist of reading books and watching TV.

Peter was an auditor and his work gave him a pessimistic view of human nature and intimate knowledge of all the forms that government corruption can take. He reeled off examples of how the ruling elite in the country were, quite possibly, benefiting themselves through government activities.

'Take the decision to move the capital from Almaty to Astana, for example,' he said. 'People close to the government would have bought up land in the area before the announcement and made a lot of money.'

'But wasn't the decision made by an independent commission?' I asked. 'I read that they looked at hundreds of possible locations before choosing this one.'

'Well, that's the official story.' He didn't sound convinced. 'And all these new public buildings being constructed. You can be sure the work is being done by firms with links to people in the government.'

After listening to him for a while I wondered if it was possible for any government to be free of corruption.

After dinner, back at the apartment, the sun was still shining as if it was the middle of the day. There were now two pile drivers in the neighbourhood, one on each side of the river, in a perpetual race. They started synchronised but one pounded a fraction of a second faster than the other and they were soon beating a syncopated rhythm until, after a few minutes, they were briefly working in unison again.

I surfed the local TV channels. The Russian language program was a version of *Big Brother*, which added one more to the list of *Big Brother* programs I'd seen around the world in the original Dutch, German, French, Polish and even Arabic.

Between the variety shows, news reports and Russian movies, the television stations also showed inspiring, patriotic community announcements. One had a Kazakh toddler climbing out of his traditional wooden crib and taking his first halting steps towards the glittering towers of the new city of Astana. A collage of images flashed onto the screen: an old Russian woman in a white peasant scarf, an old Kazakh woman in a white Muslim scarf and other scenes of happy multi-ethnic citizens smiling together followed by a brief, almost subliminal image of the president.

In the next ad, pictures of traditional Kazakh horsemen riding across the steppes and women in funny hats symbolised the qualities of the local brand of beer.

•———•

OUR OFFICE WAS on one side of the central square of 'old' Astana. The century-old town market once stood on this site but had been demolished in the 1920s. In its place there was now a swanky shopping centre full of luxury name-brand stores.

There was a gushing fountain and a statue in the centre of the square, which Azhar told me represented the legend of the first Kazhak, who'd been raised by a wolf. The statue shows him as a chubby little boy standing on the back of the wild wolf, giving orders. He's wearing the first Kazakh hat, a high topped sombrero, and nothing else.

Across the square, the new Museum of the First (and at that stage only) President of the Republic of Kazakhstan had just opened in the former presidential office. The office had been built just seven years before when the capital was founded, but it had recently been superseded by a new presidential building further down the river.

Azhar and I decided that a visit to the museum could be classed as work because the museum service was one of the government programs we proposed to evaluate as part of our pilot evaluation program.

It was the middle of the summer holidays and crowds of Kazakh citizens were queuing for a chance to see displays about the life and activities of the president. The building itself, although modern on the outside, was decorated inside in a faux-Versailles style with grand arches and columns, pastel pink, green and yellow wallpaper, and imitation antique furniture.

The tour was in Kazakh so Azhar translated for me. According to our guide, it had recently been discovered that the president was, in fact, distantly related to a renowned Kazakh warrior hero of several centuries ago. The president himself, however, had been born into a humble family and started his career as a steelworker. He soon rose through the ranks of the Kazakhstan Communist Party and when the Soviet Union collapsed, had deftly side-stepped into the role of president of an independent Kazakhstan.

The museum's displays included the slightly shabby furniture in his recently vacated former office, including a collection of old ring-dial telephones. One large hall was devoted to a collection of medals and decorations bestowed upon the president by foreign governments, mostly from other ex-Soviet dependencies, but also an expensive-looking chain and medallion from Pope John Paul II, and the Order of St Michael and St George, presented by Queen Elizabeth II.

The Kazakh visitors in our tour group were suitably impressed by the displays and listened intently to the commentary by our guide, but I was sure I detected a few sniggers and smirks at her attempts to glorify the president. The state propaganda campaign hadn't completely eradicated independent thought.

ONE EVENING, TOWARDS the end of my six-week visit, Shaizada took me to see the newest extension to the city—a huge open space surrounded by monumental buildings, most of them still under construction. The builders were racing to finish before winter started.

As the light of day gradually faded, floodlights illuminated the buildings.

'Does it remind you of anything?' she asked as we stood in the middle of the central plaza. 'The Mall in Washington, maybe?'

She may have thought I was American and would immediately know what she was talking about. It didn't take long, however, based on my one visit to Washington a few years before, to recognise the layout of parallel avenues, central gardens and reflecting pools, flanked by large public buildings. Definitely like Washington, although on a somewhat smaller scale.

At one end of the grand plaza, the new Office of the President looked very much like the US Capitol Building, but with a blue and gold dome. Facing it at the other end, where the Lincoln Memorial would have been, was the headquarters of the state oil company—a sinister building that resembled the set of a Batman movie. Along each side were libraries, museums, government offices and the half-completed future embassies of foreign governments.

In the middle, more or less echoing the Washington Monument, with some influence from the Eiffel Tower, was a tall white structure with a huge gold ball on top. Shaizada explained that it represents the nest and egg of a mythical Kazakh bird. The Kazakh government was clearly very effective at mining local folklore for symbols to support its regime.

From inside the gold ball, high atop the narrow tower, we had a view in all directions around Astana—miles and miles of flat, empty nothing. On the level above, the main attraction was a block of gold metal with, supposedly, an imprint of the hand of the president. Local tourists lined up to have their photo taken with their hand in the president's oversized palm.

The most beautiful building in the whole complex was the Islamic Centre—a gift from Saudi Arabia, all white and gold and brightly illuminated. When sunset finally arrived, the call to prayer, at full amplification, shattered the evening. It was the first time I'd heard the Islamic call to prayer since I'd left Kabul. It brought a sudden, unexpected wave of nostalgia.

Shaizada, however, although a Muslim herself, was appalled. She vented her disgust at the growing Muslim influence in the country and the increasing number of women wearing Muslim headscarves.

'This was never part of our culture,' she said. 'The Kazakh women never covered their hair. They wore it long, in plaits, trimmed with jewellery, and when the country was under attack, they rode horses and fought alongside the men.'

At last, the end of my assignment was in sight. Just one more week of this tedium. I went to the Ministry of Economy and Budget Planning one last time to hand over my finished work to Dina and to say goodbye.

I didn't feel that I'd contributed much to the reform of the budget process in Kazakhstan. In fact, I thought the staff in the ministry could probably have worked it out for themselves with a bit of textbook reading and some internet research.

But Dina seemed very satisfied, particularly with the detailed training manual and class exercises I'd prepared.

'When will you be able to come back to deliver the training?' she asked.

My heart sank. I would die of boredom if I had to spend any more time in Astana.

Peter, my hero, gently lowered her expectations. 'We'll need to discuss that with head office. And have a look at the budget.'

In the end, it was Doug, who I'd met on my first day in Kabul, who was sent to do this job. I was off the hook.

Before the meeting, while we'd waited for Dina outside her tenth-floor office, I'd been gazing at the grey clouds and rain rolling in from the north and absentmindedly watching the young people at their work stations of pale timber with matching cupboards and bookshelves, engrossed in their flat computer screens—all well-dressed young men and women with smart hairstyles. The scene was not much different from the government office I'd left in Canberra a few years ago.

Then I remembered where I was and it suddenly seemed all wrong, like one of those spooky movie scenes where you realise that everything is not what it seems.

Of course, there's nothing particularly weird or sinister

about Kazakhs sitting at computers in a well-organised office, but I found it strangely disturbing.

Why shouldn't the people of Kazakhstan have all the modern things that we have, like clean offices and state-of-the-art computers, fashionable clothes, iPods and mobile phones and flat-screen TVs and their own version of MTV? We should be pleased that they'd come so far from the backwardness Peter and David had described.

The experience made me question some of my ideas about the work I'd been doing and the nature of foreign aid. The aid projects I'd worked on until then had been based on the assumption that people in other countries were incapable of doing things without our help. But there was no sign of a lack of capacity in the Kazakh administration.

I WAS MORE than ready to get out of this strange, surreal place, but leaving was not that easy. The day before my flight, I glanced in my passport and realised my visa had expired. I clearly remembered giving my passport to the office assistant two weeks earlier and getting it back with her assurance that the visa had been extended, but somehow it hadn't been and I'd been there for a fortnight without a valid visa. I couldn't leave until it was renewed.

This was starting to feel like one of those nightmares where you keep running and running but never get anywhere.

Shaizada pulled out all stops with the government bureaucracy to get the problem solved the next morning, even though it was Saturday. I was a few hours late, but at last, I was on my way to Almaty to join the endless midnight check-in queue, the even longer immigration line and finally, my escape to Frankfurt.

The Orange Revolution Turns Sour
Kyiv, Ukraine, September 2005

I arrived in Ukraine in late 2005, less than a year after the 'Orange Revolution' in 2004 that had forced out a corrupt regime and supposedly brought democracy.

By then, however, the Orange Revolution was already running out of steam. Its two charismatic leaders, Viktor Yushchenko, who had become president, and Yulia Tymoshenko, the new prime minister, were finding it difficult to work together and the government lurched from crisis to crisis.

The city of Kyiv was glorious in the last days of September. The golden domes of ancient churches glowed in the autumn sunshine, the leaves were just starting to fall from the trees along wide, cobble-stoned boulevards, the footpaths were crowded with café tables and coloured sun umbrellas, and the main street was lined with emporiums of designer goods from the west.

Like most parts of Europe, Ukraine has a complicated history. Kyiv was first settled by Scandinavian Vikings in the 800s and, at various times since then, the country has been conquered or ruled by Mongols, Lithuanians, Poles, Turks and Swedes, divided between Poland and Russia, and fought over by Austrians and Russians and Nazis and Bolsheviks.

For many years it was an important part of the Soviet Union, until in 1991, as the communist bloc was falling apart, the government in Ukraine declared itself independent. However, most of the old leaders stayed on, the economy crashed, and corruption and shady business deals became the norm.

Capitalism flourished in this environment and Kyiv now had luxury fashion boutiques, classy restaurants, cinemas showing Hollywood movies and a wealthy elite who drove around in big, shiny black cars with dark-tinted windows, apparently exempt from traffic regulations.

It was clear to me that my assignment in Ukraine was a direct consequence of the Orange Revolution. The new Yushchenko/Tymoshenko government was more pro-west than its Russian aligned predecessor and the US Agency for International Development had seized on the change of government as a chance to expand its influence in national government ministries.

I'd been recruited to provide the Ukraine Ministry of Finance with advice on modernising their budget processes. Once again, this meant introducing program budgeting, something I was starting to become an expert on.

It soon turned out, however, that this might not have been the best time for this particular policy innovation.

The USAID project was based in an office in an elegant apartment block near the city centre. Most of the rest of the building was inhabited by elderly ladies and their cats. The women would sit on a green park bench outside the front door each morning, gossiping and feeding the cats. Then they would go back to their apartments, shuffling slowly through the foyer, and the cats would follow them into the lift. The foyer smelled of cat's piss.

It was a relatively small office and most of the employees were Ukrainian. Many, despite working for an American company, didn't speak English. In most places, English would be the first requirement for a job like this.

Some of the staff were former Ministry of Finance economists who produced analytical reports on the Ukrainian economy and the government's budget on much higher salaries than they'd received from the government. Others were trainers who travelled the country delivering seminars on program budgeting to municipal bookkeepers. Some of these people became good friends while I was in Kyiv. Some of them didn't.

Robert, the 'chief of party', was Slovakian. He'd come to Ukraine by way of Yale on a US passport but he spoke the local language fluently. At the time I'd assumed that this was Ukrainian, but in retrospect, I realise it was probably Russian. I was never sure whether people were speaking Ukrainian or Russian. Although Ukrainian is the official language, Russian is also widely spoken and they sound much the same to an outsider.

Robert didn't seem to have a strong understanding of the purpose of our work, and the only issues of concern to him appeared to be 'What will USAID think?', 'Will I get into trouble?' and 'Who can I blame?' I could almost see these three ideas revolving around in his head as he wrung his hands anxiously whenever a problem arose. He had an uncanny capacity for pushing all the wrong psychological buttons to make a manageable situation unmanageable.

The only other non-Ukrainian there at that time was a remarkable African American woman called Marcia. She'd already spent several years working as a local government adviser in a remote oil mining town in Kazakhstan. Having been to Kazakhstan I could appreciate how difficult that must have been.

After that, she'd taken a job in Basra, which had soon become one of the more dangerous towns in post-Saddam Iraq. Now she was working with regional municipalities in Ukraine where almost no one spoke English and they'd rarely met a foreigner, let alone an African American.

We became friends by necessity and I came to admire her self-sufficiency in this foreign environment. When things went badly on the project, which they soon did, she was supportive. She waved her hand dismissively in the direction of the chief of party's office, clicked her tongue and tossed her head. 'Don't you worry about him. Just put your head down and produce the work.'

Unfortunately, in this case, her strategy didn't entirely work.

Our involvement in the Ukraine Ministry of Finance was facing problems even before I arrived. The president, after less than a year on the job, had decided to dismiss the entire cabinet. It was not clear, therefore, who the Minister of Finance was at that moment, and whether or not whoever it was would continue to support the US-sponsored reform program. The deputy minister was still in his job, however, and Robert had scheduled a meeting with him the morning after I arrived.

The deputy minister's office was in a Stalin-era, neo-classical building in the centre of Kyiv. A semicircle of gigantic Greek columns dwarfed the limousines and police vans parked in the forecourt.

We were met by a shy young man from the protocol department who led us along a semi-circular corridor to the ministerial conference room on the top floor. The room was fresh and bright with cream walls, cream curtains and a row of tinted sepia photographs of former ministers on the wall. A number of people were already arranged along one side of the table, waiting for us.

The deputy minister came in quietly, without fanfare. He was dark-haired and good-looking and seemed young for his senior position in the government. He sat between two women, both blondes, who looked at him solicitously like two middle-aged guardian angels.

The meeting was tediously slow. Every sentence had to be translated from English to Ukrainian and from Ukrainian to English, although I could tell that the deputy minister and some of the others knew English fairly well.

It was only my second day in Kyiv and I'd been given no prior information on who we were meeting, or what the agenda was, or even what my role in the project was, but Robert suddenly turned to me and asked me to make a presentation on what I planned to do. As I hadn't yet had a chance to discuss this with anyone, I had almost no idea. Marcia was also caught off-guard.

I quickly stuttered some generalities and vague principles, furious at Robert for dumping me in this situation. The people on the other side of the table didn't look happy.

On the whole, things went downhill from there.

I FOUND A place to live in a grand old apartment block in a lively area in the centre of Kyiv, at the top of Red Army Street. It had large windows facing the morning sun and had recently been painted in a bold scheme of lime green, lilac and apricot.

The building itself was not as well cared for as the apartment. The foyer was unlit, the floor tiles were damaged, and the row of metal letterboxes looked as if they'd all been broken into more than once or twice in their long lives. The metal cage around the lift was furry with decades of dust and the lift itself made alarming grating noises as it went up and down. All the privately-owned apartments, however, had new front doors, state-of-the-art security locks and video intercoms.

Undaunted by the disastrous first meeting with the ministry and the ongoing chaos in the government, Marcia and

I proceeded to arrange meetings with Ministry of Finance officials. Most of the senior staff we met with were women, mostly blondes, obviously bright and capable.

But I met them rarely. As in Kazakhstan, I didn't have ready access to ministry buildings and staff. Every meeting had to be booked long in advance and was likely to be cancelled at short notice if something more urgent came up, and that happened often.

There were other obstacles also. I soon became aware that Ukrainians are keen on 'methodology'. Everything required a methodology and nothing could possibly be done until the methodology was approved, preferably in the form of a legal document. This meant that the implementation of even the smallest new idea was deferred indefinitely while working groups, committees and consultants worked on developing the methodology, then getting it approved by the minister, the cabinet or parliament. Until this was done, nothing could change.

Legislation was also important. Everything had to be put into the form of some kind of legal document. Even an invitation to a training course was written as a formal order signed by the Deputy Minister for Finance. The idea that people might turn up at a training course because they want to learn something, and their bosses might let them go for the same reason, was apparently unknown.

Despite these challenges, I managed to organise a training program for government staff. The Ukraine Institute of Scientific Financial Research provided the venue and the deputy minister duly signed the decrees ordering people from the Ministries of Finance and Economy to attend.

The institute was some way from the centre of town. The historical grandeur and touristic attractiveness of Kyiv faded rapidly out there. The elegant buildings and gold-roofed churches gave way to rows of apartment towers, concrete public buildings, traffic-choked intersections, crowded bus stops and unrepaired footpaths. On this grey, glum day it was all unbelievably ugly.

When we arrived, we were met by a white-haired and dignified doctor professor who introduced himself in a way that made it clear he was well above the humble level of this seminar. His photo, adorned with numerous medals and ribbons, was prominently displayed in the foyer. The trainees selected by the ministry for the seminar were middle-level, middle-aged men and women. A man from the Ministry of Economy with curly brown hair and a large ginger moustache looked as if he'd just arrived from the mid-1970s.

Our Ukrainian trainers presented most of the sessions. They'd already been doing the same thing for all the municipalities. After a lunch of various potato-based dishes in the institute's restaurant, the attendees went home duly 'trained' in the concepts of program budgeting and we were able to tick off another milestone in the contract.

It was rush hour by the time we finished. The quickest way home was to join the crowds flowing into the vast hall of the local metro station. The escalator to the platforms below moved at several times the speed of normal escalators, hurtling us deep underground. A uniformed driver, sitting at the top, looked down on the crowd and controlled the speed. Beside us to the right, hundreds of other people moved in the same direction on a parallel escalator, while to the left, hundreds more came up from the trains. People congregating around the base of the up escalator were quickly and efficiently sucked into the upward-moving stream.

The train carriages were old and somewhat toylike, but after an initial lurch, they moved off at speed. After only two stops, we got out and went flying upwards on the escalator as if we were on a fun park ride and found ourselves in the centre of Kyiv. The trip cost the equivalent of ten US cents.

OUR PROJECT OFFICE had now also become the home of a USAID-funded Civil Society Development Project in neighbouring Belarus. Visiting representatives of local non-government organisations from Belarus met in our conference room on weekends to discuss their common interests, including how to ensure that the forthcoming elections there would be free and fair.

The project to support civil society in Belarus was based in Kyiv and not in Minsk because foreign organisations such as USAID were not welcome there, and because if the same people had met together in Belarus they would probably have been arrested. The chances of the election in Belarus being free and fair seemed remote.

AS AN OUTSIDER who didn't speak either Ukrainian or Russian, I knew little about what was going on in local politics at the time. I got most of my news from the Kyiv Post, a free English language weekly handed out in restaurants and bars which made its money from many pages of ads for escort services and introduction agencies.

I also picked up some insights from random discussions with English-speaking Ukrainian colleagues. Over lunch one day, Bohdan, a Norwegian Ukrainian, gave me a short lecture on the subject.

'The first thing you have to understand,' he explained, 'is

that almost everyone in Ukraine is corrupt. Some are just more corrupt than others.

'Everyone knows, for example, that votes in parliament are for sale. The price depends on the importance of the issue.'

He went on to explain that there were more than 400 members of parliament who nominally represented political parties, but it was easy to register a political party and most were little more than a name and a contract with a PR consultant. They had slogans, advertising campaigns and focus-group-tested election promises paid for by wealthy backers but little real community support.

Getting your name on a party 'list', therefore, depended on how much money you could stump up for the party leaders rather than any process of pre-selection by the membership.

The old communists were the only party with any kind of grassroots structure behind them. Soon after I arrived, the Communist Party held a rally in central Kyiv. They gathered at one end of the main street and marched to the now-famous Maidan Nezalezhnosti—Independence Square—where they stayed all afternoon making speeches and playing heroic-sounding music.

There were only a hundred or so of them, almost lost among the Saturday shoppers, but they positioned themselves strategically across the road and waved a mass of red flags marked with the hammer and sickle or red stars. From a distance, they looked like a vast crowd.

Every policeman from the Kyiv region seemed to be on duty for the event, standing three-deep, a wall of dull blue, overwhelmingly outnumbering the marchers. A group of riot police in helmets and body armour loitered a little further away.

The issue that had brought the communists onto the streets was the new government's proposal to recognise the veterans of the Ukrainian Insurgent Army, a World War II nationalist paramilitary group that had fought against both the Nazis and the communists. But it was clearly not an issue that most people in Kyiv felt strongly about. Passers-by went on with their shopping.

Both the current president, Mr Yushchenko, and the prime minister, Mrs Tymoshenko, and almost everyone else in the current Orange Revolution government had also served in some capacity in the previous pro-Russian government of Leonid Kuchma. Yushchenko was, at one time, prime minister and Tymoshenko had been deputy prime minister. This seemed strange to me given that the Orange Revolution had been based on opposition to Kuchma and his cronies.

The Revolution had begun as a protest against a rigged presidential election. Young protesters had camped in tents in Independence Square in the centre of Kyiv under the glare of international scrutiny. Viktor Yushchenko's pock-marked face—the result of dioxin poisoning in a failed assassination attempt—had been a frequent sight in international news bulletins.

Yushchenko had eventually won the rerun of the presidential election with fifty-two percent of the vote. It wasn't a resounding victory, but many believed it meant the people of Ukraine had thrown out the old guard of corrupt leaders and elected a new, clean government.

However, the ascension of the Yushchenko/Tymoshenko government had apparently not done a great deal to change the corrupt politics in the country. One of President Yushchenko's close supporters, Petro Poroshenko, a cabinet minister, was under investigation at the time in relation to a large apartment block development on prime real estate by the river. Kyiv City Council had granted permission to construct a fifteen-storey building. The developer, however, had decided to make it twenty.

When Yushchenko had been elected, he immediately stopped construction, but there were suggestions that Poroshenko had asked for a share of the profits in exchange for allowing construction to resume. This allegation was made by an ally of Yulia Tymoshenko, the prime minister, and was one of the reasons Yushchenko dumped the entire cabinet, including Yulia, at the beginning of September.

Meanwhile, the developers waited to find out whether they would have to demolish the top five floors of their building (the Kyiv City Council's proposal), the whole thing (the president's plan), or whether they would eventually be able to finish the building and make a fortune selling million-dollar apartments within walking distance of parliament house. My money was on the latter.

By November, the mild late-autumn days were over and the temperature dropped to minus twenty-five Centigrade in the middle of the day. Although I only had to walk one block to the office, the skin on my face was screaming with pain by the time I got there. It was like sticking my cheek against the inside of a freezer.

No one walked slowly in this weather. Women wore fur or sheepskin coats with big fur-lined hoods or fur hats. The men pulled tea cosy hats over their ears and turned their collars up.

I went to Kyiv's biggest department store with Alla, a translator from the office, and bought a featherdown-filled coat in avocado green. I looked like a sleeping bag with feet but it was much warmer than the jacket from Marks and Spenser which had been sufficient for winters in Kosovo and Kabul.

Clouds of steam billowed from the entrance to the metro

station every time a train went through. The metro was the warmest place to be and the underground passages around the Maidan and Tolstoho stations were lively with young people setting up guitars and amplifiers and standing in puddles drinking beer.

The temperature in the apartment got a little colder each day as the building's heating system reached its capacity and the outside climate started to win the battle. The large rooms, high ceilings, polished floorboards and stark modern furniture no longer seemed like such a good idea. A warm radiator, thick curtains and a comfortable sofa would have been preferable.

But I was luckier than some of my colleagues who lived in modern Kyiv apartments. One woman woke in the morning to find the water in the glass by her bed had turned to ice.

The cold weather went on for weeks and the daily temperature rarely rose above minus twenty.

The gym at the Premier Palace Hotel, however, was warm and only a short walk from the office. The membership fees were astronomical by Ukraine standards so there was rarely anyone else using the equipment.

Sometimes a large, thuggish man would arrive with his bodyguard who inspected the room carefully before taking up his position in the corridor outside. The man himself, with his closely-shaved head and thick arms, looked more dangerous than the bodyguard. The young gym instructor, who obviously knew who he was, danced attendance on him like a fawning puppy dog.

Although the gym itself was usually empty, the luxurious women's changing room was often filled with attractive young women making use of the showers, the large mirrors and the suntanning cubicle. I wasn't sure whether they were the trophy wives of Ukraine's wealthy elite, or professional ladies taking a break between appointments in the hotel rooms.

They were all formidable beauties; tall, leggy and long-haired with all over suntans. They came out of the showers naked — not even pubic hair for modesty—looked at themselves appraisingly in the mirrors, lavished body lotions and perfumes on their skin and brushed their glowing hair. Then they put on skimpy lace underwear and pulled themselves into tight black pants and long boots and bosom-enhancing shirts.

Ukraine is famous for beautiful women. They are one of the country's major exports.

OUR BUDGET REFORM work at the Ministry of Finance really started to go off the rails in the new year. The most cooperative Ministry of Finance officials, including the deputy minister, resigned and moved to other jobs. In their absence, the head of the budget department refused to work with us.

My main contacts in the ministry, Inna and Natalia—the two guardian angels from my first meeting—were sympathetic, but too junior to have any influence. Winter did not suit them, or perhaps they had been working too many long hours. They both looked tired, had put on weight and their hair was no longer blonde.

My presence in Kyiv was beginning to feel a bit pointless. During most of my days in the office I just filled in time, waiting for documents to be translated to and from Ukrainian, and drafting reports and recommendations that might possibly never be read. Coming so soon after my tedious days in Kazakhstan a few months earlier, I began to lose confidence in my ability to do this kind of work.

My evenings and weekends were equally dull. Living in

Kyiv was no different from being a newcomer in any large city, but with the added problem that I didn't speak either of the local languages. I'd met a few other expats and we sometimes went out for drinks, but there was nothing like the camaraderie and shared interests of life in Kosovo or Kabul.

Most of the men I met were involved with Ukrainian women or were looking for one. I'd already been warned that a single western woman couldn't get a date in places like Ukraine. The competition from glamorous young blondes who also have engineering doctorates was too strong. Compared to previous postings where there'd been a significant excess of available, if not necessarily single, men relative to the number of single women, the socialising opportunities were quite restricted.

Kyiv was, however, one of the first places I'd worked where I could imagine becoming close friends with local people. The line between 'us' and 'them', which had been fairly clear in places like Kosovo and Afghanistan, was less distinct there. I got on well with some of the women in the office and now regret not getting to know them better.

Halya, the office administrator, introduced me to her hairdresser, far out in the outer suburbs of Kyiv at the end of the metro line, which provided adventure as well as a haircut. One of the several Svetlanas in the office helped me in my futile quest to learn Ukrainian.

My translator, Alla, shared with me her concerns about her son and her need to get him out of doing national service.

'If you knew my son,' she said, 'you would know that he would not survive the army.'

But she had a plan. She had arranged to see the army medical examiner. 'Only fifty dollars should be enough.' She came back to the office later in the day looking satisfied, confident her son would get a suitably adverse medical report.

Mostly, however, my evenings and weekends were quiet.

At least politics was always interesting. The president had now appointed new ministers to replace the ones he'd dismissed in September, but a few months later, the parliament, in its turn, decided to dismiss all the new ministers.

The government said this was unconstitutional and the ministers demonstrated that they were still doing their jobs by attending a Ukrainian Orthodox ritual which involved immersing themselves in the frozen waters of the Dnipro River. The event was reported on the evening news—a group of overweight middle-aged men in small swimsuits jumping into a hole in the ice.

One of the other top stories at the time was the imminent privatisation of the Kryvorizhstal steelworks, the biggest and most profitable state-owned enterprise in Ukraine. It had already been privatised once, just a year earlier, by the previous government.

Two local businessmen, one of whom was the son-in-law of the then-president, Leonid Kuchma, paid $900 million for it. Several international steel companies had also put in bids, most of them much higher than this, but to their surprise, were disqualified for contravening some aspect of the government's tendering procedure.

After the Orange Revolution, the new government re-nationalised the company and put it on the market again. They were depending on the money to finance increases in the minimum wage and welfare benefits. The steel mill was eventually sold to an Indian multinational for $4.8 billion, somewhat more than what it had gone for the first time around.

•———•

BY THE END of March, our program budgeting project had completely fizzled out, with not much achieved for all the time and money spent. USAID decided to pull the plug on it.

This was when Robert's skill at finger-pointing and blame-shifting was on full display.

The company in Washington wasn't happy. They'd lose money. A senior executive flew out to Kyiv to try to salvage the project and managed to calm everyone down. Robert succeeded in saving his own job but there was no further need for Marcia and me. The local staff would stay and continue to do what they'd been doing and would no doubt do it well.

While I was getting ready to go home, Ukraine was preparing to elect a new parliament. The March 2006 election would be conducted under a new electoral law which Bohdan described as the worst electoral system in the world.

There were no longer any geographically defined electorates. Ukraine would be a single electorate, voters would vote for parties rather than individuals, and seats in parliament would be allocated according to each party's share of the vote.

Members of parliament would, therefore, no longer have any responsibility to a local constituency of voters who had elected them but would be even more beholden to the party leaders and oligarchs who had sponsored their campaign.

When the party lists were made public a few months before the election, even the most cynical Ukrainians were surprised at some of the names that turned up as candidates. They included business tycoons who had never shown much interest in party politics but were suspected of having been involved in illegal activities under previous regimes. The reason for their sudden interest in politics was simple—members of parliament were immune from prosecution for previous crimes. Buying a seat would keep them out of the courts for at least a few more years.

By mid-March, election fever reached a climax. Party tents and booths went up around the entrance to my local metro station and commuters ran a gauntlet of people handing out leaflets. There were flags on every corner—yellow, light blue, green and, of course, orange—waved above the crowds and traffic on long poles beside matching coloured tents. The main street seemed to be lined with orange flags.

The opinion polls suggested that the voters narrowly favoured the party led by Yanukovych, the guy who'd lost to Yushchenko in the rerun of the presidential election not much more than a year earlier. Most of the people I spoke to at work, however, seemed to support Yulia Tymoshenko, the recently dismissed prime minister, who appeared on television each night in folkloric embroidered costumes with her long blonde plait wound around her forehead like a golden crown.

The final results of the parliamentary election didn't come out until after I'd left. The opinion polls had been right. Yanukovych's party won the most votes and, with some support from the socialists and the communists, he became prime minister. Yulia Tymoshenko's party came second. President Yushchenko was clearly on the nose with voters by then and his party won only fourteen percent of the parliamentary votes.

The map of electoral results clearly showed Ukraine's geographical divisions, with the south and east, dominated by ethnic Russians, supporting Yanukovich, and the north and west clearly for Tymoshenko.

Four years later, in 2010, the Russian-aligned Yanukovich was elected president. He won a run-off vote with his nearest competitor, Yulia Tymoshenko, 48.9% to 45.4%. The remaining 5.7% of voters presumably went to the polling booth specifically to say 'none of the above'.

In the end, I was sad to leave Kyiv. The weather had become much warmer and the snow had melted away. Once again, I could go out in comfortable clothes instead of voluminous coats and heavy boots and I could walk the streets without worrying about falling over on the ice.

I'd also become close to some of the people I spent my time with in the office each day. It was difficult to say goodbye to Alla, Halya and the Svetlanas.

I'd also developed an affection for Ukraine. It had a sophisticated culture and a well-educated population, good infrastructure, reliable electricity, an efficient public transport system, bohemian cafés, successful businessmen and Eurovision-winning pop stars. The people in Ukraine didn't lack education, application or ability. They should be capable of solving their own problems if they were given the opportunity and motivation to do it.

I packed up my apartment and spent my last night in Kyiv at the Ukraina Hotel, which provided another perspective to the Ukraine experience. The Ukraina was a former state-run hotel still stuck in the last days of socialism. Although it was now operated by a private hotel chain called Best Eastern Hotels, not much had really changed. In particular, the concept of customer service hadn't yet caught hold.

The dimly lit lobby retained its 1970s décor and the reception desk resembled a post office counter, including narrow benches for filling in the registration forms with pens tied down with string. Upstairs, a floor supervisor sat at a desk at the intersection of several wide corridors to safeguard the keys and observe the comings and goings of all the guests.

Despite the luxury hotel room rates, I'd seen better rooms in youth hostels. Breakfast was served holiday camp style with the guests seated at long tables strictly in order of their arrival. The plates of cheese, meat and bread were already laid out and, from the texture of the bread, had probably been there most of the night. At the far end of the restaurant, an abstract mural in unappetising red and green colours appeared to represent either the glories of the people's revolution or the torments of hell.

It was all a reminder that, although Kyiv appeared to be a city of good restaurants and expensive boutiques, of flashy advertising and rampant capitalism, in some respects it hadn't come all that far since the days of the Soviet Union.

AFGHAN BOY SCOUTS
Kabul, Afghanistan. September 2006

Dubai Airport at five in the morning once again. A year and a half after I'd last said goodbye to Kabul, I checked in for the first of several more visits to Afghanistan.

I seemed to find it difficult to say no to entreaties from consulting firms who were having more and more trouble finding willing employees as the deteriorating security situation made work there less attractive.

By late 2006, Dubai's Terminal 2 had become the staging point for all Middle East war zones. The departure board that morning listed two flights to Kabul, one to the US airbase at Bagram, three to Baghdad and one to Kuwait. The lounge was full of American accents and khaki clothing.

Several new private airlines now flew the lucrative daily route to Kabul, but all their flights left in the early morning, in time to return in the afternoon, ensuring that no aircraft had to spend more than a few hours on the ground in Kabul.

The attendants on this flight were blonde Russian women in short skirts and stiletto heels. It was still summer holidays in Europe, so many of the passengers were families coming home to visit the old country. Teenage girls in tight T-shirts and hipster jeans disappeared into the aircraft toilets and came back transformed into modest Afghan women in scarves and long skirts.

During the flight, I listened to a podcast on my MP3 player (a recent innovation in travel entertainment). It was an interview with an Australian woman who worked for an Afghan charity. She talked about how the situation there had deteriorated, about the number of her staff who'd been murdered, and how a colleague had been kidnapped.

And I was about to land there!

Friends at home had been concerned when I'd told them I was going back. Australia now had soldiers deployed in Afghanistan so they heard a lot more about it in the news and everything they heard was bad. The daily emails I received from my employer's security adviser in Afghanistan were full of alarming stories. Just a few weeks ago there'd been a suicide bomb attack near the US Embassy only a few blocks from where I used to live.

The plane made a steep, corkscrew descent into Kabul, spending as little time as possible within range of any ground-to-air rockets that might be nearby.

At the airport nothing seemed to have changed. The tarmac still swarmed with unauthorised visitors and the arrival hall had, if anything, deteriorated, with half the fluorescent lights now out of action and the glass in the windows cracked and dirty.

Driving into town I recognised some streets and it began to look comfortably familiar. The afternoon traffic of bicycles, scooters, mini-buses and suicidal taxis slid around our car, paying no attention to the foreigners inside. Kabul was going about its business as usual.

Then we drove through the area where I used to live. The quiet suburb of tree-lined streets and modest houses was now barricaded and patrolled by armed sentries. Almost all the houses were surrounded with concrete blast walls, Hesco barriers and rolls of barbed wire. The embassies and military bases were now fortresses.

I was on a different project this time, working for a different company and a different donor in a different government ministry. The project was funded by the Danish aid organisation—Danida—and implemented by a British consulting firm which had carved a niche for itself working almost exclusively in dangerous places like Afghanistan, Iraq and Somalia. The beneficiary this time was the Afghan Ministry of Education.

The accommodation arrangements, however, were much the same as they'd been before—a group house with guards at the gates, swarms of servants and little privacy. At least in this house we each had our own bathroom.

The Kabul building boom had continued since I'd left and some districts were now full of multi-storey mansions and small palaces built specifically to be rented to foreigners. Although the houses looked luxurious from the outside, with their elaborate colonnaded balconies and ornate decoration, they'd been hastily constructed and the workmanship was shoddy. One of the many things Afghanistan desperately needed was good trades training.

The concrete front yard was full of vehicles and generators and the street outside was an unpaved dirt track. The psychological torment of sharing domestic life with half a dozen strangers was also much the same as it had been before.

On the bright side, Tony, a former colleague from Kosovo, was also working on this project, helping the Ministry of Education write its strategic plan. Until recently, he'd been trying to reform public finances in Baghdad and had hair-raising stories to tell about the experience. He'd decided to leave when he was no longer allowed to visit the Ministry of Finance to work with local staff.

'Also, the minister had a torture room in the basement. That was another reason,' he added.

Not long after Tony left Iraq, an IT expert he'd worked with was kidnapped from inside the Ministry of Finance building, along with his two security guards. The IT guy eventually made it home. His security guards didn't.

The Afghanistan Ministry of Education was one of the largest and most important ministries in the government. A few years before, when the Taliban had been in power, there had been less than a million children attending school, all of them boys. The Taliban had banned girls from attending school, but there had also been fewer boys because female teachers were no longer allowed to work so there was no one to teach them.

Now, only a few years later, there were more than six million children at school and a large proportion were girls. There weren't enough classrooms for all of them so many schools operated in tents and, as in Kosovo, often ran classes in two or even three shifts a day.

A new Minister for Education had recently been appointed; the fifth in five years. Hanif Atmar, with a degree from a UK university, had previously been the Minister for Rural Reconstruction and Development where he'd built a reputation among donors as someone who could get things done. They were now hoping he could fix things in education. He was also being touted as a possible future president.

I met him once, during a meeting with provincial education officials. He entered the room in a blaze of light. The door from his office, backlit by the east-facing windows, silhouetted him against the morning sun.

He was a suave young man, at that time still in his thirties, wearing a dark suit and leaning on an aluminium crutch. He'd lost a leg somewhere in the past, like so many others in Afghanistan. He was a charismatic charmer, treating each person as if he knew them well, shaking hands with everyone and switching languages from Dari to Pashto to English.

The Afghan government, with a lot of help from the World Bank, had recently developed a sophisticated and wordy National Development Strategy—a weighty document setting out a wonderful future for the people of Afghanistan.

In education, for example, it forecast huge increases in the number of children at school over the next five years and significant improvement in the quality of education.

The Ministry of Education was in the process of preparing a plan to put the National Development Strategy into action. The resulting Education Strategic Plan was also a weighty document, written largely in English, mostly by foreign advisers. In fact, much of it, I gathered, had been drafted by a team attached to UNESCO sitting in an office in Paris.

The strategic plan listed everything the Ministry of Education wanted to do over the next five years. Some of it was essential and sensible—build more schools, train more teachers, write new textbooks.

A lot of it, however, was fanciful. There were plans to construct playing fields and gymnasiums in every one of Afghanistan's thousands of schools, an Olympic-sized swimming pool in each major town (in a country where both men and women are expected to keep their bodies covered from ankle to neck at all times), and a long section on expanding the activities of the boy and girl scouts, including buying uniforms at thirty-five dollars each, which was about the monthly salary for one teacher. The middle-aged ministry officials responsible for this proposal turned up at the budget meeting dressed in their own scout uniforms.

There was no chance the money would be available in the foreseeable future to do most of these things. In the meantime, the usual problems continued—many teachers didn't get paid regularly, schools had no money to spend on repairs, and Ministry of Education representatives couldn't visit half the provinces for fear of being killed by the Taliban.

The main purpose of the strategic plan, in reality, was to make the donors happy. A good-looking and well-written plan would inspire them with the confidence to commit money to development. To the extent it achieved this it might not have been a complete waste of time.

My job was to help the Ministry of Education rationalise the big ideas in the plan, work out how much it would cost, and develop a sensible budget. This involved days of tedious meetings with all the program managers going through their 'pie in the sky' list of projects and attempting to remove or at least scale back the more ridiculous and absurd.

Most of the Afghans we were dealing with at the Ministry of Education spoke fluent English. That was largely because the ministry was full of 'national advisers'—smart, well-educated young Afghans, many of them returned refugees, who were doing government work on much higher salaries than regular government staff would earn.

The local program managers were, of course, reluctant to lose their pet projects—the scouts and the gymnasiums and swimming pools, the 346 literacy schools and the hundreds of boys' and girls' madrassas.

We sat with them for days, coaxing them to calculate the cost of their grand plans. Most had never had to do this before and, like many public servants everywhere, they'd underestimated the true cost of doing things and overestimated their ability to get things done. As a result, they'd produced a long list of tasks and projects that were all due to be completed in the first half of the following year; a physical impossibility even if the money miraculously became available.

Meanwhile, the Department of Education had other important things to worry about including building 5000 new schools, organising new textbooks for every student, and reviewing the qualifications, and indeed the existence, of all the teachers on the ministry payroll.

CONDITIONS IN THE Ministry of Education building were much the same as they'd been in the Ministry of Finance three years before, including dirty stone-floored corridors, badly painted walls and dusty windows. The woodwork had so many layers of paint, roughly applied over so many years, that the door frames appeared to be made of plasticine. A hideous smell came from the men's toilets and muddy footprints led from the open door down the corridor.

Our foreign advisors' office, in the executive wing of the ministry, was somewhat better. It had new carpet, vertical blinds on the windows and new furniture.

Several local staff were already working with us. Iqbal was a Pashtun doctor from Jalalabad who, like most Afghan doctors, was working as an interpreter for much more than he would earn as a doctor.

He showed me photos of his wife on his mobile phone. She was an attractive young woman and, from the dreamy look in his eyes, he was clearly besotted. In some of the photos her hair was uncovered and I guessed he didn't show them to his male friends.

They'd been married for three years already, although she was still only nineteen, and Iqbal was worried that she hadn't become pregnant yet. 'Next week, I'm taking her to see a specialist.'

Our other interpreter, Azifa, was at an advanced stage of her third pregnancy. Her first baby had lived only a few months, the second just one week. Now she'd found out she was expecting twins. My colleague, Tony, gave her the money for a doctor's appointment and then a scan. Women in Afghanistan don't normally go to the doctor just because they're pregnant.

The twins arrived soon afterwards, two months premature. Azifa was back at work almost immediately. Three months later, in the depths of winter, the babies, with their weak lungs, developed chest infections. Azifa rushed them to hospital in the middle of the night but the emergency room was too busy and turned her away. She tried other hospitals but each one was crowded with people waiting to see a doctor.

Finally, she found somewhere that was able to admit them and the babies stayed there until their lungs recovered. They had avoided joining the fifteen percent of Afghan children who die in infancy.

Despite the ever-increasing security precautions, life in Kabul for foreigners seemed to go on much as it had before. We still went to restaurants and bars, had dinner parties and barbeques, shopped in Chicken Street, went for walks on the strange little hills that dot the city, and drove out to the King's Palace for sightseeing trips. The Lebanese, Mexican and French restaurants were still busy, although they were all trading behind higher walls and with more security guards.

Life for the Afghan elite in Kabul was also coming along nicely. The modern new malls with their shops full of gold jewellery seemed to have plenty of customers, the number of large cars on the road had increased dramatically and the construction of extravagant houses continued apace.

In early 2007, we were ready to submit the education budget proposal to the Ministry of Finance. I finished the long and complex submission forms with great difficulty, struggling to make the constantly changing numbers add up. About forty documents had to be submitted, in both English and Dari.

By then, however, I'd become skilled at preparing spreadsheets in Dari, with columns of numbers reading from right to left lined up with the correct province or program. I could read just enough Dari to cut and paste words like 'budget', 'total' and 'dollar Americani' into the table in the correct places. The need for translation was reduced to one or two headings.

Then the minister decided that he wanted to see how the budget would be allocated to each province. He sensibly told his team of Afghan senior advisers they must do this themselves and not expect foreign advisers to do it for them.

Dr Ghaznawi, the deputy minister responsible for the strategic planning exercise, convened a meeting of the senior advisers and technical staff to discuss how to proceed. Dr Ghaznawi was, we estimated, about ninety years old and had spent most of his life in Paris where he did a PhD in French literature.

He'd read Proust's *À la Recherche du Temps Perdu* from cover to cover in French and was also fluent in a number of other languages. He was, however, renowned for his lack of interest in budget matters or anything else involving numbers. His eyes glazed over as soon as the discussion turned to finance and he was inclined to close proceedings at that point, assuming that nothing important remained to be decided.

I was asked to come to the meeting to explain what needed to be done to fulfil the minister's request for provincial budget data. I showed them a blank table with the names of the provinces down one side and the names of the programs across the top.

Dr Ghaznawi looked at it in puzzlement. 'But these boxes are blank. They should be filled up. There should be numbers across and down.'

'Exactly,' I said, pleased that at least he had grasped the concept. 'We will fill in the form as soon as your staff give us the numbers.'

The Afghan advisers assured him that all was in hand and set off to do the analysis required to determine in which provinces the planned new schools, madrassas, teachers' colleges and literacy centres would be established during the coming year.

I was expecting to have to provide assistance, in spite of the minister's instructions that they should do it themselves, but when I visited their offices I was delighted to find the Afghan advisers and their technical staff gathered around computers working on the spreadsheets.

•———•

WITH WINTER OVER, NATO, with a fanfare, launched its latest offensive against the Taliban, assuring us that this year they would be defeated.

Meanwhile, in Kabul, workmen added another metre to the top of the already high security wall around the Serena Hotel. The Serena had previously been the bomb-damaged old Kabul Hotel, down the road from the Ministry of Finance. Now renovated, it provided four-star accommodation to visiting dignitaries, and international meals in its restaurant, although without any alcohol service. Armed guards stood in front of the heavy main gates, and the door that was to have been the grand front entrance from the street was now bricked up.

Our Ministry of Education building was also being fortified. Hescos had been erected inside the front wall and around the entrance to the car park. But the building itself stood on a busy city street, facing the central city park, with its large windows above the passing traffic; an easy target for a missile.

Taliban terrorists and missiles were not the only security issue we now had to deal with. In the city, the Afghan police themselves had also become a potential danger, setting up roadblocks at night and demanding money from foreigners.

The twenty-first of March is traditionally the Afghan new

year and the start of spring. It also marked the end of the first phase of my assignment in the Ministry of Education and I was getting ready to go home.

The weather was fine and the air was clear. The normally brown and dusty hillsides around Kabul were coated with young green grass and the tiny tree seedlings that had been planted the year before had started to grow. It looked as if they would survive and, in five or ten years, the barren hillsides would again be a forest.

That afternoon the hills were dotted with people climbing the slopes; a new year custom. Families were dressed in their best clothes, women in colourful scarves and dresses and heavy make-up, little boys in white Afghan suits with gold embroidered waistcoats, and men in sequined skull caps. The ice-cream seller on his scooter, the carts selling fresh coconuts, and the man with a bunch of inflated balloons all did good business.

On the roads, whole families crammed into small cars. Groups of boisterous young men cruised the streets in a good mood and called out to us in English as they drove past. These days everyone their age learnt English.

Our driver, Ramin, warned us to be careful because some of the men might have been drinking. We pretended to express surprise. 'Surely not alcoholic drinks!'

'Yes, of course.' Ramin laughed. All the government's prohibitions on the import and sale of alcohol apparently had little effect on the supply available to locals.

The city was full of new buildings. Old ones were being painted and renovated. There were new shops, new businesses and lots of cars. And there were women on the street. I left Kabul feeling optimistic about the future.

By the time I returned more than a year later, however, things seemed considerably worse.

It was mid-2008 and there'd already been several serious terrorist attacks so far that year. In January, the Taliban had stormed the Serena Hotel, one of the most heavily fortified buildings in the city. Men with guns and suicide vests had forced their way past the security guards at its metal gates and had roamed the building, randomly shooting people who'd simply been sitting in the lobby or exercising in the gym, before blowing themselves up.

Then, in April, President Karzai had almost been assassinated during a military ceremony, in spite of the intense security at such events. The areas of red and yellow on the UN's risk assessment maps were steadily expanding, making more and more areas of the country out of bounds for aid workers and government officials.

Nevertheless, first impressions when I arrived at Kabul airport were good. The immigration and baggage handling services had improved greatly and a new terminal building next door appeared to be almost finished. It was due to open in a few months. Work on a new car park had also been completed.

But the driver who came to pick me up had a grim expression on his face. 'There's been an explosion,' he said. 'We have to take the long way.'

A massive car bomb had been detonated in front of the Indian Embassy, killing about fifty people. It was the largest bomb in Kabul for some time.

So we avoided the most dangerous route from the airport by taking a new road that now circled the edge of the city—a wide highway lined with new shopping centres, apartment buildings, modern service stations and gigantic 'wedding halls'. Whole blocks of suburban houses appeared to have been bulldozed to make way for it.

The road was divided by a garden of recently planted grass, trees and rose bushes. Various new and old monuments and sculptures sat in the centre of the traffic circles.

Eventually, we turned towards the old part of town and things changed. When I'd last been in Kabul, I'd thought the city couldn't possibly be more fortified and battle-ready. Now, however, there were even higher concrete blast walls and more blocked off and guarded side streets in what used to be leafy suburbs. We had to negotiate half a dozen boom gates at checkpoints manned by different security companies to reach my new accommodation.

Our company now housed its consultants in two huge buildings side by side in a treeless concrete car park surrounded by high walls and barbed wire. There were security notices and maps on the walls in the living room, gym equipment in the lobby, and catering supplies stacked everywhere. The people who lived there were nice enough, all thirteen of them, but it felt more like a warehouse for people than a residence.

The focus of my work this time would be the Ministry of Education's regular budget department and its thirty-nine Afghan civil servants. Up until then, all the budget preparation work had been done by foreign consultants and Afghan advisers without any serious input from actual ministry staff, apart from some routine paper shuffling. It was more than time to think about developing their skills for when the highly-paid advisers inevitably left.

I recognised Abdullah, the budget director, as one of the wrinkled old men from many previous meetings at the Ministry of Finance. He remembered me too and shook my hand.

The staff of the budget department were sitting two to a desk around the edges of the room, facing the door. The three women were huddled together at one desk. Abdullah had a circle of visitors and hangers-on sitting on the sofas around his office, and the chowkidor sat on his chowki next to the kettle. It reminded me of the Ministry of Finance offices when I'd first arrived almost five years earlier.

These days staff in the Ministry of Finance sat at new desks working on computers. They also had more interesting work to do and better salaries. Their equivalents in the Ministry of Education seemed to have been left behind. Most likely, their jobs consisted of filling in and copying and checking numerous paper forms and ledgers, work which was now done mostly by computer or on a few spreadsheets.

Several donor-funded Afghan consultants with good English had also been assigned to the budget department. Zia, the most senior, had a Bachelor of Business Administration from Pakistan and a raffish appearance, like a young Clark Gable, with a neatly trimmed moustache and strands of Brylcreemed hair curling onto his forehead.

He told me his family had a profitable business in Pakistan so he was already rich and was just working in the ministry because it was interesting. That sounded familiar. It was more or less what Jo Truschler had told everyone in Kosovo before he stole 4.5 million Euro from the Kosovo electricity corporation. Of course, in this case, it might have been true. I never had any grounds for thinking Zia was anything but honest, although he didn't strike me as particularly hard-working.

Zia was supported by Faraidoon and Habib, two well-educated and good-looking young Afghan men. Habib was married to an American woman he'd met in his previous job.

'We were attracted to each other,' he told me, 'but it's not like America here. You can't just date. So she converted to Islam and we got married.'

Every afternoon the young Afghan men said prayers in the corner of the office, just slipping off their shoes, stepping on to the communal prayer mat and bobbing down to the floor. I never quite got used to this.

One day Zia and I were deep in discussion about budget administration issues when he suddenly stood up and walked away to the corner to start his prayers, as casually as if he was making himself a cup of coffee.

I found all the public praying embarrassing. It seemed wrong to be watching what, to me, seemed such a private ritual.

Our chowkidor's name was Kaka, which means 'uncle'; a term of respect for an old man. After the first few weeks, however, Kaka refused to work for us anymore because we wanted him to stay until five pm. Most civil servants in Kabul finished work at 3.30.

We offered Kaka an allowance for the extra hour and a half but it didn't sway him. He explained to Zia that many people in the ministry are paid overtime, but they still leave at 3.30. It wouldn't be fair if he actually had to work late.

He was reassigned to another office while we looked for someone else.

The main thing I hoped to achieve while I was in the budget department was to get the ministry's new expenditure management database up and running. It had been in development for almost a year; an impressive piece of programming by bright young people at a local IT firm.

The ministry had finally overcome procurement delays and funding obstacles and the general inertia of the bureaucracy and we were on the verge of putting it into operation. It would revolutionise the ministry's financial management. It would churn out all the forms and documents, the purchase orders and the payment requests required for financial transactions, replacing dozens of manual ledgers and numerous spreadsheets, and would provide reliable information on the state of the ministry budget.

But it would only achieve this if it was used properly, and that was the big worry. We would need clearly documented procedures, adequate security measures and lots of training.

This was something I could do as a foreign consultant that could really make a difference. Besides, no one else seemed to have the time or the interest.

Meanwhile, a large amount of the ministry's resources and expertise was directed to producing new textbooks for all the six million or so students.

The Danish government had provided funding to write and print textbooks for the new curriculum. They would replace the old books that had been in use since the Mujahideen era, originally produced by the US government, which had included maths problems based on adding quantities of Kalashnikovs and grenades.

The textbook project had, however, become a monumental stuff-up. The Danish aid agency had followed best practice in development funding by providing the money directly to the ministry so they could arrange the printing through their own administrative processes. The objective was to build the capacity of local staff in carrying out tasks like this. Unfortunately, this had interfered with the other objective of the funding, which was to produce textbooks.

The minister had insisted that the contract be given to an Afghan firm but no Afghan printers had the capacity to produce forty-three million books locally so they'd subcontracted to other firms, who in turn subcontracted, taking a profit margin each time, so there wasn't enough money left to actually produce books at the quality that was expected.

When they eventually arrived from various print shops

in India, the donor-funded books were poorly produced on flimsy paper and badly bound and cut. They were unlikely to last one school year.

Storing the textbooks and delivering them to schools was the next problem. The warehouse the ministry had leased for them had burned down. Luckily, because production was so far behind schedule, there were no books inside at the time.

Then we learned that in remoter areas the books were being transported by public bus, stacked under the seats beneath unsuspecting passengers. In areas with poor security, being caught by the Taliban with any government document could cost you your life.

The ministry arranged to purchase a number of trucks but they soon became embroiled in Afghan politics. President Karzai was still signing numerous decrees and instructions each day on all sorts of things and one of the documents he'd signed was a limit on the maximum engine size of government-owned trucks, presumably an attempt to save fuel costs.

I'm not sure who knew about this rule. It appears the Ministry of Education didn't because they'd arranged to buy trucks that exceeded the legal limit, and President Karzai had duly signed the contract.

The fact that the president of a country of this size with this many problems is required to sign every government contract is itself a problem. The fact that he signed a contract that contravened one of his own decrees was fairly typical.

The attorney general, Abdul Jabar Sabet, had detected the inconsistency, decided it was an illegal contract, and impounded the trucks. Sabet claimed to be leading the fight against corruption in Afghanistan and had brought some high-profile cases into the newspapers. It was rumoured, however, that if you paid him enough, the accusations would go away.

A few weeks later, Sabet announced his intention to run for president the following year and Karzai promptly sacked him. Shortly afterwards, the new trucks appeared in the Ministry of Education carpark.

Of course, the whole exercise would have been much easier if the aid agency had just printed the books themselves and given them to the ministry as a gift. In the end, this is more or less what happened. When the new books hadn't arrived well into the school year, Minister Atmar called up his contacts in the US government who organised and paid for the printing and distribution by US military transport of a complete set of forty-three million textbooks. They managed to do it in ten days.

●———●

WHEN THE BUDGET management database was about to go live, I visited the staff in the accounting department to talk about who would operate it and to arrange training for them.

The accounting department staff, like those in the budget department, were not on the high salaries the young Afghan consultants received. They administered the budget, paid the teachers and, if there was anything left over, paid other bills.

Their west-facing office was hot in the mid-afternoon sun. Four elderly men sat behind a table piled high with ledgers and record books and pieces of paper, laboriously writing letters by hand.

In the room next door, other men transcribed figures from one ledger to another, and a row of middle-aged ladies sat with open account books in front of them waiting for forms to be delivered for their attention.

I was worried that there would be trouble when the young, computer-literate staff controlled the database and the old men realised that their work on the ledgers and forms was redundant.

Shafi, the database coordinator, didn't share my concern. 'That won't be a problem,' he assured me. 'They think the computers are just typewriters.' As long as the database printed out nice official-looking forms for them to sign, the old guard will be happy.

The introduction of the new budget management system was just one of the signs that we were making progress in the task of developing government capacity. One afternoon, I followed the red carpet down the corridor to the minister's conference room where all the senior Afghan advisers were crammed around the shiny boardroom table for a presentation on strategic planning.

As well as the young men in their suits and ties there were now a few young women in colourful headscarves. I was one of the few foreigners.

The teaboys, who in the minister's suite wore smart suits and ties, squeezed around the room delivering a cup of black tea and a sugar cube to each person.

It was now almost two years since the ministry's first strategic plan had been published and the minister wanted it reviewed and updated. The planning department staff handed around neatly prepared agendas, timetables and instructions and made a slick presentation with PowerPoint slides in Dari.

The questions and comments were also in Dari, but they found it difficult to express ideas like 'cross-cutting issues', 'millennium development goals', 'anti-corruption strategy' and 'crisis management' so the whiteboard was soon covered with words like this in English.

The whole meeting was a convincing demonstration of the increasing competence of the government and the potential for the future. It was true, of course, that these people were from the small educated elite and earned high salaries. They were perhaps not a representative sample, but they were young and would no doubt make a positive contribution to the country in future.

I left the meeting feeling optimistic. I hoped that the revised strategic plan would this time be written in Dari by Afghans rather than in English by advisers.

The economy seemed to be improving too, if only marginally. One day I looked at the things sitting on my desk and realised that the mineral water was bottled in Kabul and the box of face tissues was manufactured in Mazar. I was surprised. I'd always assumed that everything we bought here was imported. A bottle of water and a box of tissues are not much, but they were a small sign of hope for the economy.

The pine trees planted on the hills around the city were still growing and made dots of bright green on the vast brownness. The huge Russian-built grain silo across the river, which had for years been a sad concrete shell, had been restored and painted yellow and its factory was again producing solid, Russian-style loaves of bread for sale all over Kabul. Things seemed to be looking up.

•———•

A FEW WEEKS later, however, it all went downhill again. In mid-August, three foreign women were killed while they were travelling on the road towards Kabul.

According to the news reports, about forty men had

blocked the road and shot at the car, killing the women and their driver. It must have been terrifying. The women had been travelling in a clearly marked International Red Cross vehicle, but Red Cross neutrality hadn't protected them. The Taliban don't differentiate between aid workers and military. They regard them all as foreign invaders.

It happened on a Friday and they'd been only an hour away from Kabul. I wondered what they'd been planning to do there. Were they looking forward to a Friday night of bright lights in the big city? Dinner at one of the foreigners' restaurants with a bottle of wine, perhaps? Or maybe they'd been on their way to the airport? They would have been in time for the two pm flight to Dubai.

The incident was the beginning of the end of my infatuation with Afghanistan and I began counting down the days to the end of my assignment, looking forward to going home.

Shortly before I left, old Mr Abdullah finally retired. He was almost certainly well past retiring age, whatever that was in Afghanistan. He received a retirement payout and, apparently, then took up a contract job in another part of the ministry, a deal that was no doubt necessary to get him to move on.

Young Najibullah, one of the Minister's Afghan consultants, was appointed in his place. Najib was only twenty-three but he was bright and hardworking and had studied computers and English at a private college in his spare time. My colleague, Faraidoon, was appointed as adviser to the new budget director and sat at a small desk beside Najib's big one.

On the first day without Mr Abdullah, Najib and Faraidoon called a staff meeting. It was possibly the first staff meeting ever held in the budget office.

Faraidoon was excited about it. The civil servants were excited too. During the two months I'd been there I'd seen them sitting in their offices with mugs of green tea on their desks and almost nothing else. Now Faraidoon and Najib had drawn up a new structure and assigned new responsibilities to everyone.

Two of the women told Faraidoon they'd been employed in the office for years and no one had ever given them any work to do. Now they were being trained to type letters on the computer. They looked happy.

ON MY SECOND to last day in Kabul, there was a dull thump as we drove through the city on our way to work. It sounded like an empty metal drum falling over, but it wasn't. It was a suicide bomb about a kilometre away in the busiest part of town; one more indication of the deteriorating security situation.

Yet almost every day another foreign diplomat or a US defence official expressed confidence that the Taliban could be defeated and backed up their statements with news about increased troop numbers and more aid to strengthen the government and improve people's lives.

From where I sat, in the isolation of the foreign advisers' office in the ministry and the protected foreign residents' compound, I found it difficult to tell which way things were really going—whether the country was on a downward spiral to instability and war or whether it was crawling slowly towards a safer and happier future.

I was relieved, however, that I'd soon be home and once again watching this most recent episode in the long history of the country from the sidelines.

The next time I came here, I decided, it would be as a tourist and that wouldn't be until it was possible to travel safely throughout the country. At the rate things were going, however, that might mean never.

As the brown honeycomb of Kabul's suburbs disappeared below the aircraft window, I sealed the city up in my memories with all the people I knew and all the people in the little mud houses who did not have the option of leaving at the end of the assignment and hoped they'd be safe there.

SERIOUSLY WEIRD
Manila, Philippines, November 2007

I was packed and all ready to leave for Manila in late November 2007 when my new employer, a consulting firm in Sydney, sent an email, as a courtesy, to let me know there'd been a *coup d'état*.

The message didn't provide any further details and the online news reports weren't much more enlightening. They mentioned the Manila Pen, which turned out to be the luxury Peninsula Hotel, and GMA, which meant the Philippines' president, Gloria Macapagal Arroyo. It was clear, however, that coup d'état was a slight exaggeration. A handful of malcontent soldiers and their supporters had barricaded themselves inside the city's best hotel and demanded the president resign.

A luxury hotel seemed an unlikely base from which to overthrow the government but I was soon to discover that a lot of things in the Philippines are unusual. When the general population of Manila didn't rise up in their support the rebels soon gave up, but only after the army had driven a small armoured vehicle through the front doors and across the marbled hotel foyer. A young couple about to get married in one of the hotel function rooms decided to go ahead with the ceremony in spite of the minor interruption.

By the time I arrived, two days later, it was old news and the Peninsula Hotel, with its cascading fountains on the corner of two broad avenues in the business district, was back in business.

This was my first exposure to the weirdness of politics in the Philippines. It became more unfathomable during the few months I was there.

I arrived on a Saturday evening. The temperature was a

balmy twenty-eight degrees Celcius and the air smelled pleasantly of wood smoke. My knowledge of the Philippines at that point was limited to Imelda Marcos's huge shoe collection, Cory Aquino's People Power Revolution, and the large number of Filipina mail-order brides who now called Australia home.

I soon learned that there's a lot more to the country than that. It had been colonised by the Spanish in the 1570s, at a time when a trading outpost in East Asia was as remote from Europe as a colony on the Moon. The main legacies of Spanish rule today are conservative Catholicism and the feudal politics that endure in many rural areas.

The Spanish lost the islands to the United States in the Spanish-American War of 1898. The Americans believed they had the best of intentions in annexing the country and, over the next fifty years, they brought English, capitalism and US-style democracy. The US influence is still obvious. Light switches are upside-down, dates are back to front and fast food restaurants dominate the landscape.

•———•

My employer had booked me into one of the best hotels in the best part of the city. It was a significant change from the run-down apartments in Kosovo and the shared houses of Kabul. My one-bedroom suite was about the same size as my flat in Sydney and much better furnished. From its windows the next morning I looked out at sleek, shiny skyscrapers.

Manila seemed to be a flourishing, modern metropolis. The sprawling air-conditioned shopping centre next door was full of familiar names—Giordano, Esprit, Speedo, Bodyshop, Gap, Gucci, Subway and McDonald's. Its arcades were crowded with shoppers and noisy with piped music.

In an open space between Starbucks and Marks and Spencer a priest prepared for Sunday mass and rows of plastic chairs filled up with worshippers. Uniformed security guards with holstered pistols on their belts checked bags at every entrance, including two who stood side by side at the point where the Landmark Department Store joined the Glorietta Shopping Mall, one checking people leaving Landmark to enter Glorietta and the other checking people leaving Glorietta to enter Landmark.

For the first time, I was working for an Australian company on an Australian aid project. I'd been appointed team leader—a position which didn't include any extra pay, but the company assured me it wouldn't be much work. This turned out to be a lie.

The other advisers on the team arrived on Sunday afternoon and we met for a few beers and a Thai meal deep in the windowless shopping mall.

Dean and Phil had been among the people I'd shared houses with in Kabul at one time or another and the others were former public servants from various countries now starting their second career. We would each be working on different aspects of 'consolidating and embedding' the reforms the Philippines administration had supposedly made to its public finance management practices.

THE FIRST THING on the project work plan was a meeting with officials from the government agencies we would be working with. The venue was in another part of Manila, not far on the map but a long taxi ride in bumper-to-bumper traffic on a Monday morning.

Manila was not so sleek and shiny from this perspective.

The congested highway was flanked by high concrete walls and the air was grey with exhaust fumes. Above us, super life-sized models in flimsy lingerie leered out over the traffic from sky-high billboards, next to ads for fast food restaurants, high-end fashion labels, cosmetic surgery and skin-whitening lotions.

The taxi driver had religious icons arranged on his dashboard and rosary beads hanging from his rear-view mirror. The radio station playing soft rock paused every now and then to urge us to 'pray the rosary' and some of the apartment towers we passed had 'In God We Trust' in neon on their rooftops.

The meeting took place in a function room at a swish hotel, close to the huge complex of the Asian Development Bank headquarters. It was more formal than I'd expected. Important-looking Filipino men and women sat around tables decorated with pleated satin. The hotel staff served each person a late breakfast of a poached egg and a thin slice of ham on a dainty piece of bread.

The Australian aid representative made some opening remarks about the long history of cooperation between our two countries and a few of the government officials added appreciative comments.

Then I was called on to speak. That's one of the hazards of being team leader. I introduced my colleagues, thanked everyone for their input and said how much I was looking forward to working with them. Everyone seemed satisfied with that. Then the meeting was over. The point of it all was largely lost on me.

The project was part of an ongoing and possibly never-ending process of reforming and modernising the budget procedures of the Philippines government. The World Bank had started this particular set of reforms in the late

1990s and the Australian aid program had picked it up since then and inherited the pet ideas introduced by the World Bank consultants.

One of the reforms was called the Organisational Performance Indicator Framework, which was a version of program budgeting, but because this was the Philippines, it had a different name. Dean and Phil and I were there to explain how we'd implemented more or less the same thing in Australia and to figure out how to make it work in the peculiarities of the Philippines' financial management system.

The next day we started our work at the Department of Budget and Management. The department had been established in 1936, the same year that John Maynard Keynes published his *General Theory of Employment, Interest and Money*, as the secretary of the department apparently liked to point out. I don't think the two events were related.

The DBM building was just down the road from the presidential palace in old Manila and I was told the building had been designed by Imelda Marcos herself. It had been constructed in the 1970s although it looked to me as if it could have been the 1936 original—a squat, grey structure with a vaguely Spanish look about it. The interior was panelled with timber and the windows were hidden behind lime green Venetian blinds.

As it was November, the offices were decorated for Christmas. Tinsel was draped across the ceilings, baubles hung from light fittings, and Christmas trees, Santa Clauses, candles and stars sat on desks and filing cabinets. There were more Christmas decorations than you would see in most department stores. This was in addition to the regular collection of saints, crucifixes, rosaries and bibles set up on small tables wherever there was space.

The open-plan office was cramped but spotless. The

Philippines is a country where it's possible to pay a lot of people very little to do trivial tasks so there were cleaners constantly sweeping and wiping and polishing and emptying bins, and support staff who photocopied and collated and stapled, ran errands and carried briefcases for senior officials.

We were given a room to work in and our team soon became part of the daily routine of the office.

DBM staff had an official colour-themed dress code for each day of the week. Even the most senior staff followed it. Monday's colour was red and most people wore red T-shirts or polo shirts. They looked like a sports team. Tuesday was green day and everyone, both men and women, wore at least one item in some shade of green—a pale green shirt or tie, a blouse or a cardigan. Wednesday's colour was yellow, Thursday's was blue, and Friday was 'washing day' when there was no colour theme and staff were free to wear anything presentable.

In each bureau, at lunchtime, the staff pulled plastic picnic tables out from corners and sat in their workgroups sharing the meals they'd brought from home. Then the fluorescent lights were turned off for siesta. Some people draped handkerchiefs over their faces while they slept, others played computer games until the lights came back on.

After lunch, the women all went to the ladies' restroom together with their plastic carry baskets of soap and toiletries and waited two-deep for their turn to wash their plates and vigorously and thoroughly clean their teeth.

•———•

AT THIS STAGE, I was still working out exactly what I was supposed to do. I had terms of reference and a long statement of objectives, outcomes and milestones, but what it all meant in reality was a different matter.

I started meeting with the Budget Bureau directors to find out what they were expecting. The Philippines is another place where budget management is regarded as an exercise in good housekeeping and the directors were almost all women. Most had made their offices into extensions of their homes with bright cushions on the chairs, ornaments and family photos on the bookshelves, a kettle and a microwave on the filing cabinets and a fridge covered with fridge magnets.

The question I really wanted to ask the directors was why they needed foreign advisers. The senior officials and middle-level staff I'd met in the office so far all seemed competent and knowledgeable about their work and how it could be improved, despite the fact that they all had names like Bingle and Amlet or Peach, Zemma or Jobele. The men I met were called Elmer or Aldwin or Delfine and there were at least two Bongs.

It's possible the main reason the staff I spoke to seemed competent and knowledgeable was that, unlike most government officials I'd worked with in other countries, they all spoke excellent English. Once I was used to the strange accent and a few peculiar phrases it was no different from dealing with any public servant in Australia. In fact, many of the staff soon told me about their university studies in Australia in places like Armidale or Wollongong, on Australian government scholarships.

If any of them had stayed in Australia after graduation they could well have had successful careers as Australian bureaucrats. But in the Philippines, for some reason, it was assumed they needed outside help to do their jobs.

I did my best to help them, but my time was taken up with a larger than expected amount of team leadership duties. I'd negotiated a contract with a driver, for example, in almost total ignorance of the going rates for cars and drivers in this part of the world, and also written a 'mobilisation report' for the project, which largely restated what we'd said in our original plan but with different dates. It was clear, for example, that ambitious proposals to run training sessions in the weeks before Christmas would have to be reconsidered.

I also held meetings with each of our local Filipino consultants. We were supposed to have twelve of them. Mostly they were retired senior government officials who still had useful contacts in the bureaucracy. One of the younger ones couldn't make it to the office during the day to meet me so I arranged to see him in my hotel room in the evening. When he arrived, I was embarrassed as I ushered him into the long white-tiled corridor of my luxurious hotel suite.

'Isn't this hotel amazing!' I gushed. I didn't want him to think I took this for granted.

'Yes, I know it well,' he said casually. 'My wife and I stayed here for a few months while we were looking for a house.'

I was shocked. These rooms cost hundreds of dollars a night. How could a young Filipino family afford to live here?

In the end, he turned out to be too busy to fit us into his schedule and never did any work with our project, but through my meeting with him, I started to comprehend the extent of the inequality in this country. One person could casually spend a few hundred dollars a night on a place to live while others were lucky to earn that much in a year.

The World Bank had estimated that twenty-seven million Filipinos, perhaps a third of the population, were living in poverty. I was told there were children suffering from malnutrition just a few blocks from my comfortable hotel.

Whenever our driver took a short cut through side streets, we could see for ourselves the cramped houses and makeshift shanties of the low-income workers and impoverished squatters who made up a large part of the population of the city. The jumbled-together timber or concrete houses and apartments were wrapped in tangles of black power cables and cluttered with posters advertising fast food and local politicians.

The back streets were crowded with children swarming around the motor tricycles and hawkers' stalls and the ubiquitous jeepneys that seemed to growl like chained beasts, pawing at the ground as they revved their engines and strained against the brakes. Some of the poorer shanties were little more than cardboard shelters built precariously at the edge of rubbish-choked canals or above evil-smelling drains.

But there was vibrant life in these streets and a strong sense of community pride. There were meeting halls and community noticeboards announcing organised functions and activities. I saw people playing bingo, sitting at small tables in the narrow lanes between the shanty houses, karaoke parties under shade tents on the footpath, and sometimes mass being celebrated, or an open coffin displayed for a wake. In spite of the poverty and squalor, the people seemed cheerful as we barged past in our air-conditioned vehicle.

I hoped my work in DBM might in some small way help the Philippines government do something about the crushing poverty of most of the population—assuming they wanted to.

The basic issue, as always, was how to ensure the government spent its money wisely on things that would help the country, rather than on white elephant projects or schemes to benefit their political supporters. That was the idea behind the reform initiatives. They were meant to make government agencies explain what they were doing and report on what they'd achieved.

I could see already, however, that it might not have the revolutionary effect on government performance that we hoped for. The existing budget process was already complex and work-intensive and involved manipulating and reporting on thousands of budget items. The new system simply added another layer of complexity to the process, without reducing any of the existing workloads, and with no apparent benefit to the people who were doing the work.

It was more than likely government agencies were simply going through the motions of complying with DBM demands for output descriptions and performance information without improving anything.

But this problem was insignificant compared to the many other flaws in the way the government dealt with its budget, most of which were outside our terms of reference. Unlike most countries, the administration of public finance management was divided between four completely separate government bodies, each with a different idea about how things should be done, each determined to protect its territory, and each with its own politically appointed leader fiercely defending his position in the administrative hierarchy. There appeared to be no superior body willing or able to knock people's heads together to achieve sensible procedures.

Each of these agencies, for example, used a different system for classifying budget transactions. DBM and Congress used one set of budget codes, while the Commission of Audit demanded expenditure reports based on its own completely different and incompatible set of accounts.

Meanwhile, each government department or agency was responsible for its own financial management, through its own bank accounts, and had little incentive to provide up-to-date reports to anyone on what happened to the cash in these accounts.

In 2007, most government organisations still did their accounting in ledger books. In this respect, they were not much more advanced than Afghanistan. Even if they'd wanted to report on time it was almost impossible.

It was not surprising, therefore, that no one was sure where the government's money was going or that up to one-third of it simply disappeared in fraudulent payments and inflated invoices. Compared to all these problems, my little project seemed rather marginal.

•——•

CHRISTMAS OFFICIALLY ENDED in early January with the Feast of the Three Kings and all the Christmas trees and decorations suddenly disappeared.

The next thing on the religious calendar was the festival of the Black Nazarene. About three million people came out in the centre of Manila to see a small black figurine paraded through town. It took eight hours for the procession to pass through a relatively small section of the city and two people died from heart attacks in the crush. The parade passed close to our office and we could hear the hubbub and the fireworks a few blocks away.

By then, I had moved to a slightly more modest serviced apartment a few blocks away from the hectic shopping mall. I was on the twenty-sixth floor with a view across the western half of the city, although twenty-six floors didn't seem high next to the office towers around me.

Not far from my apartment, a multistorey concrete car park was being slowly demolished to make way for another construction project. Teams of men with large hammers pounded on the concrete slab all day, progressively turning it into rubble, leaving a tangle of exposed metal reinforcing rods behind.

Manila sits on a thin peninsula and, on a clear day, I could see water in both directions. Manila Bay, to the right, was dotted with fishing boats, and to the left, the huge lake of

Laguna de Bay shimmered in the distance.

Straight ahead was the airport and the elevated highway, undulating away to the horizon, whisking those who could afford the toll above the congested traffic.

In the other direction, I could see the large houses and quiet tree-lined streets of San Lorenzo village. It was one of the gated suburbs that surround the business district, hidden from the main road behind high walls and metal gates and protected by security guards, out of bounds to cars and pedestrians unless you had the right sort of ID card or diplomatic number plates. There was no traffic inside San Lorenzo, just an occasional morning jogger or a child on a bicycle.

•——•

By February, we were ready to present our recommendations on the next steps for the Organisational Performance Indicator Framework to senior DBM staff. They were almost all women, as usual, with brains as sharp as razor blades. It was Wednesday—yellow day—so they sat around the table like a posy of jonquils.

The two men who lumbered in late, also in pale yellow shirts, were clearly not in the same class—their minds as flabby as their waistlines, struggling to keep up.

Our proposal involved changes to the way government departments classified and reported on their budgets, to give the public a clearer idea of where the money was going. The meeting went well. These senior women understood what we were talking about and came up with useful suggestions. Things seemed to be going to plan.

A few days later, we made the same presentation to a much larger group of staff in a frigid air-conditioned auditorium with harsh white fluorescent lights. The audience, sitting on white plastic chairs at plastic tables, was a pea-green sea of Tuesday-coloured outfits.

This meeting didn't go so well. Many in the audience had been in training courses for a week already and they looked bored and exhausted. Others were too junior to know what we were talking about. When we were planning the workshop, I'd queried the need to include such a large number of people, but Mario, the senior official we reported to, had insisted.

We had to provide morning tea and lunch for everyone who attended. This was a feature of office life in the Philippines. Whenever more than two people were in a meeting room together at any time of day, food would be provided. Unfortunately, we hadn't been aware of this when the budget for the project had been drawn up.

Dean and I had just begun our presentation when attendants started handing around morning snacks and we had to suspend proceedings while everyone dealt with their Styrofoam boxes of spaghetti in a pale pink tomato sauce and plastic sachets of orange juice.

Eventually, I returned to my PowerPoint slides and used the microphone to explain what we wanted the department to do and why it was a good idea. The acoustics in the auditorium were bad and the loudspeakers sent my voice back to me distorted and unrecognisable. The DBM people didn't have the same problem. When it was their turn to speak they crooned into the microphone like nightclub singers.

Officially, everyone who works for the government speaks good English. I could see from the frowns and blank looks from some in the audience, however, that this might not be completely true. Many of those who did understand what I was saying looked unhappy.

When I opened the floor for questions they made their

concerns clear. As I'd suspected, they simply saw the changes we were proposing as extra work. 'We're suffering from reform overload,' one of them said.

There was a rebellion brewing by the time we closed the meeting. We conferred with the budget bureau directors and decided we needed to go back to the drawing board.

Since I'd arrived, I'd been trying to follow Filipino politics by reading the local newspapers. It was clearly very complicated.

There had been three attempts so far to impeach the current president, Gloria Macapagal Arroyo—the previously mentioned GMA—on grounds of corruption. She herself only became president when the previous incumbent, 'Erap' Estrada, was forced out for the same reasons. And it wasn't that long ago that the People Power Revolution had overthrown President Ferdinand Marcos. To lose one president in this way is unfortunate, to lose three in two decades is serious.

A few months into 2008, politics became even more interesting. At DBM, instead of snoozing through their siesta, staff listened to live radio broadcasts from the Senate. In the hotel gym that evening the attendant, unusually, switched the television from the pop music channel to the Filipino language station showing the same Senate meeting.

I had to spend a few hours on Saturday morning with a collection of the week's newspapers and a list of acronyms and nicknames to work out what was going on. The excitement revolved around the Senate's inquiry into an alleged attempt by the husband of President Arroyo to extract a $130 million commission from a proposed government project to build a national broadband network.

The president's husband, who was known as the First

Gentleman (or FG for short), denied everything. But the Senate was pressing ahead with its inquiry and was in the midst of hearing evidence from a star witness, Rodolfo Lozada Junior (or Jun for short).

Lozada's part in the affair was perplexing. He was, at the time, CEO of the Forestry Corporation, a body mainly concerned with re-afforestation and environmental conservation. Nothing to do with broadband networks and internet technology at all.

Lozada was, however, a former executive of Alcatel, a telecommunications company, so he did know a little about these things and had apparently been providing technical advice to the then chairman of the National Economic Development Authority—a friend of his—free of charge.

The other people who seemed to have a major role in cooking up the NBN project were the secretary of the Department of the Environment and the head of the Electoral Commission. These were also, you will note, not bodies that normally have much to do with communications technology projects.

Getting Lozada in front of the Senate committee hadn't been easy. He'd been due to testify a few weeks earlier but had found a sudden need to go to Hong Kong that day. When he'd returned, he'd managed to disappear from the airport somewhere between the door of the plane and the immigration counter where officials from the Senate's sergeant-at-arms' office were waiting with an arrest warrant.

His wife and family said he'd been kidnapped and claimed he was being held prisoner in Malacañang Palace, the official residence of GMA and the FG. The Philippines National Police eventually admitted that they had him in safe-keeping, at his request.

Two days later, Lozada suddenly turned up at De La Salle College, a Catholic institution, and gave a press conference at two am, surrounded by priests and nuns, promising to tell the truth to the Senate committee the next day. He was then escorted to the Senate building in the pre-dawn hours by a dozen or so nuns who dramatically formed a protective circle around him as he walked out of the college in the glare of TV floodlights.

On Friday everyone in Manila was glued to the radio while Lozada gave eight hours of testimony. Our budget department colleagues were particularly interested, of course, because it involved the budget, and also their bureaucratic rivals in other arms of the government.

The original purpose of the NBN had been to provide distance education services for poor students in rural areas, especially in Mindanao in the south, where a Muslim insurgency had been bubbling away for several decades. The initial price estimate was fairly modest and it was proposed that the private sector could build and operate it with the government as a client.

At some stage, however, that idea was scrapped and GMA popped over to China and signed a contract with a Chinese company to build it at about three times the original price, plus an agreement to borrow money from the Chinese government to pay for it. The big increase in the cost was apparently due to all the kickbacks and commissions for the go-betweens and facilitators who had helped the Chinese to get the contract, including the FG and the other influential gentlemen already mentioned who had suddenly developed an interest in broadband technology and the learning opportunities available to rural students.

The only one in the news reports who didn't appear to have a nickname was Benjamin Abalos, who had been chief of the Electoral Commission at the time of the 2004 presidential election which GMA won, but which was widely believed to have been rigged.

The 2004 election had already generated the 'Hello Garci' scandal that arose from the revelation of a secret recording of GMA phoning Virgilio Garcillano, another senior official of the Electoral Commission, to discuss his part in manipulating votes. The president's cheerful greeting, 'Hello Garci', became a popular ring tone on Filipino mobile phones. I heard it all day in the office.

It was assumed that GMA and the FG owed people like Abalos and Garci for their help in fixing the election, which was why the kickbacks for the NBN deal had to be so big. According to Lozada, the normal kickback on all government projects (and he named some of them) was only twenty percent, but for this project, it was inflated to forty percent.

Mr Lozada had clearly been part of this scam and I wondered why he'd decided to spill the beans on his mates. 'He probably wasn't getting a big enough share,' one of my colleagues suggested.

None of this was a revelation to anyone in the Philippines. It did, however, give my daily newspaper, *The Star*—apparently not a fan of the current regime—an opportunity to publish another in its ongoing series of cartoons showing corrupt politicians and officials as fat crocodiles, preying on the poor Filipino peasant, weighing him down with Chinese debt to fund their snappy clothes and cigars.

All the newspapers were full of outraged letters to the editor demanding that the president resign. TV commentators speculated about a possible coup. A few cynical opinion writers, however, suggested that a coup would just be an attempt by someone else from the political elite to muscle in on the profits to be made from running the government.

Moreover, in spite of all this controversy, it seems that the Philippines economy was booming under GMA's administration. She does, after all, have a degree in economics and apparently was at university in the US with Bill Clinton. Foreign businessmen at the World Economic Forum at Davos had heaped praise on the president's sound economic management.

The anti-GMA movement organised a rally on a Friday evening. The government was clearly expecting trouble. When we arrived at the office that morning several empty shipping containers had appeared on the street blocking off side lanes and ready to be dragged into position to block the route to the palace.

The rally itself, however, took place at the intersection of the two widest avenues in the Makati district, in the space between HSBC, Citibank and the Manila Stock Exchange. Both the mayor of the prosperous Makati local government area and the leaders of the Makati Business Club were active supporters of the anti-GMA campaign so it was hardly the start of a proletarian uprising.

The rally was only a few blocks from my hotel so I strolled in that direction after work to see what was going on. I got within a few hundred metres but the roads were barricaded, overhead footbridges were closed and there was total confusion at street level.

I had a much better view at home on the television. Cameras on top of skyscrapers provided a bird's-eye view of thousands of people thronging the intersection while shredded paper rained down from office windows. As it became dark, they seemed to be standing in a snowstorm.

The event was billed as an interfaith prayer rally so there were several bishops and other church dignitaries leading the speeches. Two former presidents were there also. One was Corazon Aquino, who became president after Marcos was thrown out of power by the People Power Revolution. The other was Erap Estrada, who had himself been overthrown by another People Power revolt a few years ago. The TV reporter noted that some people, especially non-Filipinos, might find that a bit strange. Well, yes, indeed we might.

IN MARCH, WE held another mass seminar in the cold, white, echoing DBM auditorium.

An official DBM circular had recently announced that red Monday would become pink Monday, or white for men, so the audience no longer looked like the support crew for the Ferrari racing team. Instead, it resembled a flower garden with everyone in a variety of shades of pink and floral patterns. The snack this time was a cold croissant filled with chicken and mayonnaise salad.

This meeting went better than the first. We were able to focus on the more senior staff and didn't invite people who had little interest in what we were doing. Our proposed changes were duly accepted. The objective had been achieved and our work could wind up.

AT THE START of my last week in Manila, I read in the paper that the head of the legal department of the Electoral Commission had been shot dead in downtown Manila at lunchtime by two men on a red motorbike. His predecessor in the same job had also been shot dead, just last November.

The strange thing was that this news was reported on page seven of the paper. Surely a murder in broad daylight in the middle of the city should get more attention than this? But murders seemed to be extremely common. The lead stories in the papers that day were the news that Cory Aquino had colon cancer and the arrival home of a local boxing hero who'd just won a fight in Las Vegas to become the world champion of small skinny boxers. Journalists obviously thought these things were more important than political assassinations.

The scandal of the NBN kickbacks and rumours of coups seemed to have been pushed off the front pages. The current top story every day was now about rice. There was, apparently, a shortage and the price was going up.

The government made a new announcement every day about its emergency strategy for dealing with the crisis. They repackaged subsidised rice into one-kilogram bags, supposedly to make it harder for traders to steal. They set up a special police unit to check for people who might be 'hoarding' rice. Queues of poor people formed outside the office of the National Food Authority to collect their cheap rations.

I was sceptical about the sudden panic and the constant flow of government announcements and initiatives. Filipinos clearly cared about rice more than they cared about broadband networks or corruption and this crisis pushed all talk of a change of government off the agenda.

As one of my final tasks I was asked to write a report on what needed to be done next to reform the Philippines' budget system. Luckily, there were already numerous other reports on what should be done, so that was fairly easy.

My last working day on the project was stressful, as they always are. The project debriefing meeting at nine am on a Friday morning was much like the first meeting back in November, with all the government officials and local consultants and Australian government staff there to hear my report on what we had achieved.

The meeting went well. Amazingly, the client and the counterparts seemed fairly happy with what we'd been doing.

As usual, I was sorry to be saying goodbye to some of the people I'd been working with, but at the same time, I was looking forward to going home to a place that was just a little less weird.

I still had a report to write, the driver to pay and the accounts to balance before I started packing, but by the following morning, the stresses and anxieties of the project had already started to drift away.

Expat friends I'd made in Manila took me out for a final meal—the buffet lunch at the Hyatt Hotel. We drank bottomless glasses of champagne and sampled food from every cuisine, from smoked salmon and medium-rare steaks to Chinese dumplings and chicken feet.

We were surrounded by tables of well-off Filipino families while outside the air was still polluted, the traffic still snarled and most of the people of Manila were in their overcrowded houses lunching on plain rice.

Adventures in Abayaland
Qatar, May 2012

The Budget Department in the Qatar Ministry of Finance looked, on the surface, like any modern government office. The work stations and partition screens, the computers and filing cabinets, the electric jug and tea bags on the coffee table could have been in any office almost anywhere.

But there was one big difference. The workers in this office were all women and they were all wrapped in long black gowns and tight black headscarves. The doors to the office were firmly closed. No men were allowed into this part of the building.

The women in their black abayas did all the things that civil servants normally do. They wrote reports, entered data into computers, held meetings, made phone calls, and brought cakes to celebrate birthdays. But if they needed to leave their office, even simply to walk across the corridor to another closed door, they completely covered their faces with their scarves so that no one could see them.

The men of the ministry, in long white tunics and white headdresses, were just a few metres away. They sat in offices with their doors open to the corridor where they could be seen drinking coffee and tea, watching sport on TV, playing computer games, burning incense and sometimes also writing reports or making phone calls, although not, it seemed to me, very often.

The two groups rarely met and when they did, in meetings and training courses, the women sat separately with their faces covered. Most of the time, however, email and telephones eliminated the need for face-to-face communication. In this respect, the five weeks I spent in Qatar count as one of the more unusual experiences of my career. In other ways, however, it was one of the most normal.

I'd been invited to Qatar by email at short notice, as usual, to work on yet another program budget project. On the short flight up the gulf from Dubai, I sat next to a man from New Zealand who was travelling to take up a job with Al Jazeera, the Qatari-funded international news broadcaster.

The capital, Doha, was a modern city of wide highways and towering skyscrapers, many still under construction. Hundreds of imported workers from South Asia toiled on building sites on the edges of the rapidly expanding town. New buildings lined the Corniche around the bay as we drove to the hotel, each one an architectural masterpiece of glass and steel. A huge IM Pei designed Museum of Islamic Art appeared to float on the calm water of Doha Bay.

In this case, there was no well-meaning donor pushing the idea of budget reform and providing the funding. Qatar is a wealthy country with no need for foreign aid. Its natural gas deposits, discovered in the 1970s, have funded rapid development and high incomes.

The Qatari government, or at any rate, a young senior adviser to the Qatari Minister of Finance, had initiated this budget reform project and was funding it from the national budget. The government wanted Qatar to have all the attributes of a modern public financial management system, including IMF-compliant accounting classifications and program budgeting. The local branch of an international accounting firm had been contracted to implement the project and had recruited Lebanese consultants to do a large amount of the work. They'd gone to their US head office for people with more specialist skills and had ended up with several Australians.

Once again, after travelling halfway around the world, I found myself working with someone else from Canberra. I'd never met Tania before but she knew some of the people I knew. That didn't mean we had anything in common or were destined to be friends, but as the only two foreign women on the team, we had to work together. For those few weeks, we managed to get on well enough.

We were staying at the W Hotel, a stylish new twist on the Westin chain which played techno music in the elevator and was full of young staff of various nationalities who greeted me like an old friend whenever I met them in the corridors.

I hated it. Lovely though the staff were, it felt to me like an air-conditioned high-security prison. It was surrounded by building sites and sandy vacant blocks in the still-developing West Bay area, kilometres from anything of interest or anything green.

It was only May but already the temperature during the day hovered around forty degrees Celsius. In spite of the soaring heat, workers still laboured on the building sites around us. In the coming months, the temperature would reach as high as fifty degrees.

Only about thirteen percent of the residents of Qatar are actually Qataris. Almost all work is done by foreigners. There were several different strata of expatriate workers.

At the top of the tree were the well paid and comfortably housed professionals who run Qatari businesses and provide advice to the government. Small businesses seemed to be operated by Indians, or by Arabs from elsewhere in the Middle East. Most of the shop staff were Filipino, and domestic helpers and nannies were from South East Asia, especially from Muslim Indonesia.

At the bottom of the heap were the workers from Bangladesh, India and Nepal who were delivered to building sites by truckloads each day, or dangled from ropes high above the street, constantly washing desert dust from the glass-walled skyscrapers.

The rights of foreign workers are strictly limited. I'd travelled to Qatar on a tourist visa and a few days into the assignment I asked about the process I assumed would be in place to get a work permit.

'No. No. No. You definitely do *not* want a work visa,' I was told emphatically by my colleagues. 'You don't want to have to get written permission from your employer whenever you want to leave the country. No, thank you!'

So most of the foreigners working on our project were on tourist visas, even though some had been there for years.

GOVERNMENT ADMINISTRATION WAS one of the few areas where Qataris held most of the jobs. The Ministry of Finance building was not as new or as remarkable as many of the more recent constructions in the city, but it was modern enough. It had a vast marble entrance foyer and large windows with a view of the bay.

Everyone in the ministry spoke good English. Qatar had been a British protectorate until independence in 1971 and the men of the ruling family have traditionally done their military training at Sandhurst.

Tania introduced me to the women of the budget department—Haya, Lulwa, Manar, Aisha, Maha, Najla and Fatima—and we started discussing work.

The ministry had issued instructions to government agencies to present their budgets in program format and their submissions were now due, but the budget department staff weren't exactly sure what they should do with them. I was there to help.

I was assigned a desk behind the closed doors of the women's office and started working out what they needed from me.

Our workday in Doha started early. We were in the car by seven, crowded together with a couple of other foreign consultants in the morning rush hour traffic. Most ministry staff were also delivered to work by drivers; some women accompanied by Asian maids who carried their bags.

The lifts in the ministry building were largely monopolised by the female employees. Men and women could not, of course, be in the lift together, so the men had to wait.

The workday didn't seem overly demanding or arduous and finished at 1.30 pm. In the secluded budget office the women worked, gossiped, talked about their children, about movies they'd seen, about shopping and diets. At 11.30 am they all went to wash their feet in the bathroom at the end of the hall and pulled out their prayer mats beside their desks and prayed towards the back corner of the room.

Every few days there was a reason for someone to bring a cake or some other treat to celebrate a birthday, a son's school graduation, or the latest victory of Barcelona Football Club, Najla's favourite team. They were not just any ordinary cakes but large and extravagant, or small and beautifully decorated. For the Barcelona celebration, Najla brought cupcakes in BFC team colours.

At the end of the working day they pulled their black scarves over their faces, picked up their handbags and took the lift down to meet their waiting chauffeurs.

At first, the women's black gowns all looked the same to me—plain, dull and uniform. In fact, they were each decorated in subtle ways with strips of colour, or sequins or embroidery. Haya's gown had slits sewn into the fabric which parted to reveal red satin beneath the black as she moved.

Najla, the youngest member of the group, was still single and wore the most conservative outfit. Every afternoon she got ready to go home by taking her niqab from the hook beside her desk and tying its various sections over her existing head covering so that the veil fell over her face, leaving only her eyes visible through a narrow slit.

Najla was planning to spend the summer months in Europe. She and her sisters were going to travel to Spain and Italy. I wondered how her long black gown and niqab would be received in the tourist spots of Europe.

'They'll leave all that stuff behind,' Tania said. 'They'll wear normal clothes when they're abroad.'

I wasn't entirely sure this was true and I never had a chance to ask Najla.

For these women, their black outfits were normal. It was just what they wore. There was no sense that they felt oppressed by them.

Their discovery during a conversation one afternoon that I had worked in Kabul generated an intense discussion between them, in Arabic, about the Afghan burqa. I could guess what they were saying from their gestures and frowns.

These Qatari women, who pulled a black cloth over their face simply to walk across the corridor, tut-tutted over the plight of Afghan women who were forced to view the world through the blue mesh of a burqa. When I explained the Taliban's rules against girls going to school or women working or visiting a male doctor they seemed incredulous.

From a feminist point of view, the dress restrictions and separation of women from men in places like Qatar is a form of oppression, no matter what the individual women think of it. But so are high heels and tight skirts and uncomfortable bras and 'shapewear' and so many other impractical, inconvenient and expensive fashions and behaviours that women in the west choose to inflict on themselves.

You could almost argue that the voluminous black gowns were preferable. Under their abayas the women wore all kinds of outfits that no one outside their family or female friends would ever see, ranging from scruffy tracksuits to jeans and T-shirts and, yes, tight skirts, high heels and lacy push-up bras.

These women enjoyed a privileged and comfortable lifestyle within their large extended families, in spite of the restrictions of separation and covering. I doubt they'd ever suffered financial hardship. They had servants. They drove expensive cars or were driven in limousines. They travelled abroad frequently, especially in the hottest summer months. As women they could drive, study, work and travel. The Filipina housemaids and the Bangladeshi men who laboured on construction sites in the fifty-degree heat were arguably much more oppressed.

●─────●

THE MINISTRY BUILDING was empty by two in the afternoon. If we were still there after then, perhaps conferring about our work plan yet again, the security guards would come around and tell us to leave.

There wasn't a great deal to do in Doha outside work hours. A large shopping centre, a one-kilometre walk away in the heat, provided relief from the tedium of the hotel room. Shoppers of every conceivable nationality and ethnic group—tall, pale Europeans, African families and Indian women in saris—filled the supermarket aisles and queued outside the Western Union office to send their wages home.

In the centre of town, Souk Wakif was the old Arab market area, although it wasn't that old. Established 100 years ago, it was nevertheless one of the oldest places in the city. It had been renovated for tourists but wasn't completely sanitised. It was still possible to become lost in the narrow alleyways of small shops selling spices and sweets and dried fruit and handcrafts.

A large part of the souk was given over to restaurants serving Middle Eastern food and elaborate, calorie-filled fruit drinks. Alcohol was only available in the big hotels and the hotel staff checked identities at the door to ensure we were *bona fide* foreigners and not errant Qataris looking for a drink.

The Villagio Shopping Mall, a taxi ride away in a suburb of high-walled villas, was another shopping option. It was spacious, luxurious and maze-like with an interior decorated to resemble the streets of Venice, complete with water-filled canals, stone bridges and a summer blue sky with convincing fluffy clouds painted on the ceiling.

Women in black face coverings with their children and hijabed nannies in tow strolled around the luxury brand stores and disappeared into the change rooms with armfuls of designer ball gowns. Groups of them met at coffee shops, lifting their face coverings just far enough to eat spoonfuls of exquisitely expensive cake. Men in pristine white gowns strolled together, holding hands and fondling their worry beads.

On weekends, in the cool early morning, I would explore the West Bay neighbourhood on foot, passing the waterfront mansions on embassy row and the other high rise international hotels along the seafront, or turning away from the sea into quiet streets of large villas draped with bougainvillea.

The route back to the hotel followed the Escher-like streets which appeared to be going somewhere but doubled back on themselves, winding around the not-yet-finished buildings. I was surprised to see spray-canned graffiti on some of the walls of the neat, regulated streets, and by one of the vacant blocks I noticed several discarded syringes in the gutter.

GOVERNMENT DEPARTMENTS IN Qatar turned out to be no more willing to comply with Ministry of Finance deadlines than anywhere else in the world, but eventually, their program budget submissions started rolling in.

It was clear that many agencies were well ahead of the Ministry of Finance in adopting the concepts of 'modern' budgeting. Most were, after all, crawling with foreign advisers who were experts at describing their corporate vision, objectives and performance indicators with no need for guidance from the budget department. Others didn't take it at all seriously.

I provided the staff of the budget department with guidelines for identifying the good submissions and how to respond to the ones that needed much more work. I also made suggestions for improvements to the process for next year and started planning a workshop to discuss the issues, resigned to the fact that it would have to be run twice—once for the women and once for the men.

As in most places I've worked, the staff in the ministry were divided on the subject of change. Some embraced it enthusiastically. Most of the women I was working with seemed to be in this category.

Others were resistant. The Qatari Ministry of Finance had its share of people who saw change as a threat to their hard-won position of authority and foreign advisers as a transitory disruption to business as usual.

Towards the end of my assignment, there were indications that the conservatives were gaining ground. The project manager called us into his office to tell us the completion of the program budget reforms would be deferred until the following year. The smart young adviser to the minister seemed to have fallen out of favour.

We were, in any case, almost at the end of our contract. We finished the last items on the work plan and started writing our exit report.

•———•

A FEW DAYS before I was due to fly out, at the end of May, I turned on the television after work to the surprising scene of senior Qatari government officials, some of them members of the country's large ruling family, conducting a disorganised live press conference.

At first, it was not clear what it was about. Eventually, I understood that there had been a serious fire at the Villagio Mall. A number of people had died, many of them young children who'd been trapped in an upstairs childcare centre.

It was a tragedy for their families, but also an embarrassment for the Qatari government. Doha's modern buildings and luxury lifestyle had been revealed as a façade hiding inadequate fire safety standards and corruption in the licencing of childcare facilities.

'This is really significant,' one of my colleagues said as we watched the news conference on the television in the hotel bar. He'd been working there for a while so I assumed he knew what he was talking about. 'It's unusual for government officials to appear on TV like this and answer questions in public.'

Since the days of the 'Arab Spring' in other parts of the Middle East, neighbouring authoritarian governments, like Qatar, had been warily balancing pressure for more openness and accountability with their determination to remain in control at all costs. The press conference could have been a sign that the ruling elite was becoming more responsive to the public.

But then again, perhaps it didn't. Qatar was still an absolute monarchy with a consultative assembly appointed by the ruling emir, despite provisions in the 2003 constitution for an elected legislature.

IN THE DAYS before our departure, Tania and I set out to Souk Wakif to buy a farewell gift for our Qatari colleagues. Having seen the extravagant treats the women in the department routinely brought to the office I felt the large basket of chocolates we'd organised might not make much of an impression.

Tania wasn't concerned. 'They realise we can't afford the same things they can.' I'd never heard anyone say that on previous assignments. Usually, my pay had been a fortune compared to the salaries of locals.

On our last day, we delivered the basket of chocolates to Haya's office and she accepted it graciously. Tania wanted a photo.

The women laughed. 'What for? You won't be able to see us.'

She took it anyway; the women all standing in a row with their faces covered.

I'd enjoyed working with these women during the brief time I was there. The seclusion of the budget office gave them the opportunity to work without the scrutiny, competition and derision of men—a situation women in the west can only dream of.

At my last meeting with the project coordinator, he told me I'd achieved more in one month than some other advisers had achieved in a year, although to me it didn't seem like I'd achieved much at all. I told him I'd be happy to come back for the next phase if there was one. Apparently, however, there wasn't.

The last I heard of Tania she was roughing it in South Sudan.

Into a Black Hole
Tripoli, Libya, March 2014

It seemed as if I was the only woman on the Emirates flight to Tripoli; certainly the only non-Arab woman.

The man sitting next to me was listening to a recitation of the Qur'an on the in-flight entertainment system. I could see the list of surahs displayed on his video screen. It seemed to go with his white hat and his long beard with no moustache and the fact that he hadn't acknowledged my presence.

I felt uncomfortable sitting next to him, but as we were leaving the plane, he bade me a friendly goodbye in fluent English and wished me a good visit to Libya.

There were no signs in English in the airport, in fact, no Latin script of any kind, and everyone was male, except the dark-skinned young girl on duty inside the windowless women's toilets.

I'd arrived on the day Tripoli Airport returned to normal operations after fighting a week earlier had prompted all the international airlines to suspend their flights. Luckily, I'd known nothing about this when I boarded the A380 in Sydney. On a busy Tuesday afternoon, it seemed like any other relatively modern airport.

A security officer from the World Bank was waiting for me. Instead of the usual scrappy piece of paper, he held up his iPad screen with my name on it. Not that it was difficult to find me. I was still the only foreign female in the crowd and Mark seemed to be the only non-Arab male.

The airport's Foreign Exchange Bureau was closed, perhaps permanently, but a group of men milling in front of it were ready to sell Libyan Dinars for US dollars. The World Bank's armour-plated SUV with red diplomatic number plates was parked on the footpath outside.

As I strapped myself in, Mark, sitting in the front passenger seat beside the local driver, began his safety spiel. Even in this place, I was dealing with another Australian.

'It should be an uneventful trip,' he said, 'but there are a few things you need to know. This thing on my belt is a GPS tracker.' He pointed to a black pager-type device with a red button. 'If anything happens to me, you need to press this emergency button for three seconds to get help. OK?'

There was another red emergency button beside the handbrake and a sophisticated piece of communication equipment bolted to the dashboard. The driver radioed our movement to the control centre and we drove into Tripoli's hectic traffic.

Mark continued his 'welcome to Libya' speech. Tripoli International Airport, like most places in Libya, he explained, wasn't controlled by the government. It was held by one of the many militia forces and was a lucrative source of income for them.

Other areas of the city were also controlled by different military factions.

'Normally diplomatic vehicles like ours aren't stopped at the checkpoints,' Mark explained as we sped past sentry points marking the boundaries between the militias' various territories.

Our route took us around the outskirts of the city, through flat, dry countryside and small towns of sand-coloured buildings built on sand along sand-dusted roads. In each town we drove past fruit stalls, furniture emporiums and small shops where men drank coffee at tables on the street. At each intersection, the battered cars jostled with each other for right of way.

During the drive, Mark briefed me on the situation in Tripoli. 'You'll probably hear a lot of gunfire, especially at night.

Mostly it's just what they call "celebratory fire"—people shooting into the air for the hell of it. Or it could just be fireworks.

'But the main threat to safety,' he said, 'is traffic accidents.'

Just as he said this a young man in a small sedan slalomed his way around the cars on the crowded two-way street at about 100 km an hour.

When Mark started explaining the economic situation I found myself finishing his sentences.

'Foreign companies are reluctant to come here to do business,' he said.

'Because they're worried about the lack of security.'

'Yes. Particularly if they're doing business with the government.'

'They have to pay bribes.'

'And even if they have a contract, the government is unstable.'

'So they might not get paid.'

'Exactly!'

THE PALM CITY residential development, on the coast about twenty kilometres from the centre of Tripoli, had been built before the overthrow of the Gaddafi regime and was meant for tourists. Now it was home to foreign diplomatic staff and advisers. The EU and the World Bank both had their offices there. A black and white police car was stationed permanently opposite the front gate, next to a mobile ATM machine in an armoured van, and a Thai restaurant.

At the gatehouse our vehicle was checked for hidden bombs and the electronically activated bollards sank into the ground to let us into a world completely different from the villages we'd just been driving through. It was a bizarre toy town kind of place. Rows of identical houses with perfectly manicured gardens lined empty winding streets. Identical Toyota Landcruisers with bull bars and whiplash antennas were parked outside each villa, and maintenance staff whirred around in modified electric golf carts.

My World Bank 'task team leader' opened the front door of his villa and looked for a moment as if he had no idea who I was or what I was doing there, although we had exchanged many emails about the details of my visit.

He then launched into a thirty-minute introductory monologue which covered topics ranging from the work I would be doing, the domestic arrangements in the house and dozens of other useful and not-so-useful pieces of information, threaded through with grievances and complaints about the World Bank.

We did a quick tour of the main points of interest in Palm City. During the day the place seemed like a ghost town. The inhabitants were out on their missions to meet government officials or supervise aid-funded engineering projects. We visited the deserted sports centre and swimming pool and the equally deserted 'piazza' with its empty coffee shop. In the supermarket the same catchy pop song played on an endless loop while I studied the limp parsley, wilting lettuce and shrivelled carrots on offer.

In my upstairs bedroom that night I listened to the screeching of cars driven too fast and stopping too quickly on the street outside the walls of Palm City, and the pop and whistle of fireworks ignited on the waste ground next door. At least, I hoped it was fireworks.

●━━━●

It was almost three years since the people of Libya, in the flush of the 'Arab Spring', had overthrown Muammar

Gaddafi, the man who'd ruled the country as his personal domain for forty-two years.

While the people no longer lived in fear of the erratic dictator, the new life they'd hoped for had still to be achieved. One of the obstacles was that there was no agreement on exactly what the new life should be like.

In 2012 the voters had elected a moderate government and many saw the future of the country as a western-style secular democracy. A large part of the population, however, thought it should be a conservative Islamic state, and some of those in the eastern part didn't see a future in Libya at all but wanted a separate independent nation which, incidentally, would contain much of the country's oil resources.

A couple of weeks before I arrived the prime minister, Ali Zeidan, had lost a confidence vote in parliament and had fled the country fearing arrest over accusations of 'financial irregularities'. He blamed Islamists for his downfall. The defence minister, Abdullah al-Thinni, had been appointed interim prime minister but it wasn't clear for how long.

Given the political uncertainties, reforming the Ministry of Finance might seem a bit premature, even trivial, but the foreign aid organisations were busily trying to create the type of society they hoped most Libyans wanted. They had set up offices in government ministries, delivered new computers and software, provided training courses, and sent senior officials away on study tours.

The World Bank and the IMF had written several reports on what needed to be done in the Ministry of Finance, some by experts who reportedly never left the safety of their four-star hotel. My assignment was to assess the organisation and staffing of the ministry and suggest how it could be restructured to make it more efficient. My visit would add one more report to the pile of helpful advice.

The next morning jet lag woke me at five am so I had ample time to prepare for my first day of work. Sometime later, another consultant emerged from the third bedroom in our home office—a rotund old man with curly white hair and the daintiest little feet. He came down the stairs slowly and with great difficulty as if his tiny feet were too feeble to carry his weight. He introduced himself in heavily accented French as Danny.

It was only later, after he'd left, that I realised he was a well-known World Bank expert, the author of many of the reference books and research papers I used in my work, and the closest thing there is to a public finance celebrity.

At 8.15 our car, with another local driver and another World Bank security officer, arrived to collect us. Central Tripoli was a modern city with tall buildings, wide streets, multi-lane expressways and the type of rush hour traffic you would expect in a place with cheap petrol and no public transport. It also had no effective police force so cars drove on the footpath, took shortcuts across concrete dividers, and ignored speed limits and traffic signs.

The city skyline was littered with unfinished building projects; legacies of the previous regime's grand development plans. Abandoned cranes stood sentry over vacant apartment blocks and large empty shopping centres.

It took almost an hour to travel from Palm City to the main Ministry of Finance building, but nevertheless, we were early. We waited for our local staff on the garden terrace of a coffee shop, drinking cappuccinos. A caged bird sat on a table chirping at the morning sun.

Ahmed arrived first—a good-looking young man in a smart suit and black-framed glasses carrying an iPad in a leather portfolio. It was his first day at work with the World Bank.

Ahmed had grown up in the UK, the son of immigrant doctors, and had given up a job with HSBC in London to return to his hometown of Benghazi when the revolution started. He showed me a photo on his iPhone of him and his brother in khaki Kevlar vests taking a break during the fighting in 2011. They looked like two young men on a camping holiday but he assured me the fighting was real and terrifying. I thought about his mother, miles away in a northern industrial town in England, and the terror she must also have experienced.

The Ministry of Finance occupied three buildings in central Tripoli. We visited the one where the minister and his deputy had their offices. It had suitably impressive marble floors, elaborate beige curtains, large varnished desks and brown leather sofas.

Ahmed and I spent an hour with the minister's grey-bearded senior adviser, Dr Ahady, who recounted the problems of the Libyan public sector and the particular woes of the Ministry of Finance.

The story was not much different from the situation in some of the other countries I'd been to. The government was the largest and, it seems, almost the only employer in the country, but a government job may not involve actually working or even turning up. Salaries are low and there's not much difference between the pay of high-level officials and the wages of their staff. With regular 'promotion', a long-serving junior officer can eventually take home more than his boss. Various allowances and perks, such as committee sitting fees, are used to top up take-home pay.

This may explain why so many people I interviewed over the next few weeks were so keen to set up committees to deal with any problems.

The Ministry of Finance, with perhaps 700 regular staff, is considered small compared to the tens of thousands employed by many other ministries. Exactly how many staff there are, however, wasn't clear. Staff files were out of date and there were no attendance records. The number had certainly increased since the revolution because people who had been dismissed by the previous regime in an efficiency drive had demanded their jobs back. And some people could have been getting a salary from several government agencies because there was no central control of civil service employment.

Ahady also believed that many people were not qualified for the jobs they held.

'But it's impossible to dismiss anyone,' he said. 'Not in the current situation.'

Nevertheless, he had hopes for the future and rattled off a list of reforms and improvements he wanted to implement.

The second Ministry of Finance building, which we visited next, was nowhere near as opulent as the minister's offices. It had a gloomy foyer, a lift that didn't work and piles of shabby ring folders piled on the floor.

The head of treasury sat at a large desk in the centre of a large room. He was a gentle man with sad puppy dog eyes and a subtle sense of humour.

A constant stream of people came with papers for him to sign and matters they urgently needed to talk about, interrupting our discussion about staffing and workload and reform options. The same four or five men reappeared in rotation.

'I know the situation here is not good,' he told Ahmed, who translated for me. 'I don't need a report to tell me.'

Like Dr Ahady, he also had a list of things he would like to see changed in future. But he shrugged. 'What can I do?'

After the meeting, we decided to go out to get something to eat. Our World Bank guard looked slightly alarmed at the idea of walking anywhere in this town but didn't object.

The street of high-walled houses, parked cars and shuttered shops was deserted during the mid-afternoon lunch break, but the takeaway food shop was open. We stood around a high table eating spicy chicken rolled in flat bread. It looked to me like most Middle Eastern takeaway food.

I asked Ahmed what it was called.

He consulted the shop owner. 'It's an enchilada!'

We arrived back at Palm City to find Danny, the overweight Frenchman, in a state of panic. He was due to leave the following day but Alitalia had suspended its services to Tripoli indefinitely and his flight home had been cancelled.

It was not so much that he might have to stay longer in Tripoli that bothered him. It was the fact that the day after returning to Paris he was due to fly out again to Togo, or some similarly obscure part of Africa. In his late seventies and barely able to walk, I wondered why he didn't just stay home.

He was on the phone to a travel agent trying to arrange an alternative flight to Paris and having some trouble making himself understood in his dense accent.

'I am To-ma-si. Dan-ee-el. Pleez can you 'elp me? My flight to Paree eet az been can-cel-led!'

Eventually, staff in an office several time zones away arrived at work and booked him a flight to Paris via Tunisia. Lufthansa, Austrian and British Airways had also cancelled their flights. Now only Middle Eastern and North African airlines like Tunis Air, Egypt Air and Emirates still flew to Libya.

AHMED AND I spent most of the following weeks trying to organise meetings with each of the department directors in the ministry. Ahmed had a list of the people we needed to see and their mobile phone numbers.

The Director of Administration and Finance should have been first on the list but we were told the chances of meeting him were slim. He'd recently been kidnapped. His captors had released him after a few days but he hadn't come back to work yet.

Ahmed wasn't clear why he'd been kidnapped. It could have been a family matter or a tribal dispute, but it could also have been because he was the person responsible for all Ministry of Finance employment and all its contracts with the private sector.

Most of the other directors also seemed to be busy, out of the area, or simply not there but eventually we managed to track them down. In the midst of the political upheaval and everyday danger, they were continuing with their work as best they could.

The Ministry of Finance had many problems to deal with. Most of Libya's revenue had always come from oil, but the rebels in the east had blocked the ports and closed down the pipelines so the stream of easy money had dried up. For the first time, the government had to pay attention to what it was spending. The situation wasn't helped by the fact that four months into the financial year, parliament hadn't yet approved that year's budget.

I managed to get a meeting with the Director of Accounts, Mr Almehdi, simply by turning up in his office on the off-chance he would be there. The accounts department, several floors above the treasury office, comprised room upon room of vacant desks and boxes of dog-eared papers and folders.

Mr Almehdi's room, like the treasurer's, was large and replete with brown sofas and coffee tables. Once we'd cornered him in his office, he was pleasant and helpful.

He explained as best he could the role of the accounts department.

'We collect information on the financial transactions of all the government spending units. Then we analyse and check the data and, after the end of the financial year, we prepare the annual financial reports.'

It sounded straightforward enough.

At the moment, however, he admitted they were a little behind schedule. They'd only just finished the accounts for 2008, six years before. These had been sent to the National Audit Authority for checking and until they got the results of the audit, they couldn't start work on 2009.

'We can't prepare the accounts for the next year until we know the opening balance,' he explained.

With my limited knowledge of accounting processes, I thought there was probably a way around this if anyone had been seriously interested in understanding the government's financial position. In the meantime, the boxes and files of budget information from 2009 to 2013 sat on the floor in the office and the desks were empty because there wasn't much to do so most of the fifty-six staff didn't come to work.

The World Bank was in the process of introducing an automated accounting system to consolidate the financial data managed by the ministry and it would be able to produce the end of year accounts almost at the push of a button. It would make much of the accounts department's work irrelevant. But the new system would only work if spending data was collected and entered every month, not five years later.

Mr Almehdi assured us that the Accounts Department would do it, but we were several months into the financial year and, so far, there'd been little progress.

At least the staff in the ministry knew all about computers.

Each department had its own database or spreadsheet which they used to record the information they needed. And each department duly re-entered the information it got in reports from the other departments, checking and re-analysing it and adding their own information, and then passing their printout to the next department.

The idea that all this information could be in one system which they would all share was proving difficult to communicate. Information is power, and each department believed that their information was better, more accurate, and more reliable than any other department's, and they didn't want to lose control of any of it.

The new system would also mean that much of the work they'd been doing would be redundant. Some of the directors I met with weren't worried. Their staff were already flat out and there were plenty of other things for them to do. Others, however, were clearly not so comfortable with the idea.

IN THE SECOND week, I finally met a woman with a responsible job. Ms Mofida managed the ministry's personnel database. She was about forty with a smooth, chubby face wrapped in a bright purple headscarf.

She showed us the type of information held in the database—staff names and photos, qualifications, job titles, employment history and banking details. All very useful.

'Alas, we don't have all the records up to date at the moment.' Ms Mofida turned her palms elegantly towards us and shrugged. She promised to give us a printout of what she had and disappeared.

After a considerable wait it seemed she was having trouble getting the computer to produce the report we needed. She suggested that Ahmed come back the next day to collect it.

Her colleague, however, kept his own records separate from hers, on a spreadsheet. Regrettably, it turned out that this was also not up to date and the total number of staff he'd recorded was significantly different from Ms Mofida's totals.

Ahmed finally managed to get his hands on the official data several weeks later. Based on this, it seemed that most of the staff in the ministry were quite old. Fifteen percent were over sixty, and there was apparently no one under the age of thirty, although that may have been a measure of how out of date the records were. Only twelve percent were women.

Most of the women seemed to be located in the administration building, the third of the ministry's three locations in Tripoli. When we visited all the male officials we met had a female receptionist sitting in their outer office.

We proceeded from floor to floor in the claustrophobic little lift to meet the department directors. Each of them had a large desk, a lot of sofas, and a number of hangers-on who sat in on our discussions.

The enthusiastic head of financial control explained the role of the 200 or so ministry staff that were outposted to government agencies to check and approve all their transactions. He was about to launch a comprehensive training program to ensure that future recruits to these jobs would know more about government accounting than the current crop did.

Down two levels, the head of financial institutions was disappointed I didn't speak French as he'd become fluent during his time as Libya's representative in Senegal. He explained the work he did in trying to negotiate the repayment of loans the Gaddafi regime had generously offered to impoverished African countries like Chad and Burkina

Faso in the 1970s. He was still hopeful of collecting on some of them one day.

The head of financial resources, who looked like an Italian gangster in his black shirt, silver tie and spiv moustache, was responsible for monitoring and forecasting all sources of government revenue, including oil export receipts and the profits of state-owned enterprises.

Finally, we met Mr Miloud, the head of the 'follow up' department. His was the newest department, set up to provide the financial reports none of the other departments were able to supply. He had a neat moustache and shiny slicked-down hair. In my notes, I nicknamed him the Brylcreem kid.

He kept us waiting for several minutes while he finished reading an important-looking report, then leant back in his chair to talk to us. The sofas in his office were occupied by a larger-than-usual number of onlookers. There was a vase of artificial roses with glitter-covered petals on the coffee table and a large plastic ficus tree in the corner.

If information is power, Mr Miloud was the most powerful director in the ministry. His staff collected all the available revenue and spending data from other departments and compiled it into a massive spreadsheet to produce quarterly reports. But the new accounting system would do exactly the same thing, with much less effort, making his spreadsheet irrelevant.

Mr Miloud didn't seem worried. 'When the database is operating,' he assured me, 'I'll be able to produce my report every day.'

I'm sure he realised, however, that the new system would mean he would no longer have a monopoly on information. Every other director would also be able to get reports if they wanted to. I was certain he would be scheming to make sure this didn't happen.

At the end of the conversation he dismissed us and picked up another report from his desk, examining it intensely as we left the room.

All the directors we spoke to were educated, thoughtful and informed about the rest of the world and they shared similar opinions about the problems of the ministry and how they should be solved. Better human resource management was number one on their list, followed by better staff, more training and higher salaries. They also wanted more teamwork, more consultation and cooperation, and open-plan offices.

Every evening several of us squeezed into the back seat of the World Bank vehicle for the long, slow drive home, with our security officer sitting in the front seat by the driver.

Our security procedures meant we took a different route each day and, as a result, I never had any idea where I was. After a while, a few landmarks made an impression. Sometimes we drove along the Tripoli waterfront, past cargo ships and ferries, parks and children's playgrounds, the ancient forts and buildings of the old city centre, and the modern towers of the business district.

Not long before, cruise ships had stopped in the port and tourists roamed the old town where streets still had Italian names from Libya's time as an Italian colony. But this was as close as I got to the tourist sites as they whizzed past. Even taking photographs was discouraged in case someone took offence, so I could only snatch a few blurred shots from the back seat of the car.

Further down the road, we passed the complex of office buildings known to foreigners as the Johnny Walkers because they resembled upside-down whisky bottles. The name was particularly ironic as Libya, unlike most Islamic countries I've been to, really did enforce a no-alcohol policy.

There were several large western hotels, including the Radisson on the waterfront and the shimmering filigree metal skin of a newly constructed Marriot hotel. No doubt the Marriot's investors had hoped for a boom in tourism after the change of regime but the hotel's opening date had been pushed back while the developers constructed a three-metre-high security wall that had not been envisaged in the original plans.

At the end of March, the World Bank was suddenly deluged with visiting 'missions'. Several women came from Washington to discuss the electricity situation and some Scandinavian consultants arrived to assess plans for political decentralisation.

It seemed the security of our little team was now not such a high priority and our security staff were reassigned to look after the visitors. We were left in the hands of Aseem, a young Libyan driver.

As it happened, this was the week that protesters decided to block most of the main roads in and out of the city. The reasons for this were never clear to me, but it caused a major traffic jam when all the city workers tried to return to their homes. This made Aseem very distressed. He was determined to find an uncongested back street that none of the thousands of other drivers travelling in the same direction had found yet and raced down any empty piece of road triumphantly before screeching to a stop at the next blocked intersection.

Suddenly, he saw a road that was apparently, mysteriously, uncongested and headed down it, in spite of the fact that all the other cars were turning around and driving in our direction. He cursed them for obstructing his way but they waved frantically back at him.

Looking ahead towards the empty street I could see why. A black vehicle was parked across the road and a black-clad, black-bearded man was brandishing a large gun.

Eventually, Aseem realised the danger he was driving us towards and turned the car around.

•———•

I WROTE UP my report for the World Bank before I left, although I expected the chances of anything happening in response to it in the foreseeable future were slim.

The report listed all the problems that had been identified by the people I'd interviewed and made suggestions about how the ministry should function. It included organograms and flow charts and dot points on short-term decisions and long-term actions. Ahmed provided statistics and graphs on the employees. I carefully didn't suggest that any departments should be abolished or that any jobs be lost.

If my report could have said what I think the problem really was I would probably have used the word 'trust'. The most significant impact of more than forty years of capricious dictatorship had been the destruction of trust. Trust between the people and the government, between neighbours, between bosses and workers, and between work colleagues. Lack of trust was reflected in the fact that no one wanted their photo taken because they didn't know what you would do with it, and in the way no one in the ministry wanted to share information or work together to solve problems.

It would take a lot more than a new financial management information system and a new organisation structure to rebuild the trust needed to run an effective government.

The day I left Tripoli, Abdullah Al-Thinni, the new prime minister, resigned. This was less than a week after he'd been formally appointed to the position by parliament. Evidently, an attack on him and his family the previous day had convinced him to give up the post.

The same day, Emirates Airlines decided that it would no longer risk sending an expensive Boeing 777 to Tripoli. My flight was delayed while they arranged a substitute plane—one so old it still had ashtrays in the armrests.

Several hundred passengers queued patiently at the check-in counter for three hours waiting for an announcement to explain the delay while we calculated the flow-on effect of our missed onward connections.

A few weeks after I'd left, fighting broke out again between militia groups at the airport. The last of the international airlines cancelled their services and Libya's main link to the outside world was closed.

Over the following months, the fighting escalated and consumed the whole country. Foreign embassies evacuated their staff. So did the World Bank.

I had an email from Ahmed. He said the country seemed to be heading into a black hole. The better future the people had fought for in 2011 appeared further away than ever.

A Glimmer of Hope
Kismayo, Jubaland, Somalia, November 2014

Kismayo International Airport looked freshly painted, shining white and blue against the red dirt and grey scrub of Jubaland.

Our twin-propeller Embraer aircraft, operated by Blue Sky Airlines, taxied up to the small terminal building and was immediately surrounded by waiting Somali families and passengers ready to board for the next leg to Mogadishu.

It was still early. Our journey had started in the dark, at five am, in the muddy car park at Nairobi's ramshackle second airport. A small group of Somalis waited for the flight under the fluorescent lights of the snack bar, the women and girls wrapped in voluminous black gowns with only their doll-like faces showing.

Our aircraft sat on the tarmac among a sea of Cessnas and zebra-painted safari planes. While we waited to board, two big unmarked jets roared down the runway, taking off to deliver daily supplies of fresh khat leaves from Kenya's fertile highlands to traders in Somalia.

My neighbour on the flight was a Somali doctor, now retired in California, returning to volunteer at the Red Cross-run hospital. Another passenger, a man in his late twenties, was coming back for the first time since he was a child. An elegant young woman with striking black eyeliner and thick false eyelashes was decorated from fingertips to elbows with elaborate henna tattoos.

Inside the terminal at Kismayo, we queued to pay our fifty dollars for a visa and then waited while a young woman in a purple gown thoroughly searched each bag looking for contraband goods such as alcohol.

The Somali passengers then left to travel into town. The three of us working for the Somalia Stability Fund turned back towards the runway. Our accommodation was a few metres across the gravel, behind a high wall with a large sign—'Camp Kismayo'.

The blue and white airport terminal and the scrubby horizon beyond was as much as I would see of Somalia during this visit.

Camp Kismayo was a testament to the power of the profit motive. Even in this dangerous and unappealing corner of the world, there was money to be made by people with an entrepreneurial spirit and an appetite for risk. Camp Kismayo had been set up to accommodate and service the gradually growing number of aid workers and consultants visiting the newly-created state of Jubaland.

Its outer walls were large canvas tubes filled with red dirt, creating a row of melting pillars, like the archaeological remains of an ancient fortress. Inside, rows of white shipping containers provided small rooms with basic furniture, powerful air-conditioning and a reasonably effective internet connection.

It was blazing hot and the sun glared on the red gravel. There was a communal ablution block with cold salt-water showers, a steel-reinforced 'safe room', and a dining hall which also doubled as a meeting room where visiting foreigners consulted with officials of the Interim Jubaland Administration without leaving the protected compound.

Until two years before, the town of Kismayo had been controlled by Islamic Al-Shabaab militants. They'd been steadily forced out by the UN-sponsored, African Union-led, AMISOM peacekeeping mission, consisting largely of Kenyan, Ugandan and Ethiopian troops, and the new Federal State of Jubaland had been created. A local warlord had been named as 'leader' of the interim administration, although everyone I spoke to called him 'president'.

Al-Shabaab still held large areas of territory, however, and travel was risky for foreigners. Most organisations that delivered aid to Somalia were therefore based outside the country.

I'd spent the past few days in the office of the Somalia Stability Fund in the Kenyan capital, Nairobi, being briefed in preparation for my visit. Once I was in Kismayo, I stayed within the confines of the AMISOM-guarded airport and the interim administration's ministers and officials came to me. It was considered the only safe way to work.

The Jubaland officials seemed more than willing to make the seventeen-kilometre trip out to meet me. Foreigners bring the possibility of aid money to reconstruct their derelict public buildings and to employ returning Somali professionals on rewarding salaries.

The 'Minister for the State Presidency' arrived a few hours after we landed, accompanied by two of the president's political advisers. They were all Canadian citizens.

'I was a telecommunications engineer in Canada,' the minister said. 'The United Nations asked me to come here to work for them. I said no. It took a lot for them to persuade me, but eventually I agreed.'

That was a few years before. Now he'd become one of the most senior officials in the new state

We were meeting to talk about how to set up the civil service for the Jubaland administration. The new government had recently created a Ministry of Finance and installed a financial management database so they could assure the donors they had sound finances. Now they needed to demonstrate that they could manage their staff and payroll effectively. At stake was money from the World Bank.

The World Bank wanted them to establish a 'Civil Service

Commission', but exactly what this meant needed to be clarified. There are numerous models of civil service management around the world. The basic objective is to have a civil service which is apolitical and recruited on merit, but this is a novel idea in many countries where finding government jobs for friends, family and supporters is one of the main objectives of going into politics.

An independent Civil Service Commission is supposed to prevent this. The trick is that the commissioners need to be powerful enough to stand up to ministers who bend the rules, but not so powerful that they can disrupt the government or benefit their own friends, family or clan.

I talked about these issues with the minister and his advisers. How would the civil service commission fit with the interim administration's political structure, and what were their own expectations? Who should the commission report to and who would appoint the members? How many commissioners did they need and what sort of people should they be? What exactly would they be responsible for?

The minister's ideas were a bit vague and we discussed the pros and cons of a few options. A body reporting to the president seemed to be what was required. And given that the bureaucracy was still small and its abilities unknown, centralised recruitment and HR management by a few experts in the commission sounded like a practical option. I started work on a discussion paper and recommendations they could take to their bosses.

·———·

There were no lights at night inside Camp Kismayo apart from some dull red globes in the bathrooms, so after dinner, I fumbled my way to my room by the light of a torch. Riaan, the South African in charge of the camp, had told us to turn off the light in our rooms before we opened the door at night to prevent the sudden flash that might indicate that there were indeed people inside the compound. The upside of the lack of artificial light was that the night sky in the balmy evening was luminous with stars.

Camp Kismayo was considered a temporary facility and no funds had been wasted on trivialities like mirrors, towel rails or coat hangers. The smell of sewage combined with aviation fuel permeated the compound.

In the evening there was little to do except to read a book and have an early night. The morning, when it was still cool, was the best part of the day. At 6.30 am I sat at the plastic tables outside the dining room, drinking strong brewed coffee freshly delivered in a thermos by the cook, and watched the sun rise over the blast walls.

On day two I met with the Deputy Minister for Social Affairs and Education. His main concerns were creating jobs for the large number of unemployed youth who provided a fertile recruiting ground for Al-Shabaab, and also doing something for the seventy-five percent of children who didn't have a school to go to. He didn't seem to have a strong desire to be involved in government employment issues so the proposal to give his ministry a role in examining and screening civil servants was ditched.

That afternoon almost the entire staff of the Ministry of Finance turned up—the minister, the heads of budget, revenue and HR, and a few of their local advisers.

Their big concern was salaries. They were in the process of estimating the budget for the following year and had developed a proposed salary scale to apply to all the new staff the government planned to employ.

The monthly rate of pay at the lower levels, for the cleaners and security guards and messengers, was just $200 a month. But at the senior grades, which happened to be the jobs they occupied, the salaries ballooned to several thousand dollars a month. Based on the research I'd done, this was higher than the amounts paid to federal Somali government staff in similar jobs and much more than the salaries of government staff in the states of Somaliland, Puntland or neighbouring Ethiopia.

They had several arguments to justify their proposal. 'The cost of living in Kismayo is higher than in other parts of the country,' the budget director argued. 'And high salaries will help fight corruption.'

'We want to attract the cream of the cream to come and work here,' the minister's adviser said.

I pointed out that there were so few other jobs in Somalia just then that there may not be a problem finding good people. And if they did manage to attract people from other parts of Somalia, would they stay for the long term?

Indeed, would any of the people I was meeting with stay? Most of the ministers, advisers and senior officials in the administration had other passports and other options. Like all the foreigners, if there was trouble, they could leave.

MY PERSONAL SECURITY guard, Hermann, arrived a day later, apologising profusely about the unpredictability of Blue Sky's flights from Mogadishu. It wasn't a problem. I hadn't been expecting him. I'd had no idea he existed.

Hermann was another South African, weather-beaten with nicotine-stained teeth and an impenetrable accent. He said, 'Yes, ma'am' or 'No, ma'am' in response to everything I said, even after I told him not to. His presence seemed somewhat redundant as the camp was already heavily guarded, but he sat patiently outside during all my meetings and kept track of who was coming and going.

The other guests at Camp Kismayo included Masoud, a police adviser who'd just completed two months of his twelve-month contract, and a Frenchman working for an Islamic charity.

My colleague, Suren, the son of an Indian diplomat, spoke multiple languages and had just finished a Master's degree at a Finnish university. He travelled constantly between Mogadishu and other places in Somalia, coordinating aid projects and negotiating contracts with local non-government organisations.

There were also several UN staff living in the camp, the overflow from the nearby UN compound, fifty metres away across the dirt. They included two African men who worked with the UN public relations unit to produce good news stories about AMISOM, and a Nepalese UN 'movement officer'.

A few days later, a team of UN inspectors arrived to check the assets being used by the UN's staff in Kismayo, including the cameras and microphones of the PR team which were duly brought out and ticked off on a clipboard.

Sandy, a Swede, seemed to be the only UN employee who did something of benefit to Somalia, rather than just keeping the wheels of the UN bureaucracy turning. He was working for the UN Industrial Development Organisation building a vocational training centre.

•———•

LIVING BESIDE THE runway meant we heard the engines of aircraft taking off and landing throughout the day and sometimes at night. Blue Sky made several visits from other towns in Somalia and there were regular UN Humanitarian Air Services flights from Nairobi as well as Kenyan military aircraft.

Shortly after midnight one night I was woken by the roar of large engines just outside the walls. The rough Kismayo airstrip had no lighting and the instrumentation in the tower consisted of a pair of binoculars so it was a strange time for a large plane to land. The engines continued to roar for half an hour before taking off again.

The next morning Hermann said it would have been an American military plane making a delivery. A small US military camp was hidden away somewhere down the airstrip. They had their own aviation systems and put lights out on the runway when they were expecting a flight. Another night I heard the whine of a small engine passing overhead, surely not even as big as a Cessna. The consensus over breakfast was that it was probably a US drone.

•———•

THE PARAMETERS OF any visit to Kismayo were determined by the erratic Blue Sky flight schedule. After hopping between Somali towns for four days, the airline's only plane returned to Kismayo to take us back to Nairobi.

I'd met all the people I had to meet and I'd formed a rough idea of what they wanted, or needed. Now I had to write it up in a report and I could do that much more comfortably in the Somalia Stability Fund office back in Nairobi.

We entered the little airport terminal from the airside to check in for the flight and lined up at the immigration window for our exit stamp. The immigration clerk wrote down my nationality as 'USA', possibly having no idea what

'Australia' meant and not wanting to try to spell it.

We waited in the shade in front of the building. A man with a long stick herded goats off the tarmac before our flight arrived. The aircraft taxied to the terminal to set down and pick up passengers like a suburban bus. The Minister for the State Presidency was queuing up to board with us. He was on his way to Nairobi to visit his family.

The landscape we arrived at an hour later looked identical to Kismayo—the same red soil, the same shrubby grey bushes, but we were now just across the border in the north of Kenya.

The plane landed on a long, wide runway carved out of the desert, and taxied to the small, modern Wajir International Airport terminal. It seemed to be the only building for miles around and we were the only passengers transiting there.

We paid another fifty dollars for Kenyan visas and waited for our bags to be passed through the x-ray machine and reloaded onto the aircraft. On the wall, a framed notice set out the Kenyan Aviation Authority's 'quality policy' and performance objectives. The modern management jargon seemed out of place in this remote outpost. Perhaps without these performance objectives, the queues would have been even longer and the processing of our luggage even more confused.

We reboarded the Blue Sky plane and continued our journey to Nairobi. The purpose of our detour to Wajir was a mystery.

During the flight south in the small plane, I could see the snow cap of Mount Kilimanjaro, across the border in Tanzania, on one side of the aircraft and snow-topped Mount Kenya on the other. At the lush outskirts of the city, we circled over mansions with blue swimming pools in large gardens.

Although we had already officially entered Kenya at Wajir, we were subjected to more passport processing and luggage inspection before being allowed to leave the airport. There had been several serious Somali-led terrorist attacks in Kenya in the past few years so the government was particularly cautious about anyone arriving from Somalia, even western consultants working for aid projects.

After four days living in a shipping container in the heat of the Somali desert, Nairobi's mild climate and the luxury of the Dusit hotel were particularly welcome. I spent the next few days at my temporary desk in the Nairobi office working on my recommendations.

There was clearly a long way to go before Somalia was a normal country again, but for once, I left a project feeling positive about the outcome. I wrote up my proposals for the Civil Service Commission and my draft civil service legislation based on examples from other places in the region and proposed a salary scale that tried to strike a balance between affordability and acceptability. These were all duly adopted by the new government.

Several months later, I returned to Nairobi to meet the keen young people, including several women, who'd been appointed to positions in the new administration. Their jobs would not be easy. They would have to face up to the ambitions of warlords and survive in the impoverished economy and ongoing insecurity of their homeland. I hoped the best for them.

Epilogue

Exit Report

For a long time, I thought I could keep doing this kind of work indefinitely, that the excitement of new places and the challenge of new problems would never grow stale. But eventually, after a decade and a half, it did.

When one of the 'available but not necessarily single' men I met turned out to be, in fact, single, I started spending more time at home and saying no to offers of work that took me away for too long. I tried to make sense of my experiences through academic research, and turned my diaries and notes into this memoir.

Rereading it several years later, I am appalled, firstly, at my staggering naivety and inexperience when I started my first assignment. I was catapulted into the job knowing almost nothing about Kosovo or the work I would be doing, or, as it turned out, even where my office was. In later years, I had a better understanding of what I was supposed to be doing, but I rarely knew anything about the country I was going to before my plane landed. I was sent to assignments mainly based on my availability and whether my salary level fit within the budget, rather than my prior knowledge of the project or country.

It turns out that this is perfectly normal in this line of work. Although the selection criteria for technical consultant positions may specify a need to understand the local environment, there are relatively few people who are experts in banking, legislative drafting or government accounting who also speak a local language, have a background in anthropology or history, and are willing to live away from home in a developing country for long periods.

Once they arrive in a country, many advisers tend to exist

in a foreigner bubble with limited contact with locals outside the office. Indeed, some short-term consultants spend most of their time inside their luxury hotels. A two-week IMF 'mission', for example, may arrive and depart without really understanding the most basic things about the country to which they are providing advice and opinions.

Another thing that stands out in many of the stories in this book is the smugness and sense of superiority that I and many of my colleagues felt about the local people we were working with. We were convinced that whatever was already in place in their government couldn't possibly be any good and that only we, the western experts, had the answers.

Over the years I have become more sceptical about this. I've realised that local people can solve their own problems if they have the chance to. The obstacles have more to do with poverty, conflict and dysfunctional politics than the absence of computers and modern accounting.

I've also learned that donor organisations themselves are sometimes part of the problem. Fluctuating levels of funding due to national political cycles, lack of knowledge or understanding about the local culture, penny-pinching short-term projects, constant staff turnover, and following the latest fashions in development theory all seriously limit the ability of aid donors to consistently support countries to make the changes they recommend.

My involvement in development assistance has also challenged other common ideas about the world. I've learned, for example, that there is no longer a clear border between 'us' and 'them', between the 'first world' and the 'third world', if there ever was. Almost everyone I met in places like Kosovo, Afghanistan or Somalia, had relatives abroad or had travelled to other countries to study or work. Even if they hadn't, today's communication technologies, the internet and satellite broadcasts mean they're always in touch with what's happening in other places.

All in all, the outcomes from the post-conflict reconstruction and development assistance I've been part of can only be described as mixed. In fact, some of it was probably a complete waste of money.

Nevertheless, I still believe that technical assistance is worth doing. Sometimes it works. As a result of projects I've been involved with, teachers and health workers have received their government salaries on time and in full for perhaps the first time in their careers, health clinics have the supplies they need, new IT systems have plugged gaps that used to let money leak out of the public accounts, and young people have learned new skills and have gone on to make a positive contribution to their country.

All nations that have managed to pull themselves out of poverty in the last sixty or so years, such as Taiwan, South Korea and Singapore, have had at least some outside advice, encouragement and finance.

But ultimately they've done it for themselves. In the long run, poor countries need to work out how to solve their own problems, how to build schools and roads and to provide health care and education for their people, without being forever dependent on aid. This means they need peace and security, a stable, effective government, and an economy that can generate local taxes to pay for it all. This should perhaps be the focus of our aid programs and our diplomacy. It is only when these things have been achieved that the spreadsheets and accounting systems and civil service training programs that my colleagues and I deliver can expect to make a difference.

www.ingramcontent.com/pod-product-compliance
Lightning Source LLC
Chambersburg PA
CBHW070248010526
44107CB00056B/2382